This is a collection of Owen Chadwick's principal writings on Lord Acton, the distinguished Victorian historian and founder of *The Cambridge Modern History*, in which a historian of our own times expounds the life and work of a great predecessor. Some of the pieces are no longer readily available, while one has never before appeared in English. All have been revised, sometimes extensively.

Acton (1834–1902) was born in Naples, the grandson of the Neapolitan prime minister Sir John Acton. Educated at Munich University, he sat as a Liberal MP 1859–65, was created a baron in 1869, and in 1895 was appointed Regius Professor of Modern History at Cambridge. This book explains the important aspects of Acton's complex mind and his great contribution to historical studies. Professor Chadwick, himself a former holder of Acton's Regius Chair, is the leading senior authority both on Acton and on matters of Church and State in the nineteenth century.

Acton and History

Acton
and History

OWEN CHADWICK

CAMBRIDGE
UNIVERSITY PRESS

PUBLISHED BY THE PRESS SYNDICATE OF THE UNIVERSITY OF CAMBRIDGE
The Pitt Building, Trumpington Street, Cambridge CB2 1RP, United Kingdom

CAMBRIDGE UNIVERSITY PRESS
The Edinburgh Building, Cambridge, CB2 2RU,
40 West 20th Street, New York, NY 10011–4211, USA
10 Stamford Road, Oakleigh, Melbourne 3166, Australia

© Owen Chadwick 1998

First published 1998

Printed in the United Kingdom at the University Press, Cambridge

Typeset in Monotype Janson 11/13½pt

A catalogue record for this book is available from the British Library

Library of Congress Cataloguing in Publication data

Chadwick, Owen.
Acton and history / Owen Chadwick.
p. cm.
ISBN 0 521 570743 hardback
1. Acton, John Emerich Edward Dalberg Acton, Baron, 1834–1902.
2. Historians — Great Britain — Biography. I. Title.
D15.A25C485 1998
907′.202—dc21 97–28635 CIP
[B]

ISBN 0 521 570743 hardback

WV

CONTENTS

PREFACE

A T various times I have been invited to lecture or write an article on some aspect of Acton. When these are put side by side they do not make a biography but consider weighty parts of his work. This is what this volume is. Except for chapter 1, written to explain how Acton came to be a historian, all have been published before, though one chapter (no. 5) never in English but in French. But I have not hesitated to alter by cutting our overlaps, or adding pieces where the effect seemed to be obscure. I hope that the total will give a fairly rounded portrait of the personality and his extraordinary mind even while everyone knows that no human personality is rounded and that if it is presented as rounded something rugged in it must be missing.

Chapter 2 (and part of chapter 4) were from the Herbert Hensley Henson lectures in the university of Oxford for 1976 – the subject was appropriate because Hensley Henson cared much about the relation of history to religion; and they were published by the Cambridge University Press two years afterwards, under this title but with the main title *Catholicism and History*, because the opening of those archives to the scientific historians was an important change in Catholic attitudes which was part of a wider European change to the nature and importance of history.

Chapter 3 was originally a long review in the *Journal of Theological Studies* (NS, 28, pt 2 (1977)). It describes the only time, some seven months long, when Acton hit the politics of Western Europe hard; and the result of which was to deprive him of future influence as a practical politician rather than as a political theorist, where his influence began about ten years later and remained even after his death.

The association of the Friends of Newman in France planned a conference on Newman's friendships and asked for a treatment of his links with Acton; hence chapter 5.

Chapter 6 was from the Creighton lecture in the University of London, given under the chairmanship of Sir Herbert Butterfield who was a lifelong worrier about Acton's view of history. It was published by the Athlone Press in 1976 and I am grateful to them for allowing me to republish it here. After his failure at the First Vatican Council Acton never had the least influence as a member of the British Parliament. But slowly Gladstone came to regard him as the wisest political theorist in Europe and he attained the status of a sage. The lecture sought to describe the way he won that respect, even reverence, and what were its effects upon Gladstone and others, and its trials for Acton himself. The subject was fitting for a Creighton lecture because Creighton and Acton were close colleagues, though the partnership had discomforts, in the making of the *English Historical Review* and the early development of modern and medieval history in English universities; and Acton was invited to stand for Creighton's professorship of ecclesiastical history when he left it but refused because he thought himself not properly qualified for the post. Of this fascinating relation between Gladstone and Acton we shall get a fuller picture when Professor James Holland publishes his edition of their letters.

Chapter 7 was from the annual lecture at the German Historical Institute in London which the Institute afterwards published in its annual proceedings for 1986. The question was appropriate because it touched upon one side of German influence on England during the nineteenth century, that is, the experience of historical inquiry. The problem was this: given the influence of Acton upon English historical studies, and given the great influ-

ence upon Acton of his original master at the university, the
Catholic priest and professor Döllinger, can we say whether the
attitude of Catholic historians in Germany were by this route
important in the way that English history went – and if we
cannot, why not?

Chapter 8 was a lecture, in the Senate House at Cambridge,
on Acton's professorship of history there, to which he was
appointed by Queen Victoria almost exactly 100 years before. It
was organized by the Acton Society who afterwards published it
(Grand Rapids, 1995) and I owe them thanks.

Chapter 9 was an essay contributed to the volume published
by Cambridge on the Treasures of the University Library (1998)
edited by the librarian Dr Fox and I am grateful to him for
allowing me also to include it, for the sake of greater completeness, in this volume on Lord Acton.

ABBREVIATIONS

ALL references to Acton's Papers, unless otherwise specified, are from Cambridge University Library Add. MSS; the letter numbers from the admirable two-volume catalogue of them by Dr John Wells.

Altholtz   Josef L. Altholtz, *The Liberal Catholic Movement in England*, London, 1962

Blakiston   N. Blakiston, *The Roman Question: Extracts from the Despatches of Odo Russell from Rome, 1858–70*, London, 1962

Conz.   V. Conzemius, *Döllinger–Lord Acton, Briefwechsel 1850–90*, vols. 1–3, Munich, 1963–71; and vol. 4, *Döllinger–Charlotte Lady Blennerhassett*, Munich, 1981

DD   *Lord Acton: The Decisive Decade. 1864–74*. Ed. Damian McElrath, with J. Holland and others (Bibliothèque de la revue ecclésiastique, 51), Louvain, 1970

Dessain   *The Letters and Diaries of John Henry Newman*. Ed. C. S. Dessain and others, 1961–

DNB   Dictionary of National Biography

EHR   English Historical Review

FL   J. N. Figgis and R. V. Laurence, eds. *Selections from the Correspondence of the First Lord Acton*, vol. 1, London, 1917

MacDougall   H. A. MacDougall, *The Acton–Newman Relations: The Dilemma of Christian Liberalism*, New York, 1962

Paul   H. Paul, introduction to *Letters of Lord Acton to Mary Gladstone*, 2nd edn, London, 1913

xiii

PRO   Public Record Office

Simpson   *The Correspondence of Lord Acton and Richard Simpson* ed. Josef L. Altholtz, Damian McElrath and James C. Holland, 3 vols., Cambridge, 1971–5

THE MAKING OF A HISTORIAN

A CTON was born in 1834, only son of a baronet and squire of Aldenham in Shropshire. The family owned Aldenham Hall since the fourteenth century. The first Acton to be a baronet won the title when he stood by King Charles I at the beginning of the English civil war. The future sixth baronet, rather distant by descent from the Aldenham family, became an officer in the Tuscan navy. He did so well in Mediterranean fights that he was invited to reorganize the navy of the Kingdom of Naples; from which place he was soon in control of the exchequer and then was Prime Minister and the favourite of Queen Caroline. He was the Prime Minister when Nelson moored the British fleet at Naples and first met Emma Hamilton. In the midst of this power he succeeded unexpectedly to the Aldenham title and estate. At the age of sixty-four he married his niece (the marriage needed a dispensation from the Pope) and had two sons, both of whom died young: Richard, our Acton's father, the seventh baronet who died at the age of thirty-four, and Charles who became a cardinal and died when he was forty-four. Sir Richard married a German, the daughter of the Duke of Dalberg, with her family seat at Herrnsheim in the Rhineland. But the Dalberg family co-operated with Napoleon when he broke up the Holy Roman Empire and so, when Napoleon lost the battle of Waterloo, their position was not comfortable and they were no longer a wealthy family.

When our John Acton was one year old his father died in

Paris and was buried at St Thomas' church; and the baby became the eighth baronet. As a child he was delicate and subject to attacks of quinsy.[1] He was known comically to his mother as Lord Patapouf.[2] At the age of eight was sent by his mother and new step-father Leveson (soon to be Earl Granville) to school in Paris, a rather aristocratic place for little boys under the general oversight of the most famous confessor in Paris, the Abbé Dupanloup. There he was taught by the curé of St Thomas (whom he enjoyed) and into adult life when he went to church in Paris he liked to go to St Thomas's because it was the place of his unknown father's funeral.[3]

His mother when in Paris used Dupanloup as her confessor; and an affection grew up between them, and she made sure that Dupanloup cared about her son's younger education. She received a report from Dupanloup on the boy: 'he is firm, open, decided'.

For his secondary education he was sent to the Roman Catholic College of Oscott near Birmingham. He was idle.

There were rows between the young adolescent and the masters at Oscott. But he grew; and the growth was helped by the undertaking that if he worked hard and got true academic results, they would send him abroad for a year to study; he began to work very hard, so that his step-father could even congratulate him on his new 'thirst for knowledge'.

After Oscott his family mulled half-heartedly on whether he should go to Oxford or Cambridge. At Oxford he must profess the faith of the Church of England at entry and therefore that was impossible. At Cambridge he would only have to profess the faith of the Church of England on taking a degree, and therefore it was theoretically possible to go as undergraduate to Cambridge and not to receive the BA degree; and his own uncle, who had become a cardinal, had studied as an undergraduate at

[1] 8121/6/146.
[2] 8121/6/172.
[3] 8121/7/862.

Magdalene College. His step-father, a loyal Anglican, was convinced that this Catholic boy would do better to have his higher education among other English young people so that he should not in future life be 'odd' and would be a familiar part of the society in which he would have to live as a squire. Married to a devout Catholic wife, Granville had no desire to convert her son out of Catholicism, but he wanted 'English normality' in education, so that Acton should not be different from all his contemporaries and so be at a disadvantage. But this plan of going to Cambridge depended on whether a college was willing to accept him – which meant, accepting a student who broke the college rules by not worshipping in the college chapel. And although Magdalene College had accepted his uncle on these terms, recent decades had made everyone fussy about such rules, and approaches for such exemptions for Acton were unsuccessful.

It was agreed therefore that he should go to Munich university for one year where he could learn German and study and then come back to England to try again for Cambridge or perhaps one of the Scottish universities where the same rules were flexible or perhaps London university where there were no such rules. Granville regarded it as very desirable that the higher education should be in Britain. He had no idea that when they sent him to Munich they took one of the two most decisive steps of Acton's life.

Munich had the advantage; the Arco-Valley family, seat at St Martin near Ried in Upper Austria, but with a villa at Tegernsee near Munich, and with much employment over the centuries from the Bavarian government, were related to the Actons by marriage. The Arco family was originally from the Northern Trentino in the Middle Ages and so under the prince-bishopric of Trent. Since the fifteenth century the family had served much in government service for Austria or Bavaria, often in the Italian portion of the Holy Roman Empire. The present count was Maximilian who had married Anna the daughter of the Marquis Marescalchi of Bologna and of a Brignole-Sale, a family of Paris.

Hence, when Acton became a sort of member of the Arco-Valley family, he had an easy base not only in Munich, and at the Arco-Valley chateau at St Martin in Upper Austria, but in Italy at Bologna and in France at Paris.

The Arcos could look after the young man. They arranged that the one-year student should move into an austere bedroom as a lodger in the house of the professor of church history, Döllinger. In June 1850 aged sixteen and a half Acton arrived at Munich. The bed was uncomfortable. Ever afterwards he regarded the room which he then occupied as haunted with breaths of inspiration – 'the best and happiest recollections of my boyhood'.[4]

It was intended to be a visit of a year or more before he came back to a British university and his mother and step-father did not suppose that Munich was to be his university. The meeting with Döllinger proved to be an epoch in the life of both tutor and pupil. Acton found the father he had never known, Döllinger discovered the son whom as a celibate priest he could not beget. He found a gifted boy, who earlier in his education had been idle, but now was on fire for scholarship. He made him work very hard.

And now there were two different pressures upon his future course. His Protestant step-father wanted an English education, if possible at an old university. The Catholics must take a different view. Here was the heir to one of the few great Catholic places in English society. He must be brought up a devout convinced and loyal Catholic. To send him to Protestant Cambridge or religionless London was to risk his steadiness of conviction. Döllinger had the reputation at that moment of being the weightiest defender of the Pope and the Catholic faith in all Germany. It must please leading Catholics of England that their young hopeful studied under his care.

But the argument was settled by the teenage subject of these

___

[4] 8121/7/825.

discussions. It was no longer a doubt of where best to study. It had become now a question of affection, filial. He had started to idolise Döllinger. The prospect of studying anywhere else was very unattractive.

The step-father did not give way without a fight. He was sure that it was a future disadvantage to Acton in an English life to have had a higher education outside Britain. He said so to Acton, more than once. Acton rashly argued to him that higher education produced a freedom from prejudice as its best objective and that he would be far more free from conventional English prejudices if he finished his higher education at Munich instead of Britain:

Granville wrote to Acton on 21 July 1852:

I rejoice in your hatred of prejudices, convinced as I am of the difficulty of avoiding them, especially by those who pique themselves the most on their freedom from any, but when you demonstrate that England France Italy and Northern Germany are incapable of affording you the means of continuing that course of study which you have begun so well in Munich, and that the latter place is absolutely the only one fitted for this purpose it appears that you prove a little too much.

I should regret extremely your adoption of English prejudices, but unless at your critical age you imbibe some sympathy with the peculiar feelings of the people with whom you are to act thro' life, I am afraid that you will not obtain that sympathy from them without which your powers of being useful must be diminished.

However, mother and step-father consented that he should stay for one more year's study at Munich. They hoped that he would not confine his studies to medieval history, which was Döllinger's strength and Acton's new love. Granville told him that physical science is important today.[5]

Acton later gave a picture of his own development – a young man who totally accepted that the faith in which he was brought up 'is morality and truth, absolutely without any weak point'.

---

[5] Granville to Acton (from Carlsbad), 21 July 1852, 8121/6/67ff.

Looking back he knew that at that time he had a strong tendency to hero-worship.[6]

'Endurance' was a gift which Acton attributed to his time under Döllinger.[7] It was not the only gift which afterwards he thought that he learnt in that house – also habits of thoughtfulness, patience, clearness and confidence.

It happened that Döllinger was on his academic travels. Two months after he arrived at Munich Döllinger took him with him through Switzerland to Milan and met Italian scholars and then came back through Vienna. In May 1851 Döllinger took his now seventeen-year-old pupil on a visit to the Catholics of England. They visited the new converts to Rome, Manning and Hope Scott; they called on Gladstone who had decided not to follow the others to Rome, and heard him speak in Parliament and Döllinger did not like him; they went to Birmingham and called on Newman, recently settled to make the Oratory there, and found that Newman was bothered about the crowning of Napoleon by Pope Plus VII and Döllinger defended the Pope to Newman. Then they went to Oxford and visited the surviving leaders of the Oxford Movement and dined with Mozley in Magdalene and with Marriott in Oriel; and saw Church in Oriel and Pusey in Christ Church; and lastly they went to London and saw the new Cardinal Wiseman. It was a very privileged tour for an impressionable and adolescent hereditary Catholic.[8] They were both ultramontanes. Döllinger was regarded as the historical leader of the ultramontane movement in Germany, who could show how Protestants corrupted the history of the Church. The adolescent Acton shared his master's viewpoint absolutely. Protestants were the enemies and better history could prove that they were not only wrong but immoral in their use of history.

In the next year 1852 (he was eighteen) Döllinger took him

[6] Conz., III, p. 288, June 1882.
[7] 8121/7/826.
[8] Friedrich, *Döllinger*, III, p. 105.

again into Switzerland and Italy and they visited the pilgrimage sanctuary of Einsiedeln and worked in the library at Florence. The place that was truly important to him was Venice; for the Austrians had opened the Venetian state archives and for the first time in his life Acton was able to learn history from original documents instead of other people's books. It was a lesson he did not forget. He always looked back on Venice with gratitude as an experience essential in his training as a historian.[9]

In the year after that he was in Paris and at parties heard gossip against Dupanloup who had been made the Bishop of Orleans not to everyone's pleasure, and heard rumours against the Emperor Napoleon and the Empress Eugénie, and associated with several of the leading French Liberal Catholics. But his not Liberal state of mind may be shown by his vehement assertion that Eckstein was the giant among historians; and Eckstein, despite his German name, was the historian who represented in historical work the extreme Catholic right wing in France.[10]

But he was impressed by a statesman among the French Liberal Catholics – the Count de Falloux.

Looking back he felt Falloux to be the most distinguished of them, his refinement and yet his spirit and his person 'full of point'. It puzzled the young Acton that Falloux could be a very pious Catholic and at the same time a Legitimist for the Bourbons on one side and a Liberal in politics on the other. The spectacle of Falloux seems to have widened Acton's vision of what was possible.

All this was not easy to reconcile and harmonize, and this difficulty, together with the fact that he belonged essentially to the defeated minority, developed an extraordinary artfulness, dexterity and tact, which his nobility of manner, and his religious tone, prevented from degenerating into deceit and falseness . . . He was in my opinion grossly superficial, not scrupulous, and in later years disgusted and nervous, but at

[9] Cf. to Annie, no. 126, 12 April 1896.
[10] Cf. FL I, p. 18.

his best very able, dominating, high-spirited, and the greatest statesman the Catholic party had produced.[11]

He felt later that he owed these French Liberal Catholics a good
deal 'in the way of light and help'.

Not without much doubt on the part of both Döllinger and
his step-father, lest he interrupt his education too sharply, he
went to the United States. The expedition did not lead him then
to admire the United States.[12]

In 1853–4 Döllinger gave a course in Munich university on
the French Revolution. Acton found this course to be 'a revelation' to him[13] by which he must mean that it was formative of
his historical ideals.

In 1854 he was twenty. Because of Döllinger and all that had
happened he had grown out of any form of adolescent revolt
against his mother and step-father – 'What immense pleasure',
wrote Granville to Acton, 'to see the development of all your
great qualities and I cannot say how much I feel your manner
towards your mother and me'.[14]

Acton had another chance of widening his range. Granville
was appointed the English representative at the coronation of
the new Russian Tsar. This was very interesting and an honour
but a worry because Parliament only allowed him £10,000 for
expenses – 'stingy' said Granville to Acton, and he knew that his
expenses must exceed that if he were to appear properly and had
little private money to supplement the grant. Acton went on
ahead to St Petersburg and Moscow and arranged accommo-

---

[11] To Annie, no. 64, 7 April 1893. She was trying to study Liberal Catholicism. By the
time he wrote that judgement he knew that Falloux had died in disgrace among both
royalists and ultramontane Catholics.

[12] Part of his diary in the United States, printed in *Fortnightly Review*, November 1921
and January 1922.

[13] To Jeannette Döllinger, 8121/6/645.

[14] 8121/6/68 from Aldenham, 26 December 1854. His step-father asked him about Aldenham. Under the will of his father the house and gardens were left in trust for
Acton's mother during her lifetime and she and Lord Granville were living there.
The difficulty now was that money needed spending on it and Granville saw he could
not spend money on the estate if he would soon lose it because his step-son married
and needed it.

dation and equipment including eight black horses for his coach
and a handsome harness and the hire of stables – everything for
thirteen attachés and one doctor as well as Granville's wife who
was Acton's mother.[15] There was no point in his after life when
he admired the Russian system of government.

The year after that Döllinger took him again to Italy and for
the first time Acton saw Rome. He fell in love with the city. He
felt this first visit to be an epoch in his life. He thought people
ought to go round it not with one guide-book but with three,
and not be afraid of going over the same ground again and again.
He found St Peter's the most fascinating because of its history,
(but it 'leaves one cold – can pray better in Gothic churches')[16];
Santa Maria Maggiore the loveliest, and the Minerva next most
interesting. He was in the congregation at St Peter's when the
silver trumpets carried on the high notes as the voices died away
at the elevation of the sacrament and found it a superb moment.
'It makes my heart throb when I set foot in the churches there'.[17]
It is the place, he later told his daughter, 'that I love best in the
world'.

Though he remembered that Popes had done harm, the
memory did not lessen his ecstasy with papal Rome. 'Remember
how long Rome has been the centre of religious history on the
earth, and never allow that sublime thought to be darkened by
shadows of earth, and the mass of evil and of wrong pressing on
what is holy. Edification is from God, very rarely indeed from
man.' Again and again he went back to his favourite monuments
of history – the tomb of Sixtus, the monument of Innocent, the
head of Antony, and the head of Scipio. 'Nothing helps one to
realize the past as Rome does . . . It is there I learned to find the
dead so terribly alive, that they are nearer to me than the events
of the day . . .' This was Döllinger's only visit to Rome and he
was surprised at the friendliness which met him. Acton kept a

---

[15] 8121/6/70.
[16] Rome diary, 22 June 1856; the diary was part printed by Herbert Butterfield in *CHJ*,
8 (1946), 186ff.
[17] Acton to Annie, nos. 122–3, 2–3 March 1896.

diary of the Rome visit which, a sign of discipleship, he mostly used for jotting down remarks by his teacher.

Döllinger took him to an audience with the Pope. It was the first time that Acton saw and met the Vatican archivist Theiner who was to prove so important to his historical studies. For Theiner stood beside the Pope at the audience, no doubt in case the German language should be needed – but they spoke French, the Pope speaking it badly. Acton was impressed by Theiner – he 'is more in the Pope's confidence than anybody'. Döllinger told him that Theiner had obtained permission to publish the acts of the Council of Trent, hitherto kept very secret.

A week later Acton had a family audience with the Pope – his Dalberg grandmother whom he called Nonna, two English cousins and a Dalberg cousin. Nonna was famous for her Catholic piety and known to the Pope and she presented them. The Pope knew about Acton because his uncle had been a cardinal. She made Acton talk a little; and the Pope said he 'had heard so much of our brilliancy, and of my mother's religiousness' from Monsignor Chigi (who was then the nuncio to Bavaria); and gave them his blessing.

Acton had a third audience on 12 June 1857, a month after the first. This time they talked on English affairs and English statesmen, little to the credit of Palmerston and even less to the credit of Gladstone – the Pope not knowing that he spoke to a young man who later was to be the closest to Gladstone of all the British.

Acton, ecstatic about his discovery of papal Rome, was not very impressed with the Pope: a likeable man, and kind, and generous, but fat, and taking a deal of snuff, and rather torpid, and old, and weak, and caring nothing about things of the mind, and leaving all the administration of the Papal State to his henchmen – that was how he recorded his experience of Pius IX.

Acton came away sure that the city of Rome satisfied his religious heart; and with a sense of political trouble ahead – the contrast between the holy city with its clerical government, and the showmen and gamblers and lotteries and torch-light dancers and riders or mule-drivers maltreating their animals terribly and violence in bars and 'peacock-flunkies that block up the approaches of cardinals' – could it survive as it was?[18]

That autumn he unexpectedly became the half-owner of a Catholic English periodical, the *Rambler*. The managers needed money to keep going so they approached a Catholic aristocrat with an estate. It was English and intelligent which meant not many Catholic readers (never more than 1,000), for Irish readers had other journals. So it struggled. It also struggled because bishops found its intelligence daring enough to be disturbing.

Acton had an aim which precisely fitted the goals of the *Rambler*. Educated at a first-class university in Germany, he saw the failure of Catholic higher education in England. He wanted better Catholic schools, if possible a Catholic university. It was Newman's aim, and of various of the converts who while Anglicans had been educated at Oxford. He and they did not hope to make Protestants agree with them but wanted Catholic thought not to be despised by Protestants as contemptible.

In becoming a proprietor Acton inherited another proprietor and writer for the paper – Richard Simpson, an ex-Anglican from Newman's Oriel College and a first-class mind. Posterity argued whether Simpson was bad for Acton or not. For Simpson had literary force; cared not at all whether he offended pious readers; was a deeply religious person who diminished his influence because the pen was carried away by his wit and sense of the comic. If people are ridiculous they should be exposed; and no one is exempt from this law, certainly not bishops, not even Popes, not even saints. Whether it was the ability; or the range of information; or the streak of the irreverent; or whether it was that Acton had an admiring nature for anyone who tried to think – this mind appealed to Acton and soon the pair were not only colleagues on a periodical but close friends. On his side Simpson discovered that they gained not only a young backer

[18] Cf. *Rambler*, 2 (1858), 281.

with money but a journalist with a rare range in history. The journal and the friendship were to bring the young Catholic squire, rising hope of the Church in England, into the same suspicion from the bishops. Already, by the autumn of 1858, the ill-repute reached the Pope's English chamberlain, Monsignor Talbot, who had been kind to Acton in Rome the year before. He now linked him with Simpson and Döllinger as Catholics whose work was to be doubted. And the Pope listened to what Talbot said about the English.[19]

Through an excellent editing of Simpson's letters we now know which anonymous articles in the *Rambler* were written by the young Acton, still only twenty-four when he started. He was devastating like clever young men when they begin to write for the press. Buckle's *History of Civilization*, which was a pretentious effort at social history, received no more ferocious demolition than that by the anonymous Acton in the *Rambler* ('dishonest affectation of knowledge with which he deludes his readers', 'the vulgar practice of reading the books one is to write about was beneath so great a philosopher' – and much else of such scorn). The reviewing had faults, one of which remained with him into maturity. He poured contempt on some writers because they had not read the latest German work on the subject which in Acton's eyes was indispensable. Later he grew out of this sin. But he loved also to cite learned German authorities, sometimes at length; that is, he had the habit of displaying a rare knowledge which was not necessary to his case.

But it was not all scorn. He had heroes: Burke 'the greatest statesman' – this was not only because Burke had a part-Catholic family and advocated the cause of Catholic emancipation. Burke advocated a conservatism on liberal grounds, a philosophy to which Acton was already attuned. His own teacher Lasaulx of Munich was another hero, this time overvalued ('one of the greatest modern scholars'); and these German heroes included Protestants such as Roscher ('one who has no superior among the political historians of the present day'). There is a high value

---

[19] Cf. Altholtz, p. 75 note.

put upon the Germans – for Acton was half a German – and a low value put upon the French, a nation which deserved this despotism by an incompetent Napoleon III, and was foolish enough to admire Chateaubriand (ignorant, prejudiced and immoral); with certain exceptions, the Savoyard de Maistre who was so papalist, Montalembert because he stood up against French tyranny. Already Acton had accepted the basic doctrine of the best French Liberal Catholics – 'A free Church implies a free nation' – 'He that deems he can advocate the cause of religion without at the same time the cause of freedom, is no better than a hypocrite and a traitor'. All the British historians he eyed with an unfriendly air – Macaulay because he was foolish enough to believe in progress, Lingard though he was a Catholic, Hume, even Gibbon; and Carlyle, who once did good by introducing German scholarship, is now commiting absurdities in his life of Frederick the Great.

What should Acton do? In 1859 he was twenty-five. It was evident that he had a powerful mind. He could speak French and German fluently and some Italian. He was beginning to be well-read. He could not sit back on the estate at Aldenham as an hereditary Catholic squire and baronet. Dupanloup and others had hoped that he would become a leader of the Catholic lay people in England.

There were three possibilities: go into Parliament and be a politician, enter the diplomatic service, or dedicate himself to his love of history and write. In advising him, his step-father Granville narrowed the choice to the first or last; and much preferred the first, on an excellent and unusual ground. Someone who only achieves the second rank in politics achieves things that are important, whereas someone who only achieves the second rank among historians achieves little. And to understand politics, Granville argued perspicaciously, enables the historian to understand history the better. He pressed Acton to find a seat in Parliament.[20]

A Catholic baronet, not because he was a baronet but because

---

[20] Granville to Acton, 8121/6/74, 17 March 1857.

he was a Catholic, would almost certainly not be acceptable in an English constituency. It must be an Irish seat. That he was not Irish was a disadvantage; but to the Irish his Catholicism was more important than his mixed race.

In April 1859 Granville wrote to him (he was in Germany, as much to economize on living abroad as to be near Döllinger) that if he would send £700 ('to be spent legitimately and not as bribery') he could be certainly returned to the House of Commons for the Irish seat of Carlow. The head priest of the town had been asked and was in favour. In 1859 Acton became MP for Carlow. The newspapers at first reported it as a Conservative victory but they were wrong; and when this was clear he was unjustly abused in the *Daily News* (18th May 1859) as one who was elected in his absence or because of his absence and was guilty of bad manners and impertinence.

To go into the House of Commons did not seem the obvious way to study history which was becoming his passion. To have such a man in the House was an advantage to the rarefied upper class of English Catholics. They were pleased with him. He still looked like the rising hope of English Catholicism.

But soon the contentment was less. He did not appear in Carlow for the election and for two years after the election he was seen in the town only once. Those close to him soon worried when they heard him talking of giving up his seat. He was passionate to study and do what he could for the Catholic cause by writing and politics felt to him an intrusion. In August 1861 he told his stepfather that he wanted to resign his seat. Granville was very sorry, and his letter to Acton showed that he was angry. 'Your poor mother would have been miserable at the thought of it.' (His mother died the year before.) 'If you marry it would make a difference to the position of your wife in England. All the Catholics whom I saw in Ireland thought you had a great future. Exert yourself. It would be moral cowardice to run away. It appears madness to give up the battle beforehand.'[21]

---

[21] 8121/6/113.

His contributions to the *Rambler*, and then to its successor (1862–3) the *Home and Foreign Review*, have strong characteristics. In longer articles he could bore the reader, the point is made at length. He could be crisp in shorter notes. He was very traditional in certain Catholic attitudes – the Dark Ages laid the foundations of our happiness and our civilization, when the people were truly Catholic; the Reformation caused the decline and the miseries of the modern centuries; because the Church rests on conscience it is the enemy of every form of despotism, whether wielded by monarchs or by democrats; the Church and its laws are the safeguard of true freedom. On top of these old axioms, he believed that the Germans – that includes all the Germanic tribes – were the peoples whose directness and strength linked with the Christian inheritance from Rome to beget a truly civilized world.

He showed much thought over the nature of history. It must be not only a history of events and a social analysis, but a history of mind. Several times he wrote articles on the development of history in his generation and sometimes they are profound and sometimes they leave the reader with the impression that this young historian still struggles with the nature of his craft. He was aware of the risk that every historian sees events with the prejudice which is the axiom of his own generation, and unconsciously assumes that whichever side won the victory was the better; of the fatal effect if historians make their description of the past a dry series of facts – though two of his own articles have sections which are open to this charge; of the difference made to history by the new ability to check and compare old evidence; and in Church history, of the necessity to abandon old and valued legends if the historian proves them not to be based upon reality. He had no contempt for those who valued old legend; and saw that a legend that is believed tells us something about the age in which it is valued. But history is truth and a Church accepts as part of God's gift whatever truth is proven.

He was very frank over the inadequacy of Catholic intellectual life as he found it, in England; and was over-confident that his own journal would raise its standards.

He suffered one historical disaster, the only big one which he suffered as a historian, though he might have suffered more if he had published more during his life. A forger of the eighteenth century produced a book by King Frederick the Great of Prussia, called *Royal Mornings, or the Art of Reigning*. The author hated Frederick and wished to represent him as immoral and without conscience as a politician and military leader and so put worse than the principles of Machiavelli into his mouth. When Napoleon was in Berlin his secretary discovered a copy of the text and this was what was republished and which Acton had. He accepted it as genuine and wrote a review of it as *The Confessions of Frederick the Great*.

This disaster was caused by two pieces of Acton's mind which affected his history all his life even when he was mature. In his young years he acquired the belief that all governments are bad; some less bad than others but wishing to restrict the freedoms of the individual for the benefit of the whole and all willing to accept that a moral law which applies to men and women cannot apply to their governments; that *reason of State* is a prime source of tyranny and democratic governments are as liable to misuse it as any other form of constitution. Therefore, if a king with an almost absolute power said that the only way to govern well is for the ruler to be unscrupulous, this was a marvellous illustration of a continual danger which afflicts all governments.

It mattered to Acton that this new Machiavelli was a Prussian king. He was half a Rhinelander by descent from his mother. He had many links with Bavaria and was soon to marry a Bavarian. His guide in life was the Christian leader of Bavaria. Both the Rhinelander and the Bavarian in his background resented the steps, not always acceptable ethically, by which the Prussian State worked towards its modern dominance in Germany.

The second trait which made him apt to think this forgery genuine was a natural weakness which afterwards kept reappearing. He found history fascinating and part of the excitement was the amazing events or people that happened. If he found extraordinary evidence for something, he was more likely to believe the evidence because it was extraordinary and less likely to exercise his sharp critical faculty.

Although he hardly ever spoke in the House of Commons, and worried about resigning his seat for the sake of a higher vocation, the place in Parliament was a political experience and he turned his historical fascination to the influence of the history of the peoples upon their present predicament. He began to think hard about political theory and to write about it anonymously.

This was given a sharp impetus by the events of 1859–60 in Italy.

The French Emperor Napoleon III made it possible for Piedmont to turn the Austrians out of Italy except Venice; for the Tuscans to ask to join Piedmont, for the northern Papal States to revolt against the Pope and ask to be united with Piedmont, and then for Garibaldi and the Piedmontese to overrun South Italy and Sicily and make a united kingdom of Italy except for Venice and what was left to the Pope in Lazio round Rome and the still Austrian valleys to the north of Milan and Verona.

All Catholics needed to ask what were their attitudes to the loss by the Pope of most of his historic State, including its only prosperous part, the Legations with their capital at Bologna. Acton needed to define what he thought.

He knew Bologna well. One grandmother still lived there. He was the grandson of a prime minister of a State which had just been overrun by guerrilla forces, illegally by international law. He had in his being a sense of legitimate right – sovereigns might or might not govern well, and he accepted that neither the King of Naples nor the Pope could be defended by the plea that their government was not to be improved; but they were part of the stable European order which no one ought to overturn by illegal force. Further, he loathed the Emperor of France, a usurping despot, who made all these changes possible. Further, he was a devout Catholic who honoured the Pope highly and the Pope told the world that his historic Papal States were a necessity for his spiritual office as the head of the Catholic Church. Further, he was the member of Parliament for an Irish constituency and his people identified the Pope with their religion which was part of their national resistance against the English.

But Acton was also a liberal who idolized Burke and longed for constitutional government everywhere. This inner conflict between his legitimism and his desire for freedom made him for a time very complicated to read. It was not only an inner conflict for Acton but for everyone in Europe who thought seriously about politics in the middle nineteenth century. But Acton's mental predicament was specially tense. Some paragraphs of some articles need to be read several times and at the end the reader is still not sure what he meant. He took refuge in vast platitudes; 'Duty cannot be dissociated from right' and such uninforming sentences.

Of one thing he was very sure: this new idea which runs through the world, nationality, is pernicious. The banditry which has lately united Italy is justified by its defenders on the plea that there is a tribe, the Italian nation, all of whom have the right to be members of the same State. But there are Italians in London or in Uruguay. It is a very bad State which regards it as its duty only to care for the members of the dominant race which lives within its borders. It is the duty of a State to care for all its inhabitants. Therefore, the best States are those with more than one race within them, for these preserve liberty for the minorities best – the British, the Swiss, the Austro-Hungarians.

He would not have been surprised but would have regarded it as inevitable, that the making of a nation of Italy should have ended in Mussolini and that the making of a German nation should have ended in Nazis, for whom the State's only duty was directed towards a single dominant race.

His second conviction was the Christian conviction that religion demanded the non-racialist State. It was the vocation of the Churches to encourage an international society where racial barriers were overcome, where Greek was not by race an enemy of the Scythian.

His third conviction was that which thrust him into trouble with his fellow-Catholics.

The Pope said very loudly – if it were not impossible to think of a clamorous Pope we should say that he shouted – that all his States, from Ferrara in the north to the borders with Naples in the south, had been given to the Church as a gift to God and like all gifts to God could not be alienated and that anyone who took away any part of them was guilty of sacrilege. He further said that benefactors donated these gifts to enable the head of the Church to be free in his spiritual work, which he could not be if he were the subject of any State.

Thus the defence of the Papal States against its conquerors rested for Catholics on doctrine. These lands are essential, all of them, to his work for good in the world.

Acton had two reasons for not believing this to be the correct defence. The first was that it did not convince reasonable people. Would the Pope really be less hampered in his work for God if as a secular sovereign he did not rule the city of Ferrara? Even average intelligence saw that he might be freed from a blot hampering his spiritual work if he shed some of his worldly duties.

The second was that Döllinger, the person whom Acton idolised above his other heroes, and who was famous as the Catholic stalwart of Germany, allowed that in providence it might be good for the Pope to lose his secular power at least for a time. The Papal States hurt the reputation of the Church because they have won the name of being governed badly. At this moment, believed Döllinger, they were more of a misfortune to the Church than the temporary loss of them would be. Catholics should face this. To be no one's subject was necessary to the spiritual work of the Pope. Therefore sooner or later he will receive back some kind of Papal State. But when and how this will happen, we leave to providence.

Hence Acton's defence of the Papal States was weak in the eyes of his co-religionists. You cannot defend them on spiritual

grounds, no one will believe you. The only defence is international law – this is a gross breach of European treaties and
what may happen later to public order if it is allowed? To other
Catholics this was a weaker defence than the plea that God needs
the Papal States. It identified the Pope with Bourbons and old
legitimists, a vanishing Europe populated by eighteenth century
monarchs in wigs. 'If States would live, they must preserve their
organic connexion with their origin and history, which are their
root and their stem' . . . 'Revolution is a malady, a frenzy, an
interruption of a nation's growth'.[22] We remind ourselves again
that Acton was the grandson of the prime minister of Bourbon
Naples.

Yet he accepted that secular independence is necessary to a
Pope's religious work. He accepted that it may be better
(religiously better) in the circumstances of 1860 for the Church
to lose the Temporal Power for a time and wait for providence
to restore it.

He had trouble with his contributors to the journal about this
attitude. He had trouble with his old teacher Cardinal Wiseman
of Westminster. He had trouble with his old teacher Dupanloup,
now the Bishop of Orleans. He had no trouble with his friend
Newman because he discovered to his surprise that in Newman's
eyes the Pope could cheerfully lose all the Papal States and be
stronger thereby for his mission in religion.

This powerful and often scholarly journalism came to an
abrupt pause in the spring of 1864.

In Catholic Munich there had been a public scandal. A young
philosopher at the university, Frohschammer, wrote a modest
book about the theory of the soul. The Rome Congregation of
the Index ordered it to be withdrawn. Frohschammer asked why.
The censors of the Index refused to say. Frohschammer therefore refused to submit and turned rebellious and not slowly
moved out of Catholicism. Educated Bavarian opinion had much
sympathy for him and many felt that he was unfairly treated.

---

[22] Acton, 'Mr Goldwin Smith's Irish History', *Rambler*, 6 (1861–2), 199.

The scandal raised in a perturbing form the key question of the later nineteenth century for educated Catholics – what is the relation between research and authority? – research, where the scholars go for conclusions on evidence, and take no notice if a government or any other authority tells them that they must come to conclusions which that government thinks right; and the duty of the authorities of a Church to maintain the faith and the truth which they had received.

The accepted leader of Bavarian Catholics, Döllinger, believed it necessary to study the conflict seriously. With his friend Haneberg, who was the scholarly abbot of St Boniface in Munich, he invited the German Catholic professors to a Congress in Munich to frame their opinions on this debate. The Congress, which opened with high mass at St Boniface on 28 September 1863, was less divided than might be expected because most German professors of the right, that is the side of strong Papal authority, preferred not to attend. Acton was among the laymen present.

Döllinger was peaceable. He refused to accept a motion asking for an absolute freedom of scientific research. The Congress submitted their deliberations to the infallible authority of the Church. But in the course of his speech he offended a few in the meeting, first by seeming to carry the right to free research very far indeed, and secondly because he elevated the German theology to stardom in contrast with the impoverished theologies of France and Italy and Britain. No one in Rome minded if a German denounced theology in France and Britain, they thought him correct. But to denounce Italian theology was to scorn the school tradition in Roman divinity on which the authority of the Congregations of the Church rested in safeguarding the faith.

To understand what happened next it is necessary to remember the scandal of Frohschammer. On 21 December 1863 Pope Pius IX sent a Brief to the archbishop of Munich. He thought it extraordinary and unprecedented that professors should summon a conference without the leave of authority. He said that it was the duty of writers not only to accept the definitions of General Councils and the decrees of Popes, but to submit to the decisions of the Roman Congregations.

This Brief of December was not published till March 1864. Acton could not accept it. All governments have faults. An ecclesiastical government is not exempt from this law. The interests of a Church may be identical with the interests of its government but they may not be. The Church is infallible. But the organs of the Curia are not infallible. To say so is 'monstrous error'. They are attributing to the Congregation of the Index a divine authority when their only authority rests on whether they can understand the books which they censure.

Hence he decided to close his journal. The number of April 1864, soon after the Brief was known, was the last. His reasons were public-spirited. I do not believe what the Pope says; the Brief is not aimed at the journal but if it were I could not submit to it. The journal is based upon the axiom that Catholics are as free in science and history as every other person – excepting only the doctrines recognized to be the Catholic faith and declared to be so. If the journal persists, it can only end in a hardening of the attitude of the Roman Curia and in rebellion. That would damage the Church. So close the journal before it is assailed from Rome.

This sounds reverent to the Pope and was intended by Acton to be so. But the language in which he closed the journal could not be liked by eyes in Rome. His last paragraph was eloquent:

If the spirit of the *Home and Foreign Review* really animates those whose sympathy it enjoyed, neither their principles, nor their confidence, nor their hopes, will be shaken by its extinction. It was but a partial and temporary embodiment of an imperishable idea – the faint reflection of a light which still lives and burns in the hearts of the silent thinkers of the Church.

THE MARRIAGE

While Acton lived at Munich as a student in Döllinger's house he saw much of his relatives the Arco-Valley family and at the age of nineteen began a correspondence with the Countess Margareta. This was no ordinary series of letters. Acton did not easily get on with his mother in the flesh – he once apologized for her lack of consideration with the words 'it is her Englishness' – and quickly the Countess became to him a proxy-mother in his affections. At first he always signed himself in the Dalberg Germanic way J. Emerich, at first she was *My dear Aunt*, later (before he had married her daughter) she became *My dear Maman*, or sometimes (this time in English) *My own dearest Mamma* or *My own dearest love*. He was in the habit of looking every day at her portrait which he placed by his crucifix; and wrote to her in 1857, when he was twenty-three years old, that 'The last days we passed together are the happiest I have known till now. I never knew till then how I loved you, or how surely I could trust your friendship.'[23]

The wooing of the daughter Marie did not go easily. He knew her from 1851 but began to be attracted to her, as a possible wife, some five years later. At first the wooing still had peculiarity in that Acton began it under pressure both from his own mother and from his future wife's mother that this was the person whom he ought to marry. In love with a married Countess, he at first found marriage to her daughter the best possible next step. But soon Acton had passion. Marie would have nothing to do with any plan to marry. There were agonized letters to Marie's mother.

At the beginning of 1860 they were engaged to be married though it was not announced. She even received a wedding present from Acton's stepfather. Granville even wrote his stepson a business letter telling him what his wife, Acton's mother, would do for him in the way of a small allowance on his marriage, smaller than she would like because Granville himself had a heavy debt. There was an argument whether it would be best to sell Acton's stately home Aldenham to ensure that there was enough money.

[23] 8121/7/690/1.

But that spring of 1860 Marie Arco-Valley realized that it would not do and broke the engagement.

The cause of this break, which caused torment to Acton and affected him and his work for four years, was complex. There are signs that by then Acton was suspect to Rome as disloyal and that the devout Arco family were not enthusiastic to commit their daughter to a person with such a reputation. There is uncertain evidence that a Roman monsignor who knew the Arco family, Monsignor Nardi, warned them against the alliance. In Munich a young Bavarian came on the scene as another suitor for Marie and the evidence is that in intelligence and personality he could not compare with Acton – yet Marie was attracted. She made the mistake of concealing this attachment from Acton and allowing him to go on writing love letters to her while she was in love, or seemed to herself to be so, with another. Acton could not bear this – 'she has never thought of me except as a substitute, she has never understood the affection she rejected'. 'You preferred someone', he told her angrily, 'who notoriously was unworthy of you, who had played with your honour, and committed to your family an irreparable fault'.[24]

Marie was nervous of the powerful engine which was Acton's mind; it was formidable, the speed of intellect, the accuracy of memory, the range of knowledge, the command of his opinions, the force in the personality. There is evidence that she asked herself whether she could keep up with such a partner, and to doubt whether a non-intellectual wife could be happy with so intellectual a husband. And finally, Acton did something, as yet unknown, which led Marie to think that this fiancé was not likely to make a faithful husband.

She wrote him a letter saying that she would have nothing more to do with him; and another letter showing herself very grieved:

'I see that you very rapidly know how unhappy I am at the

[24] 8121/7/812.

24

frightful sin you have committed. This last message has cruelly destroyed the hope we have expressed so willingly . . .'.[25]

At first he thought that he could keep his affections with the mother while he broke relations with her daughter. But the situation was impossible.

He felt that he had lost the only true home he had ever known – 'I feel for the first time what it really is to be an orphan.'

By November that hard year 1860 Acton had made up his mind for the break and had thrown himself into work as the only cure for a broken heart.

Meanwhile others were at work about matrimony. At the age of twenty-six Acton was the most eligible bachelor in Catholic Britain, able, a member of Parliament, heir to a great estate and a title; and several Catholic noblemen or their wives who had daughters looked at him with interest; Lady Petre was one who destined her daughter for this vocation. At the beginning of August 1861 the *Morning Post* announced the marriage of Sir John Acton to Miss Ellis, daughter of a colonel.[26] At about the same time a lady sent a message to him proposing marriage. He did not see her again for thirty-three years.

In 1864 the friendship between Acton and Marie was renewed; friendship is too weak a word for Acton's passion. They met and Acton was astonished by what happened. She had refused his advances repeatedly. The question of marriage was on again. He raised doubts with her, whether she could think him the right person. Her father was troubled because he was getting known as a Catholic who attacked what the Pope stood for; for the same reason her mother could not bring herself to trust him. He wrote to Marie, 'Since my principles will not triumph in our time at Rome, my person will always he hated there'. Or again, 'You have to ask yourself', he wrote to Marie, 'whether you can rest in full confidence in my judgment and be my companion in a career that is so little a career of triumph . . . Reflect on all this,

---

[25] Marie Arco to Acton, 14 March 1860, 8121/6/452.
[26] 8121/6/110, Cf. to Mamy, 18 and 19 April 1894.

Marie, and tell me if you are secure of our future'. If all was well they ought to announce the marriage very soon and fix it for the summer of 1865 – 'I am an insensé (mad about you). I love you with all my heart.'[27]

They announced the engagement. All was not plain sailing. 'Your grandmother cannot reconcile herself to my character and my ideas'.[28] But the love letters which he wrote during his engagement were charming – 'my own darling', 'my treasure', 'I love you with all the force of my heart' etc. and she must have loved receiving them. He always felt near to her in moments of prayer. The letters have religion in them, more than religion, a deep piety. 'Don't forget to pray for me.' He liked to tell her about his priest at Aldenham, Mr Green, and how 'scandalized' he was that Mr Green could not celebrate mass on Maundy Thursday. He liked Mr Green but found his sermons rambling. When he was in London he went to church at the Jesuits. He thought of his bride and himself receiving the sacrament side by side, and how 'I can think of nothing more conducive to piety' than that act. He told her how sorry he was that before he left Rome that winter he failed to perform an act of pilgrimage which much later in life he would have looked upon with rueful contempt – the ascending of the Scala Santa on his knees. 'This morning at communion I felt almost overawed by the wonderful goodness of Almighty God to me, and the immense promise of happiness before me. There is no love like yours, for it belongs as much to the next life as to the present.'[29]

His grandmother Nonna showered him with letters, page after page full of religious devotion mingled with care for him; worrying that her young grandson might lose his faith, praying hard in the calamity of his broken engagement, reminding him each year of prayers on the date of his father's death on 31

---

[27] 8121/7/810, 812.
[28] Acton (from London), 28 April 1865, 8121/7/843; cf 858.
[29] 8121/7/832, 877.

January; and he was thankful that she promised to give him as a wedding present a reliquary, which, he told his fiancée (20 April 1865), should hang in their room and be especially a memorial to his uncle Cardinal Acton. He was not uncritical about his grandmother – 'she is very affectionate, in spite of great selfishness, insincerity and affectation'[30] and most recipients would have been impatient with the pile of piety which came through the post, but he had his own affection for the old lady. She could not now be any 'use' to their family life, and felt herself to belong to a generation that was gone, but he and his new wife must do what they could to take care of her. He was even more critical of Marie's grandmother who was so doubtful of him as a liberal Catholic – 'do not allow yourself to be deluded' he told the granddaughter, 'by her real, ostensible, good qualities. These can co-exist with great defects, and with the greatest errors in the way of understanding religion'.[31] Of course the letters to Marie before the approaching marriage are also full of more material things, like carpets and curtains and jewels and shawls and presents to the future bridesmaids. But it pleased his heart to think of Marie passing her Holy Week that spring in devotions at Rome; and to hear how she was a little critical of all the pomp and ceremony and how she wished for a devotion less noisy and less public 'where the soul is more closely united to God, and feels His presence in peace and silence better than in the midst of crowds and spectacles', and where the mind is distracted by the knowledge that the other people are not really praying but are wondering at a show and so 'the atmosphere is not one of piety'.

But the Church is so founded by our Lord that the real edification and piety are as great in the poorest and remotest and humblest congregations, and the pulse of faith beats as strongly in those extremities as in the heart and centre, which is surrounded by all the material wealth

---

[30] Acton to Marie, April 1865, 8121/7/843.
[31] 8121/7/843.

and resources of the religious world. Perhaps you will be more deeply struck with the simple zeal of the poor Catholics in this country than by the splendours of St Peter's.[32]

One of the practical matters to be discussed was the search for Catholic servants for Aldenham – a Catholic cook-housekeeper (who was French but had been many years in England) and other Catholic servants. He was very pleased to be at mass when Mr Green announced their forthcoming marriage.[33]

He was very confident in his own intelligence, much less confident about his own character. 'You are going to marry such a selfish husband. But I don't believe my bad qualities are as great as your virtues and still hope that my new conscience and guide will teach me the way to grow better.'[34] But he somehow thought of her as a person much in need of his protective instinct. He often addressed letters to her as 'my child'. As he moved across Europe to the wedding at St Martin (26 August 1865) there was comment in the English newspapers.

During the six years after he entered Parliament, Acton's Catholic mind hardened into that of a rebel in his Church. That was partly due to the Pope and his defence against onslaughts of the world. But we cannot doubt that the agonies of a passionate emotional life had something to do with his developing psychology, and that Marie was unintentionally a little to blame for what affected not only his career as a public man but what was possible for him as a historian.

---

[32] 8121/7/843.
[33] Acton to Marie, 8121/7/882.
[34] 8121/7/868.

2

AT THE VATICAN ARCHIVES

B Y common agreement all governments restrict access to their papers. For a time at least reason of state demands that historians be allowed no access. The British government has brought this time down to thirty years – but only for that majority of papers which reason of state allows. The needs of government and the wishes of the historian conflict.

Acton, who was as personally engaged in the problem as any historian, defined it as *the enmity between the truth of history and the reason of state, between sincere quest and official secrecy*.[1]

Two different kinds of institution generate special difficulty of this nature. One is a personal monarchy. The Queen makes the Royal Archives available to authorized enquirers. But the Royal Archives contain not only some records of government but the papers of a private family, and a family is entitled to that privacy conceded to every other less prominent family. The other special case is a Church, especially the Roman Catholic Church.

Certain key-words made fanatics more fanatical: words like Pope, Jesuit, Index, Inquisition. If you open all the archives until thirty years ago, you open them to historians. You open them also to minds eager to find what discredits. Is it possible that the

---

[1] DD, p. 131.

impartiality of history is better served if the archives are closed than if they are open? Since feelings roused by religions run as deep in the human soul as passions roused by national conflict, the events of the past live in the present. Whether agents of the Church punish a man for saying that the earth went round the sun – whether the Council of Trent was no true ecumenical Council because the Pope controlled marionette bishops on invisible wires – whether a Pope was personally immoral – all these might afford matter for the obsessed, and might even affect attitudes among minds which were not obsessed. They all happen to be questions which only the archives might answer. In this argument between *truth of history* and *reason of state*, reason of state could be found arguing for a much longer closure of archives than that which advanced liberal governments came to adopt.

Modern history, sometimes called loosely 'scientific' history, made such progress during the middle of the last century that its new face affected everyone's attitudes towards the past, and therefore everyone's attitude towards the present. The principles or beliefs inherited in European tradition came under a new kind of examination. This touched all European culture. How and in what ways it affected culture is an intractable problem of intellectual history; whether it had its impact in ideals of education, or in personal approaches to literature, or in the evolutionary stances adapted from biology into other sciences, or in the analysis of politics and systems of government. To find tests of influences like these is doubtful work. The perspective towards life or society changed because people grew more informed in looking at the past. But how it changed, and how a picture of the world was altered, what difference was made to culture or viewpoint or morals, these aspects of the question are hard to test and not easy even to illustrate.

But religion is a realm where the inquiry sees results. The two akin religions of nineteenth-century Europe, Christianity and Judaism, are in their different ways religions in which history matters. The context of devotion and prayer, though of this moment, is nourished by the memory of past events. The body of doctrine is linked to men and women who lived, and to experiences which they endured, and records bearing the evidence concerning their human destiny. The Jewish and Christian memories were once identified with the historical perspectives of Europe. Religion had more sense of continuity with the past than any other element in the heritage which made up culture among the peoples. The ablest writers among early modern historians were students of Church history.

Therefore the coming of modern history, with its organization of libraries, and publication of manuscripts, and founding of learned journals, and slow creation of endowed posts for historians, could be seen to foster a view of the past which must influence religious attitudes, doctrines, and prayers. This happened in all the Christian Churches.

Among the Churches the Roman Catholic Church faced the challenge in ways which specially interest the historian of ideas. Conservative by inheritance of centuries, more conservative by resistance to radicals in the age of Reformation, ultra-conservative because in many countries a society of peasants or labourers who of all classes had minds least open to disturbing ideas, it was nevertheless a Church committed to history; that is, it could not sweep the challenge behind the door or pretend that it all sprang from infidel illusion. Some of the founders of modern history – Mabillon, Tillemont, Muratori, to mention only three – were dedicated priests. *Tradition* was important to the structure of doctrine which fed men's faith. To Protestant warriors tradition sounded like a way of closing the eyes to history – accept whatever most men believe today and refuse to ask whether they believed it yesterday. Catholic writers gave too much occasion for this charge. But tradition was continuity, and continuity was history. Commitment to tradition was also commitment to history, and a main reason why the study of Christian history was inescapable in Catholic teaching.

Facing this challenge in the realm of doctrine, Catholic thinkers began to analyse that relation between a belief and its definition in language which Newman called *development*. The idea of development had more than one ground, and was variously expressed, and had diverse consequences. But the momentous part of it was the recognition that history makes a difference to the religious understanding of the world.

A Church committed by principle to historical enquiry, and simultaneously committed by its members to conservative attitudes, must experience inward tension. The worst tension was generated by the argument over the relation between history and dogma. A lesser argument developed over the archives. Because we are committed to historical enquiry, is it our duty to allow free access to private archives, even if we are afraid that those who use the archives might change the understanding of the past, or injure the Church of the present?

The Vatican possessed a famous archive which touched the history of Europe over 1,000 years, and specially illuminated the past behaviour of Popes and other leaders of the Catholic Church. About access to this archive the argument became warm.

The political mind argued:

We have enemies in the world. Bad things happened in the past. If we open our archives, we let in not only neutrals who want to understand, or friends who have that sympathy which enables minds to understand better, but antagonists seeking to stir up dirt. Such hostile inquiry, especially if misused, hurts the institution; and in hurting the institution, hurts the world which the institution serves.

The historical mind argues:

The Church is committed to truth. The opening of archives is a necessary part of the quest for truth in an age of historical inquiry. Truth is an absolute good. No plea of political welfare can override the commitment. The Church wants to know what really happened. For the sake of that quest it must run the risk that fanatics misuse its documents. Misuse is of the moment, truth becomes a possession.

Each side had its case to advocate. Each side had inarticulate feelings even where its case was hard to argue. And if I think the historian to have the better cause, you will subtract some bias for the circumstance that it is the historian and not the statesman who must describe what happened.

From the earliest times the Pope, as head of a great administration, needed papers and books. Perhaps the example of the Roman emperor's civil service in Constantinople still ruled Rome, and the Pope kept a repository of papers in the Lateran. But, like other sovereigns of the Middle Ages, he often carried his papers round on his travels. As with secular perambulations of this sort, it was an easy way to lose letters. He probably had no systematic arrangement to collect and preserve letters and copies of letters until the pontificate of Pope Innocent III (died 1216) who was a lawyer.

The Pope, being bishop of a city, was more stable in one town than most medieval rulers. Nevertheless, even early in the fifteenth century, his main collection of papers was stored not in Rome but at Avignon.

Then the invention of printing increased the number of books, and all earlier forms of keeping books were made obsolete. Simultaneously the learning of the Renaissance began interest in manuscripts. In 1475, therefore, the Pope created a 'library' or rather extended the old library, gave a regular endowment and better buildings, and appointed a librarian, the humanist Platina, with a staff.

It was already the best stocked library in Italy. No library was yet large. It had under 4,000 volumes by 1484, but was important enough in 1527, when the emperor's army sacked Rome, to attract looters; less however for the value of manuscripts in a market or in scholarship than for seals in the making of bullets or for parchment as litter for horses. The soldiery had no idea of the value of what they tore or burnt. But several accounts describe the mass of original papal documents lying with precious manuscripts in the street. A lot was recovered later, or appeared elsewhere in Europe – one important Roman manuscript, perhaps lost during the sack, is still in the Bodleian

Library. One of the registers of Pope Alexander VI Borgia was returned in two pieces, with many pages missing, five years later.

From 1548 the status of the library was raised because henceforth the librarian was always a cardinal. But the cardinal's work took precedence of the librarian's work. The second of the cardinal-librarians was a boy of fourteen when he was appointed and, though well-educated for his age, was otherwise qualified by being a nephew of Pope Julius III. However the existence of a cardinal as figurehead of the library helped the real librarians, custodes, to get more of what they wanted.

Throughout Europe printed books poured into libraries and forced heads of institutions to build new libraries to house their growing collections. In these years the colleges of Cambridge University built their first libraries – one may be seen almost unchanged at Trinity Hall. Between 1587 and 1591, just when the old library at Trinity Hall was under construction, Sixtus V built the Vatican Library as it was to survive until near the end of the nineteenth century; Fontana's magnificent edifice. At first the change was no improvement to those who wished to consult books or papers. It took twenty years before everything was in order after the move and even then the large numbers of books were still uncatalogued. The needs of the library outgrew the endeavours of its exiguous staff, who were paid irregularly, and largely in kind.

The library was open two or three hours in the day for scholars to consult, though it was shut on frequent holidays. In 1591 Pope Gregory XIV issued a stern order against using documents without his permission. But visitors gained access easily enough and privileged scholars borrowed books comfortably. Cardinal Caesar Baronius took away a precious Greek manuscript for two months. But these freedoms varied according to the administration, and the works of scholarship which appeared were mostly due to officers of the library.

The archives were seldom accessible in this way. Only privileged members of the Curia consulted them, usually for business, but on rare occasions for history. Odorico Rinaldi used the archives to continue the Annals of Baronius, Pallavicino to write the official history of the Council of Trent.

Slowly library and archive were seen to be incompatible. The library became a treasure-house of ancient manuscripts and rare books, and clamoured to be used. The archive was full of the secret papers of government which unscrupulous men could misuse if they got copies; and the stringent precautions against consulting the archive spilled over into the attitudes to harmless scholars who needed the library. At the end of the sixteenth century Pope Clement VIII started to move archives away from the library and into the Castel Sant' Angelo. This was intended for security. But the papers were not stored in dungeons. They were needed. Busy men wished to find documents quickly. An ornamented hall on the upper floor of the castle was reserved and decorated and furnished with presses. A bull of 1593 was prepared to transfer all the archives to this repository. But second thoughts came, and the bull was never published. It was more convenient to have many of the papers in the Vatican, and the castle was considered a place of special safety for documents of exceptional value or secrecy.

The logical end was division between library and archives. In 1612, therefore, Pope Paul V reversed the policy of moving archives to the castle, but simultaneously separated library from archive as institutions. They were given separate heads. The archives were placed in a long wing of the Vatican Palace by the library. Into this building passed various groups of archives, with a nucleus in the volumes of papal registers which were hitherto kept for ready consultation in the 'wardrobe' above the Pope's apartments. Some of the papers from Sant' Angelo were carried back. But the most valuable or secret documents were still left in the castle for security.

The creation of the Archive – not called officially the Vatican Secret Archives until later – was a sensible act of administration. For until that moment papers lay about in each office. Different bureaux of the civil service still kept what they used. Therefore the new Papal archive was composed of the specially important papers in Castel Sant' Angelo (like the documents of the Council of Trent), the archive which already existed in the Vatican Library, of which the nucleus was 279 parchment registers from John VIII to Sixtus IV, the very incomplete records of the Secretary of State hitherto in the Castel Sant' Angelo, and the archives of the different offices (especially of the Treasury) which were now put, still with many exceptions, under the control of the central archive. Pope Paul V holds the honour of first creating an independent central archive which began to act like a magnet, slowly drawing towards itself the mass of various collections from various offices.

The creation of a central archive owed nothing to the notion of helping scholars to write history. It was a business transaction intended to make the administration more efficient. The Pope's major-domo was blunt in his material view of the gain. 'Old documents', he said, 'are non-military weapons for holding on to property we have acquired.'[2]

At the archives the officials could not always find the weapon that they wanted. The central collection came from various sources, sometimes piecemeal, some of them already well-arranged, others in disorder, some a complete series and others part of a collection of which the rest lay in the castle or even at Avignon. The miscellany of origin controlled arrangement inside the Archive. Occasionally papers of exceptional importance could not be found. During the weary meetings leading to the Peace of Westphalia which ended the Thirty Years War in 1648, the papal envoy Chigi wished to concoct a protest against unfavourable terms. To this end he needed copies of the papal protest against the terms of the Peace of Augsburg nearly a century before. He applied to Rome. The archivists could find no copy.

That no copy could be found might be due to ill-arrangement or negligence. The various rooms housed a lot of paper, organized by a scholarly but tiny and ill-paid staff. Since, how-

---

[2] Pastor, *History of the Popes* (English translation), XXV, pp. 101–2.

ever, they needed to serve no public enquiries, but solely the needs of the administration, they kept pace with the conflux of papers surprisingly.

The chief reason why the archives might be incomplete or copies might not be found, without any negligence of archivists, lay in the family nature of papal government. Nominally until 1692, but actually until later, popes used their nephews in the administration. A bulk of papers came to the Pope's nephew as representative of the Pope and so, when the Pope died and the nephew held office no longer, became part of the family papers. In this way important sections of the Pope's administrative records came to rest, not in the Vatican Archives, but in the libraries or cupboards of great Roman families like the Borghese, Barberini, Chigi, Pamfili, Farnese, Caetani, Albani. The papers of the last non-Italian Pope, Adrian VI, were lost altogether because at his death his secretary carried them away to Liège and they were never afterwards found. The documents of Pope Marcellus II concerning the Council of Trent, collected in fifty-four volumes, remained in his Cervini family until just before the French Revolution, when they passed into the archive of the library at Florence. Some of the Borghese papers still lie in the John Rylands Library at Manchester, whither they passed from the collection of the Earl of Crawford and Balcarres. Most of the others remained in the family until 1891 when they were bought by Pope Leo XIII.

The archives remained shut. But they did not remain unaltered. In the course of the seventeenth century the new office of Secretary of State grew towards its modern importance. Little by little the government of the Curia ceased to be a family business and became more like a civil service. Therefore the head of that civil service, the Secretary of State, steadily became more important, especially as the drafter of letters to the nuncios in various capitals and the recipient of reports from the nuncios. It was a mark of the development of the office of Secretary of State when in 1656 the Pope ordered that his records be no longer left in the care of individual secretaries but be transferred to the archives. The archives had received some records of the Secretary of State from Castel Sant' Angelo in 1614, and in 1630 the important reports of nuncios from the sixteenth century. But the decision of 1656 was a landmark in the history of the archives, for henceforth the bulk of accessions came from the office of the Secretary of State.

The archive was a different institution from the library – in name, constitution, and partly in reality. Since Paul V separated them, they went their different ways – for the library was art and the archives business. The library was headed by a cardinal, the archives only by a custos or prefect. During the eighteenth century the officers in the archives began to feel the need of some resource to whom they could turn for help, especially in the struggle for funds. They did not turn to the Cardinal-librarian, but to the Secretary of State, who now controlled the allocation of funds in the Vatican. This constitutional relation between the Cardinal-Secretary of State and the archives helped to draw the two institutions of library and archives further apart; except in the rare periods when the Secretary of State also took for himself the office of Cardinal-librarian.

The aims of the institutions were different. No one was allowed in the archive, except Pope and Secretary of State for purpose of business, or someone under their immediate orders. If the library grew more difficult of access, the archives were never in theory open to anyone outside the administration. But the atmosphere of one affected the other. The archive was a junior institution, without a cardinal at its head. In the free-and-easy age of the library, the staff of the archives were inclined to behave in a free-and-easy way; so that in 1737 Cardinal Acquaviva, who acted wholly in the interests of the King of Spain, got to see the vital letters of the Secretary of State, even those that were in cipher, on payment of a suitable fee to the staff. When the library was shut close, the archive was shut closer.

Both institutions were part of the Pope's 'family' – that is, archivists, like the staff of the library, were treated to allowances of bread and commons and received pay as members of the household. Though the institutions were already of international importance, they were both the Pope's private institutions, his collection of books and manuscripts for study or for art, and his cabinet for filing letters.

In the seventies of the eighteenth century not all was well-ordered. When the Pope needed the copy of a brief by which a predecessor suppressed the monastery of Port-Royal, he had to beg the favour of a copy from the French ambassador. Four years later the King of Saxony astonished Rome by mentioning a vicar-apostolic of Saxony, that is, the Pope's special representative as substitute for the bishop. The Curia had never heard of a vicar-apostolic of Saxony. The archivists hunted for traces of the office and found none. They must have looked either shame-faced or sceptical when the Saxon envoy produced a solemnly authenticated copy of the relevant brief.

In 1783 the last volumes still held at Avignon were moved to Rome.

Then came the French Revolution, the French armies in Italy, and French generals in Rome. Suddenly the academic world became interested in these archives, the more interested because they were inaccessible.

The Emperor Napoleon Bonaparte had a vision of a lasting empire in Europe ruled by the French. As part of his dream, he would organize the history and art of Europe, collecting the loveliest paintings into the Louvre, the fairest manuscripts into the Bibliothèque Nationale, and the archives of European capitals into a central archive to be built in Rheims or (later) Paris. He found the dream practicable, and sent orders to his governors. On 18 December 1809 the French officer in Rome, General Miollis, received the command to send the whole archive of the Pope to France. Only a few months before, the French government kidnapped the Pope.

By various convoys, beginning in February 1810 and ending in February 1811 (with a last convoy in 1813), wagon-trains filled with chests of documents passed along the roads to Turin, and over the Mont-Cenis pass to Paris. Eight chests fell into a ditch near Susa, and two carts were carried away by a flood at Borgo San Donnino. The operation cost the French government more than 600,000 francs. In June 1810 the French chief archivist, ex-Oratorian Daunou, who was an anticlerical and disapproved of popes, asked the Pope's archivist, Gaetano Marini, why some documents were missing. Gaetano Marini, who had already much experience trying to protect his archives from the revolutionary government in Rome, had to confess that he hid them in Rome before leaving; and thus the *Liber Diurnus*, then believed to be the ancient formulary which admitted popes to their office, the golden bulls which were bulls with the seal stamped upon gold for specially solemn acts, of which the Vatican Archives possessed a priceless collection of 78 ranging from the Holy Roman Emperor Frederick Barbarossa in 1164 to the Italian republic a few years before, and the acts of the Council of Trent which had always been regarded as specially secret and of unique importance, also crossed the Alps. A total of 3,239 chests reached Paris, only a few less than left Rome. The French counted what arrived. They calculated it at 102,435 registers, volumes or bundles. They omitted to ask for the records of the reigning Pope, which were buried in the gardens of the Vatican and not recovered for nearly fifty years.

This enormous bulk of paper was brought to the Palais Soubise, until the Emperor had time to build a Record Office for all Europe. In the Palais Soubise Daunou started to put the documents into new order, by making catalogues and rearranging. The rearrangement might have been excellent if it had been complete. As Daunou lost control of the archive before he finished, rearrangement was synonym for introducing confusion. The archives lost something of the piece-meal system of their old organization, without acquiring a new organization. This was not Daunou's fault. Though he was anticlerical, he was an honourable man who did all in his power to keep the archives safe and put them into order. The one danger lay in Daunou's willingness to allow scholars to use the unique opportunity to gain access to hitherto inaccessible papers, and even to allow borrowers of high rank and presumed integrity, a presumption not always warranted. But the archives suffered little loss in Paris. The damage hit them when they returned.

For Napoleon at last was beaten, and on 31 March 1814 the allied armies entered Paris. Only three weeks later the new authorities ordered that the archives be restored to Rome. In May 1814 a first load of important matter, including ceremonial necessities, the ornaments of the Pope's private chapel, a mitre given by the Queen of Etruria, a tiara given by Napoleon at his coronation, were sent off to Rome. But the archives cost 600,000 francs to bring to Paris, and no one had anything like that sum to take them back; and while the papal archivist Marino Marini (Gaetano's nephew) packed chests and wondered how much he could do for the 60,000 francs which was all the new French government would or could provide, Napoleon left Elba and landed in France; and in the hectic weeks before the battle of Waterloo, his servants found time to cancel the restoration of the archives and again put Daunou in charge. After the final fall of Napoleon, Marino Marini returned to Paris and at the end of October sent off the first load of chests by land to Rome. The chests contained what Rome most urgently wanted: part of the privy archives, the archives of Propaganda, of the Secretariat of Briefs, part of the archive of the Inquisition, and of the Congregation of the Council. Marino Marini heard that they were in danger because the escort of soldiers caused unrest among the people as they passed. He hurried after them, and caught them just as one of the chests was damaged by falling in the River Taro. He accompanied them all the way to Rome.

The archives went to Paris in 3,239 chests. They came back in about 2,200 chests. If we assume that the chests were roughly equal, about one-third of the archives that went to Paris never came back.

They went under public escort, at a cost to the European tax-payer, of over 600,000 French francs. They returned, under private contract, not always well-organized, in trouble at customs-ports, for a cost to the French tax-payer of one-tenth of that sum, some tens of thousands of francs more from the Pope's coffers – though in the interval the cost of transport rose. The losses of archives were caused not by their kidnapping but by their return.

Fragments of former papal archives could occasionally be bought in Paris shops till late in the nineteenth century.

Thirteen volumes from the Lateran registers are now in the library of Trinity College, Dublin.

The Bibliothèque Nationale in Paris sooner or later acquired groups of miscellaneous material especially concerning the canonization of saints, an Inquisition register, a register from another congregation.

The removal of the archives to Paris and their return swung the attention of the learned world to the historical importance of the archives. No one had known what they contained. During the short time that the French looked after them, the keepers started to index. The French archivists made lists, partly because they were good archivists, and partly because their head Daunou was an anticlerical looking for propaganda against popes. These indexes were neither adequate nor complete. But they were indexes, the first rough guide available to anyone except two or three men at Rome. The scholars who saw what Daunou could find published their little harvest, bit by bit, to the world. By 1820 learned Europe was more conscious of a treasure of historical documents locked away in Rome.

Marino Marini slowly rearranged the papers and got them back into better order. But the consequences of the French misappropriation were not remedied for decades. The archives hardly recovered until 1883 or 1890 the order which they possessed before the French confiscated them.

The first half of the nineteenth century saw the age of historical revival. History as subject or science came into its kingdom. Therefore historians began to press upon the doors of every important archive, from Simancas to St Petersburg. The British government, which neglected its official papers and allowed many of them to rot in a damp store, was soon forced into that course of improvement which created the Public Record Office. Berlin was the first to provide a service which satisfied scholars. Other capitals moved more slowly. If Rome moved slowly it was not exceptional. But Rome had special reasons, or fancied that it had special reasons, for discouraging enquiry.

In that same generation *nationality* became a key-word in politics. If Germany or Italy hitherto were only a political idea, and were now becoming 'nations', everyone wanted to know the meaning of *nation*, and this was best observed by students of language and of history. Every civilized country was suddenly more interested in its 'national origins'. This quest for national history made the Vatican Archives more important. The roots of modern nations were planted in the Middle Ages. Documents from that age, though plentiful in London or Paris, were less plentiful in Prague or Edinburgh or Turin. As an international supreme court of the Middle Ages, the Vatican received continual applications or appeals from all over Europe. Historians believed that, if allowed access in Rome, they might gain much light upon the history of their nation.

The Germans were first in the field. On Christmas Eve 1821 G. H. Pertz, founding editor of that noble collection which was to serve the national history of Germany, the *Monumenta Germaniae Historica*, entered Rome. He went to the Prussian ambassador, the historian Niebuhr, and said that he needed access to the Vatican Archives. Niebuhr discouraged him. He 'thought, from what he knew of the Italians, and judging by the experience of other scholars, that I should never be able to gain access to the Vatican Archives, and that it would be very difficult to obtain admission to the Vatican Library'.[3] Nine months later Pertz, to his own surprise, found that his friends had won him leave to copy documents from the archives. He might not go in, for under the rule anyone (but the staff) who went in was excommunicated. Marino Marini could not take him to the shelves.

---

[3] G. H. Pertz, *Autobiography and Letters* (English translation, London, 1894), p. 37.

But he invited him to his apartment in the Palazzo Cesi and there brought him documents for study; which a secretary might copy as Marino Marini directed, and then each extract must be seen and certified by the archivist. Naturally Pertz must pay a fee for each document.

So in the morning Pertz worked for three hours at the library, and in the afternoon for three hours at Marini's apartment.

This was an important moment in the history of history. For the first time a stranger gained access, not to the archives which would have made him excommunicate, but to documents from the Vatican Secret Archives, though he was a Protestant and though he was young and untried, solely for the interests of scholarship, and because the Secretary of State Cardinal Consalvi respected the Prussians. November 1822 may be set by July 1879 as a date in the history of the discovery of truth in history.

Other nations followed the Prussian example. The Roman Curia discovered advantage in what was happening. Since the Counter-Reformation the city of Rome was no longer a key to the politics of Europe. In compensation the popes of the eighteenth century made the city the centre of European art and archaeology. Now the Curia realized that it was also a centre of European scholarship in an age when scholarship became powerful.

The Vatican Library was an institution distinct from the Vatican Archives. But the two institutions were housed in the same block of buildings, and outsiders were not always aware that they were different. Through all the nineteenth century some applicants turned to the Vatican Library when what they needed were the Archives, and vice versa. They were under different management and went their separate ways. But because they lived side by side, and because many non-Romans imagined them to be two departments of one institution, the reputation of the library affected the reputation of the archives. As the manuscripts of the library became more accessible, men fancied that *therefore* the documents in the archive were more accessible.

For in this same age, the second quarter of the nineteenth

century, the Vatican Library first gained its true importance in international scholarship. Its prefect from 1819 to 1853 was Angelo Mai, the renovator of classical studies. To the enthusiasm of the world he found in the Vatican Library fragments of Cicero's book *De republica*. His monumental editions of classical authors and of the Fathers appeared year by year. The techniques were controversial, the editorial methods extraordinary, the person generated argument and sometimes passion. But Angelo Mai opened to an excited Europe a glimpse of the historical treasure contained in the Vatican.

Cardinals who continued to think it easy to keep inquisitive eyes away from the Pope's private papers had no idea how many hands would soon be knocking at their doors. They were like keepers of a museum who tantalized an eager public by keeping the museum shut and occasionally showing select objects through the bars of a narrow window. But to show objects brought advantage. If Angelo Mai could make the library a focus of European scholarship, Marino Marini might make the archives a focus of European history. He might also supplement an exiguous stipend with fees.

It was tantalizing. No one might enter the archives under pain of excommunication. No one could see adequate catalogues because no adequate catalogues existed. No one could check whether the copy provided by Marino Marini was faithful to its original. No one could discover whether they received a full set, or a fair selection, or even a bowdlerized selection. No one but official representatives of a government could gain even this permission. Scholars working for their governments were not confident either of the completeness or of the accuracy of Marino Marini's handiwork. Pertz observed that Marino Marini's effective staff consisted of one secretary with a tiny stipend, who could hardly decipher the simplest abbreviations in medieval manuscripts. Pertz's colleague Johann Friedrich Böhmer, was pleased with the freedom which Marino Marini allowed. Even so, delay after delay; he had to wait till the volumes, one by one, were brought to Marino Marini's apartment, where he could only work for a little more than two hours a day, and this time was reduced by gossipy conversation. 'I feel personally hurt that it is all so dreary. What a benefit to the Church as well as to scholarship if it were otherwise.' Böhmer went away and drafted a ferocious attack upon the policy pursued by the managers of the Vatican Library and Archives; in his cruellest passage accusing the staff of wanting no improvement because any improvement would make them less indispensable. He mellowed, and never published this attack, which was found among his papers after his death. But one of Böhmer's sentences, from a private letter, was destined to be quoted again and again, until it became canonized as a motto:

Please God that the next Pope, whom prophets have hoped for as a light from heaven, will look upon a truth-loving study of history as a light coming down from God to shine in our darkness and show us how we go astray in this modern age![4]

THEINER

Augustin Theiner was born in Breslau on 19 April 1804 of a German father and a Polish mother, both Catholic. He specially remembered his mother's piety, and affection, and the religious way in which she brought him up. All his life he had a special interest in the Poles and other members of the Slav races.

His elder brother Anton raced ahead as a scholar and, while Augustin was still an undergraduate, became a professor of exegesis and canon law at the University of Breslau. Anton was a young and fiery leader of the reforming Catholic movement in Silesia, and drew his younger brother with him into the assault upon the compulsory celibacy of priests, and the demand for a liturgy in the tongue of the people. The two brothers published a work in three volumes on the origins of celibacy. This book did not please authority nor escape the attentions of the Roman

---

[4] Janssen, *Böhmers Leben*, I, pp. 219–20, 326ff, 335; cf III, p. 159.

censors of theological books. But it had the effect of turning the young Augustin into a historian. In these matters the German Catholic world was more free than it became later. The elder brother Anton never submitted; and though he had to leave his professorship, he became pastor of three parishes in succession. As the young Augustin moved closer and closer to the Pope, he never lost touch with Anton; even though Anton was at last excommunicated and became a Protestant.

The controversy shifted young Augustin, for a time, away from the Catholic church and into friendly relations with Protestants. He began to react against the faith of his parents and to doubt Catholic doctrine, and to wander, as he himself described it, sadly and sceptically. But he went on with the study of history. He published a pioneer commentary on the history of canon law. The book established his repute for learning and for skill in criticizing documents.

German scholars took notice of the young prodigy. He refused an enticing invitation to join the faculty of law in the University of Berlin and instead, with a Berlin research stipend, went on his academic travels, to Vienna and then London (where he learnt especially about the Quakers and the Unitarians, 'which are so numerous here'), about the Swedenborgians, and then about the Church of England, which surprised him, and which he could only explain to himself as a survival from a feudal world. Theiner said afterwards that nowhere did he see the fruits of the Reformation in such a shocking shape as in England. In London he attended a place of worship where the preacher kept his children by him in the pulpit, whence during the sermon the children floated down paper darts. He seems to have thought the incident characteristic of English modes of worship. 'The proud individualism of the British has completed and perfected the work of proud and individualistic Protestantism' – this was only one of several harsh sayings after his visit to England. To Archbishop Howley of Canterbury he sent a letter asking for leave to consult the Lambeth Library, and received a courteous assent from the archbishop's chaplain.

Theiner went to Holland and Belgium, then to France, just breathing again after its revolution of 1830. In Paris he published researches into medieval collections of canons which he found, one in London and the other in Brussels. It was afterwards alleged that he became an agent of the French government in 1832, when the Bourbon King Charles X had just been turned off his throne.

In that year the Duchess of Berry, the daughter of the Bourbon King of Naples and widow of the murdered younger son of Charles X, who had a legitimist claim that her son was the true king of France, tried to raise a revolution by landing near Marseilles dressed as a sailor. When no one stirred she compared herself to Robert the Bruce and moved in disguise to royalist Brittany where a few hundred peasants were moved and took up arms. When her little army was more crushed than defeated, she dressed as a peasant girl and vanished into hiding with friends at Nantes. The government could safely have left her alone; but Louis Philippe's monarchy had so many enemies – royalists, Bonapartists, and former republicans of the revolution – that they were nervous and 400 soldiers worked through Nantes and the surrounding countryside in search of her.

Lord Acton always believed that the government hired Theiner to find out where she was hidden; and that he had a part when the son of the Jewish rabbi of Paris, who was a convert to Catholicism, sold the secret to Thiers the new Minister of the Interior, who had £20,000 in his hand and a loaded pistol in his pocket, and bought the information at a midnight meeting in the loneliest alley off the Champs Elysées in Paris. It was true that the convert Deutz, who had taken an oath to serve the duchess, offered the secret for sale and had two meetings at the Champs Elysées and another meeting at the Ministry of the Interior. But there is no reliable evidence that Theiner had anything to do with the shabby deal. The duchess hid behind a chimney in Nantes and was not found, though they took the house to pieces, until a cold soldier lit a fire in her chimney for his comfort. She went to prison for a year but then lived in a

mainly Swiss retirement for thirty-seven more years. The confusion over Theiner probably came from a similarity of careers;
Deutz like Theiner was a German, and had visited England, and
was a recent convert to Catholicism.

In Paris Theiner was attracted to the group of Liberal Catholics led by Lamennais, with their appeal to Christian democracy. For eight months he lived in the little community of
Lamennais at La Chesnaie. In Paris he began once again to go
to church.

He entered Rome for the first time on 1 March 1833. His
reason for going to Rome is told in two contradictory stories.
Theiner said that he had told Bishop Beauregard of Orleans that
he was thinking of being ordained and suggested that he go to
the Orleans seminary. The bishop, whose priest-brother had
been guillotined and who had almost suffered the same fate, and
who cared about scholarship, told him that it would be better
for him to go to Rome for the purpose. He had at first no desire
to change his country, or to study in a place where he did not
know the language. 'Bishop Beauregard said, *Go to Rome*. I
should have preferred Siberia!'

Lord Acton believed that he had a very different motive.
In the discovery of the hiding-place of the Duchess of Berry,
Theiner had allegedly proved his quality as a secret agent. The
French government now sent him as their secret agent to Rome
to find out what was happening and to tell them about the inner
workings of the Curia. Cardinal Bernetti was then the (very
secular) Cardinal Secretary of State, anti-French and under the
heel of Metternich and the Austrians in Vienna who had lately
saved the Pope from an Italian revolution. Acton believed that
Theiner, sent on this mission, went to Bernetti and told him
frankly what he was being paid to do and showed Bernetti his
reports to the French government before he sent them off to
Paris. Thus, thought Acton, he served two masters and betrayed
each to the other.

This again is probably a muddle with Deutz who also spent
time in Rome and was hailed there as a new convert from

Judaism and may have been used as an agent.[5] But Acton's erroneous belief that Theiner was a double-dealer over the Duchess of Berry and the French secret service in Rome caused an important English historian to suspect an important German historian of being crooked and not to be trusted.

Here was the historian Acton nodding like Homer. He may have been affected because he had a personal interest in the Duchess of Berry. His grandfather Sir John Acton served as prime minister to King Ferdinand of Naples who was the grandfather of the duchess. The historian who became the incarnation of British liberalism always had an understanding for Bourbons, which surprised his readers unless they thought about his ancestry.

For whatever reason Theiner arrived in Rome he soon settled down happily to scholarship there and won the trust of the Curia. Before the end of March 1833 he had made a public submission to the Church, repudiated all that was censored in his book on the celibacy of the priesthood, and made the Spiritual Exercises at the Jesuit seminary of St Eusebio. From being a radical of the left wing in Catholicism he dedicated himself to the Pope. He now wrote and published, first in German and later in French and Italian translations, a history of his conversion. The new status in Rome lost him the stipend which he received from Berlin for the purposes of research.

The *History of My Conversion* brought him an international reputation, not only among scholars. Pope Gregory XVI henceforth gave him constant support. Count Reisach, the young German head of the college of Propaganda and already the Pope's chief adviser on German affairs, took him up and persuaded the Pope to appoint him, though still a layman, as professor of church history and canon law at his college.

It was time to enter a religious order and be ordained. Theiner chose the Oratory, partly because he was attracted to the person of its founder St Philip Neri, and partly because the annalist of

[5] DD, pp. 133 – 4.

the Papacy, Caesar Baronius, had been a member of the Oratory. He entered the Oratory of Sta Maria Nuova in Vallicella, where lie the remains of Philip Neri and Baronius, and where the manuscripts of Baronius are preserved.

For a few years Theiner was uncomfortable in the Oratory. At one point during the early eighteen-forties he came near the point of leaving. The long hours needed by the scholar did not easily fit the monastic way of life with its frequent interruptions for worship and the duties of the community. He was held in his place by a friendship for one of the more delightful and spiritual of Oratorians, Father Carlo Rossi. Rossi was the Oratorian who trained John Henry Newman in that way of life when Newman came to Rome soon after his conversion to Roman Catholicism. Newman's letters show how weighty was Theiner in the Oratorian community in Rome during 1846–7. On Sunday 14 March 1847 Newman and two of his companions communicated at the tomb of the founder of the Oratory, St Philip Neri. It was Theiner who said mass there, and gave them breakfast afterwards. Theiner helped to bring to birth an important new venture in Catholic life.

He asked leave to continue further the annals of the Papacy. Pope Gregory XVI was so impressed by him that he gave the order that the Vatican Secret Archives should be opened for him and that he could carry away documents which he needed to his cell in the Oratory at Vallicella. He now knew that he had an opportunity granted to few historians. He had an inexhaustible quarry of documents which were inaccessible to anyone else, on a subject which the thriving historical world was eager to know. At the age of thirty-six he reached one of the key points of European historical studies, when decades of health and energy lay before him, and when he already had an idea, at least in outline, of what had to be done. For this task he was fitted by his previous training, and by a passion for the truth about papal history which can only be paralleled in Lord Acton and Ludwig von Pastor.

On 14 March 1851 Theiner became Marini's coadjutor, which

meant that he did the work for Marini and that when Marini ceased to be the archivist he would have the right to be his successor. The great scholar Cardinal Angelo Mai, shortly before his death in 1854, was reported to have said of Theiner 'He is the only man in Rome doing fundamental research. He is a great man, dedicated to the Pope, and the Pope ought to make him a cardinal.'[6]

With the office of prefect of the archives went an apartment in the Vatican. High up a winding staircase in an observatory, sometimes known then as the Tower of Galileo because Galileo was wrongly alleged to have been imprisoned there when in Rome, known now as the Tower of the Winds, the visitor reached a landing where was a private door into the archives and a way into the prefect's apartment, with a study adorned by frescoes, and a loggia with a glorious view beyond Rome to the countryside and the Alban hills. Theiner was happy to move from his cell in Vallicella to this room next to the archives. He hardly ever went out, except to walk in the Vatican gardens during the afternoon, and refreshed himself by entertaining vis-iting scholars on the loggia or in the study. He was ruthless about time.

The pay was modest. He had his free rooms high in the tower, and his academic friends were glad because, though he was still an Oratorian, his new abode got him away from the varied duties of the Oratorian rule of life and freed his hours. The stipend was 30 scudi a month, with the addition until 1859 of 12 scudi a month from two of his other minor offices. He kept a servant to do his cooking and cleaning, and paid a secretary to copy documents. These payments left little out of the 42 scudi, and for the rest Theiner lived on a small inheritance, part of which he used to help the cost of publications. He appealed sadly to the Pope for a better stipend, saying that he could hardly live in a decent manner befitting his station. Once, perhaps after this appeal, the authorities offered him a canonry at St Peter's, with

[6] Hermann Gisiger, *Theiner und die Jesuiten* (Mannheim, 1875), p. 27.

a stipend of 100 scudi a month. The money would have made him comfortable. But then he would need to perform the duty of a canon, and attend long liturgies, choral service twice a day. Grudging the hours, he asked to be dispensed from the obligation to attend the services, but authority was not willing to treat the canonry as a convenient sinecure. So Theiner preferred the gift of time to the gift of comfort, and refused both preferment and pay. Nothing interrupted his endeavours. Volume after volume, each containing hitherto unknown documents from 'his' Archive, succeeded each other with rapidity, and stood in a lengthening row on his shelves, where he eyed them with a mixture of pride and astonishment. He had a European reputation. Two kings of Bavaria in succession visited him in his tower. The Emperor Maximilian of Mexico climbed Theiner's staircase when he visited Rome to get the Pope's blessing before his fatal expedition. Theiner's birthplace in Breslau was preserved as historic.

Theiner did the traditional work of the prefect like Marino Marini. He provided Europe with historical documents, but more than Marini he knew how to present them with historical criticism. And for the rest, he allowed privileged persons to secure the copies of documents which they wanted, if or when he could find them. Usually he invited them up the 204 steps to the Tower of the Winds, to copy in the study adorned with frescoes.

In the sense in which Europe was beginning to understand the word, he was not an archivist. European scholars now thought of archivists as men who arranged and made easily accessible the papers which they wanted to see. Theiner's papers, by higher order, were hardly accessible, and he did little to arrange what he did not use. The work of a historian was beginning to be hardly compatible with the work of an archivist. This was concealed for a time from Theiner as from everyone else, because so few people were allowed into the archives that it hardly mattered if the documents were ill-ordered. The staff of the archives was still tiny and unskilled.

Theiner was a fine scholar, and gave all his time to scholarship. But he happened also to be head of one of the biggest archives in Europe, which more and more people wanted passionately to be allowed to consult. He needed the qualities of an administrator. We have no evidence that he lacked these qualities. He had no time. One of the Austrians to whom he allowed copies of documents once wrote with an aggrieved air, 'A writer is not suitable for a librarian. He is busy on his own concerns, and sometimes refuses access to materials which he wants for his private use.'[7]

From the move to Paris, with the acquisition of many papers from religious houses, the archives had never recovered. The poet Robert Browning read (1860) the old yellow book which contained the murder story of 1698 which he was to make into an epic poem. He asked in Rome whether they would have records of the case, and was told they could not be found, it was the fault of the French occupation. Browning hinted that this might be an excuse by men who were determined to release no document; and perhaps French occupation may have become an excuse for hard-pressed sub-custodians. But it was no mere excuse. Neither the equipment nor the money were available to remedy the defect. And Theiner was not the man to see that this tiny staff behaved with the required efficiency. We have evidence of documents taken from one armarium (cupboard) being put back carelessly into another armarium, and so becoming impossible to find. Whether it was the inheritance of French disorder, or the tiny staff available, or the failure of Theiner to be very concerned, catalogue revision made slow progress. The similar revision in the Vatican Library was almost as slow.

Theiner performed the customary duty of the Vatican archivist; that is, to keep the documents secure from the world, and to present to the world what it was good for the world to know. Theiner's fame, and Theiner's documents, kept telling the world what a marvellous collection of historical documents he con-

---

[7] Alois Flir, *Briefe aus Rom*, 2nd edn (Innsbruck, 1864), p. 131.

trolled. And still no one might enter the archive under pain of excommunication, and no one might freely see catalogues. They might ask Theiner for what they wanted. They might only get it if the Pope or the Secretary of State approved, and if Theiner could find it.

THE MINUTES OF THE COUNCIL OF TRENT

Soon after the Council of Trent ended its third sitting in 1563, Pope Pius IV had the plan of publishing to all the world the full acts. If he had done so, the history of European controversy would have been different. But he died, and his successor would not publish. On reflection, Rome saw that to publish the discussion which lay behind the decrees would lead to argument on the meaning of the decrees. It was better to have the decrees unadorned, part now of the laws of the Church. The Acta, diligently collected by the secretary of the Council, Angelo Massarelli, were gathered into eight volumes bound in leather with gilt edges and deposited for security in the Castel Sant' Angelo. With them were then or later deposited eighteen more volumes of reports and letters. At first the security was not very strict. About the end of the sixteenth century we find men consulting the papers for aid in their discussions. By Massarelli's diligence, no Council in Church history was better documented. But at that date, probably with the intention of silencing unnecessary discussion about predestination and grace, popes consciously adopted the policy of allowing no one to consult these papers. Not to make them available became an established rule of the Roman Curia. Papers were slowly added, under the general heading *Concilio*. By the time of the prefect Garampi in the third quarter of the eighteenth century the number of volumes had grown to 104; by 1940 it was 155.

The rule against access acquired a kind of theological defence, which survived even into the middle of the nineteenth century when it looked peculiar.

Historians have often experienced this truism, that an early, one-sided, clever and popular treatment of a large subject takes the field and thereafter hampers, often for many years, subsequent saner treatment by historians. When Cardinal Manning died, Purcell published a clever and slightly scandalous biography, with such consequences that more than three-quarters of a century later historians still could not study the Manning archives freely. This was what happened to the history of the Council of Trent. The Venetian Paolo Sarpi published, in Protestant London, his brilliant, partisan, and sometimes excellently based *History of the Council of Trent*. The book enchanted readers and became the authority all over Europe. No later history before modern times could compete. Whether they had better archives or not, whether their judgment was more impartial or not, other historians could not oust a fascinating if at times misleading book from the European field which it conquered on merit, quality of literature and of forceful aggression against popes as well as of history. Though it stood on the Roman Index from 1619, we are told that half a century later it was read by every educated clergyman in Rome.

It must be answered. Rome selected the Jesuit Alciati and opened to him (under odd restrictions against making copies) the Vatican Archives. The work was enormous; Alciati was conscientious; he knew that Sarpi could not be answered by more apologetic, but only by better history; his draft chapters tarried and finally he died in 1651, over the age of 80, with the book half-written. The Jesuit general then appointed a theologian, not a historian, to take over the work; and within five years, now with wholly free access to the archives, Pallavicino published his *History of the Council of Trent* in two folio volumes (1656).

Pallavicino versus Sarpi: if a single symbol could be taken to divine the religion of Catholics from the religion of Protestants, it was the Council of Trent. Two famous histories stated the rival understandings of what happened at Trent. Naturally the history by Pallavicino became canonized at Rome. It had better archives, far better, than Sarpi. It was nothing like so easy to read, despite or because of its rhetoric. It had no chance of driving Sarpi from his European popularity. But for the Roman theologian, who wanted to understand what happened at Trent and why the dogmatic decrees were drafted, it became canonized. It was the authentic interpretation of what happened. And therefore, more than once, anyone who suggested that more evidence should be published from the archives, was met by the arguments that more evidence could only weaken the authority of Pallavicino. The appearance of Pallavicino's book was celebrated in Rome as though it was a victory over Protestants. Nothing must be allowed to weaken its prestige.

Everywhere documents were published – except from the place where the best documents lay. Historians see the past through the eyes of the authors of the archives which they use. Pallavicino – it was later seen as a defect – saw Trent only through the eyes of cardinals then in Rome. But now men were seeing Trent through eyes in Madrid or Paris or Vienna. Pressure built up, that Rome must publish all, or at least more, of the original documents of the Council of Trent.

No project could be dearer to Theiner. He persuaded Pope Pius IX that publication was desirable if not necessary. The Pope appointed a commission with a Dominican cardinal as chairman, and the commission (April 1857) reported favourably. Theiner got the permission which he sought. He worked in the Farnese archives at Naples and among the Venetian records, then in the libraries at Turin, Milan, Trent, Padua and Bologna. The Grand Duke of Tuscany deposited forty volumes for his use at the convent where he lodged in Florence. In Bologna especially but everywhere he went, he reported enthusiasm for the project, and gratitude to the Pope and to Cardinal Antonelli, the Secretary of State. Naturally he found many documents which Pallavicino did not know. He refused access to others who wanted to see the documents, because he was working on them himself. He refused the biographer of St Charles Borromeo in words which that applicant described as few and resolute.

The course of the commission did not run smoothly. Some of the speeches at Trent, which Theiner wanted to publish, contained doubtful matter, even of uncertain orthodoxy. The Dominican chairman Cardinal Gaude asked Theiner to insert footnotes to refute what was wrong or explain what might be misunderstood. Theiner's sense of integrity was offended. He rejected such footnotes.

In the winter of 1857–8 the commission, appointed to advise, suddenly recommended that the plan be suspended. The commission saw sheets already printed, and changed its mind.

The old arguments were revived: that Pallavicino's history was classic, and must not lose authority. But a new argument, or new form of the old argument, came to the front; the necessity, as Theiner saw, the undesirability, as the commission saw, of publishing Angelo Massarelli's diary.

Massarelli was secretary of the Council of Trent at all three of its phases. He kept the minutes, and wrote as many as seven different diaries of the proceedings, diaries of unequal value. Massarelli's protocols and diaries were necessary to understand the course of the Council of Trent. No other sources, not even the reports of legates to the Pope nor the letters of national leaders or ambassadors to their sovereigns, shed so intimate a light as the papers of this efficient secretary of the Council.

But Massarelli reported what was said. He recorded the differences of opinion, the follies as well as the wisdom of the speakers, the unedifying as well as the edifying. If Massarelli's diaries were published, the decisions of the Council of Trent, sacred in so many minds, would no longer appear the unchallenged expression of a common Catholic mind, but the end of hard-fought debates over nuances of expression. Only the result had authority, not the course of events or utterances which led to the result. The upholders of Pallavicino maintained that to publish Massarelli could do nothing but weaken the authority of the canons of Trent, as well as the official history by Pallavicino.

This was particularly true of the early debates on scripture and tradition, the authority of scripture, and its canon. In the cold light of finality, the formulas look rigid against Protestants. Seen as the end of a long debate with differing opinions, the formulas have more nuance, more flexibility, than any Protestant hitherto supposed. The examining commission particularly objected to the minutes which Theiner proposed to publish, and had already in proof, of the debate on the canon of holy scripture.

A decision to suspend must grievously disappoint any historian whatever, who secured approval of a project, believed that the truth of history in this matter could do nothing but good, worked for months in the archives, and found a succession of valuable documents. Moreover, the plan was announced. Men expected it, and eagerly. To suspend it now might hurt the repute in which Theiner was held, as well as appear a further reaction in papal politics. He had already received money to print. Archbishop Hohenlohe subscribed 1,800 scudi, the Cardinal-archbishop of Vienna and the bishops of Hungary agreed to see to publication, the Austrian emperor gave 3,000 scudi.

By character Theiner was less fitted than some historians to bear so heavy a blow. Beneath the lively, friendly, likeable exterior lay the passionate son of the Breslau shoemaker. He had no patience with his critics. To the Pope he accused them of mere panic. He did all he could. He tried vainly to persuade the commission that new manuscripts, expected from Florence, might resolve their difficulty. He forced them to admit that the time must come sooner or later, when Rome would be compelled, 'blushing', to publish the acts of Trent. He appealed personally to the Pope, but in vain. His printed proofs of past were put into store.

Acton discovered how Theiner had published volume after volume of documents which no one hitherto had known. In the following year he began to write for the *Rambler* and soon reviewed a new volume of Theiner's documents. The review had a little oddity. Acton was becoming passionate to know about the history of the Popes. The person who controlled access to the main unpublished documents of the history of Popes was Theiner. It might have been expected that the young author would butter the dragon who guarded the papers which would be necessary to his work.

They were documents on the French Revolution. Since he needed Theiner, this review had high praise – each book Theiner publishes is a sign that the time is over when the Church hides documents because it does not trust that the truth will prevail. Acton could not give dishonest panegyric; he had to say that the editing left much to be desired and that Theiner printed much that was printed before. But no other person had united the power and the will to make known the papers which are protected by an excommunication. And it is best that Theiner should edit documents and not attempt to write history. If he wrote history it would be bound to have bias and would be discounted by Protestant readers as biased. 'A good conscience courts publicity.' 'Our religion will be better loved the more its character and history are understood.' And he ended by praising the Pope for encouraging Theiner to publish.

Acton began to think that more might be achieved. In May 1863 he was in a 'negotiation' with Theiner about getting copies of archives touching the history of England and Scotland. Theiner was the readier to help because he needed money to print his documents and knew that Acton would pay fees. He talked of letters of King Henry VIII and the acts of his 'divorce' trial, letters of Cardinal Wolsey and of the Scottish Cardinal Beaton, some letters of Mary Queen of Scots to Rome, the letters of King James II to Rome and the answers. He said he wanted money to publish the fourth volume of documents about the Temporal Power; that he could not get money from the Pope for the purpose; and that if Acton paid for them he would regard the money as a 'gift to St Peter'.[8]

This exchange excited Acton and made him the more determined to gain access to the Vatican Archives. He soon realized that to succeed he must have the backing of the British govern-

---

[8] Acton to Simpson, 3, 105–6.

ment; he must be seen to be an official representative of a State which was justified in inquiring into its history and ought to be helped.

The guardian of official records, until far into the twentieth century, was a senior judge, the Master of the Rolls, who at that moment was Sir John Romilly, soon to be Lord Romilly. He was doing good to the public records, making access easier and abolishing the need to pay fees. Persons who knew about the law regarded his legal knowledge as slender; and Acton's experience led him to the hard doctrine that Romilly was a goose.

Romilly was eager to help the idea that they should get copies of Vatican archives into the British records; for those which were obtained earlier, in the reign of Marino Marini, were seen as unsatisfactory. Knowing less about the situation in Rome than he ought, but aware that Acton knew his way about Rome and was an acquaintance of some of the right people and was a Roman Catholic and cared much for archives and had met Theiner, he thought it sensible to charge Acton with the negotiations in Rome. That meant that however the Curia might distrust Acton, he became a sort of agent of a respected government and should be treated fairly.

In September and October of 1866 Acton and Lord Romilly corresponded on how it was to be done. Acton told Romilly that Theiner was friendly, that the sums of money suggested would not be enough but would gain much:

It will be a matter of some delicacy, because Theiner would be giving up materials which might have served to enhance his literary fame, and because it will be necessary to establish some control and revision over copies made by his own Secretaries. Also he would be easily frightened if jealousy were awakened and an outcry raised in Rome . . . It may be well to bear in mind the uncertainty of affairs in Rome, and the chance of an unfavourable change if the Pope, or Cardinal Antonelli, or Father Theiner should disappear from the scene. The latter is growing old and his health is bad . . . The key to the archives is a very simple one, but will require some care in applying it. I shall be most anxious and happy to assist at all times with my experience of persons and things in Rome anyone whom you decide to send there.[9]

During the December of 1866 Acton, fatal bird of ill omen to Theiner, came back to Rome; now on an ardent hunt for archives in papal history and determined to try to get what he could from the Vatican Archives. He was more interested than surprised to learn that Theiner's publication of the minutes of the Council of Trent was postponed, as he said, to the Greek Kalends. Acton worked away at his manifold interests, with Theiner providing him with copies of many of the documents which he wanted. Little by little the relationship became if not a friendship a strange kind of intimacy; for Theiner a calamitous intimacy, for Acton perhaps in hindsight a damaging though an inevitable acquaintance. The alliance was necessary to Acton because Theiner controlled access to what Acton most needed for his historical work.

Not all Rome was pleased to see Acton; the pupil of Döllinger who was now suspect because of his attitude to the Temporal Power, the editor of one journal which Cardinal Wiseman had blamed, the editor of another journal who closed it because of the Munich Brief, the English squire whom the Pope's English chamberlain Monsignor Talbot distrusted. At least one member of the Curia grudged the privilege of access which Theiner, with leave of the Secretary of State, accorded him.

The ageing Theiner was impressed. He found that Acton could give information on subjects which specially concerned him, and that they shared interests in Reformation and Counter-Reformation. He had begun to need an assistant who understood the history of England. For he had collected more than 100 documents on the Spanish–English marriage of 1623. He proposed a joint venture – he should provide the documents, Acton should arrange for the publication and write the historical intro-duction. Acton was so flattered that this scholar of an inter-

[9] DD, pp. 69–70.

national reputation should want to use him, that he half-suspected an ulterior motive.

On his side Acton found Theiner an extraordinary person, perhaps the most extraordinary whom he met on his travels. Theiner's romantic career as a young man, with an alleged part as an agent to the French government in settling the Breton conspiracy of 1831–2, appealed to the man of action manqué in Acton's breast. Acton found not only an archivist with treasure at his disposal, but a man who cared as passionately as himself for archives, and for the truth to be gained from archives. He also discovered that Theiner admired Döllinger; and even though the admiration was less whole-hearted than Acton could have wished, anyone who professed himself a disciple of Döllinger was a friend of Acton.

This seemed to Acton part of the astonishing quality in Theiner. Here was a man at the heart of the Vatican who did not share, or did not seem to share, the attitudes which loyalty to the Rome of that day demanded. At little dinner parties in the room of the tower where he was host to selected scholars, he could be abrasive. He had his share of German academic pride, and something of that contempt for Italian scholarship which hampered so many Catholic Germans during the middle years of the nineteenth century. Because Pope Pius IX was determined that the Italian kingdom should not rob him of his secular monarchy over the city of Rome, the shibboleth of loyalty to the Pope, in the year when Acton arrived in Rome, was belief in the necessity for a papal state. Acton, who himself wanted the temporal power of the Pope to end, was surprised to find that this high Vatican officer felt happy if the temporal power ended. When he discovered this opinion in Theiner, he thought it a marvel. Soon he discovered Theiner's obsession. Theiner hated Jesuits.

Theiner could not forgive – few historians could have forgiven – the sudden stop upon the printing of his Trent. He suspected Jesuit machinations. As he grew older this suspicion or fear of Jesuits became obsessive in his mind.

Acton found a high Vatican official, fervent in affection for the Pope, yet hating Jesuits, admiring (in part) Döllinger, and having little use for the temporal power of the Papacy. It almost looked like a personal self-contradiction. Acton's surprise may partly account for his later harsh judgment that Theiner was a double-dealer.

By nature they were not quite made for friendship. Acton had the easy assurance of the European nobleman. Something about Theiner suggested memories of a past to be lived down, a feeling of guilt which still lingered, a shadow resting since early days upon the mature man and needing atonement. The grandchild of a prince of the Holy Roman Empire was not quite comfortable with the son of a Silesian cobbler. Theiner had a brawny air about him. When he was younger he was believed to have wielded a pick-axe as effectively as any workman in Rome. His manner lacked subtlety and delicacy. Acton was inclined to see in this roughness a cause of the defects, harshness, violence, overstatements, lack of taste, in Theiner's literary productions. He was wryly amused when Theiner gave him a draft preface for their joint work on the Spanish marriage, 'in which he proposed that I should say what a man he was, how truthful, how religious, and how generous to students'.[10] That Theiner could write books in four languages hardly impressed Acton who could use the same four. Theiner was a compiler of documents, a man who rather heaped than mastered archives. Acton decided that he was no true historian. But as a man of documents Theiner elicited Acton's warm regard. Even eight years later, when Acton believed Theiner not to be straight, he still placed him in the highest category, not of historians but of men who gave the world the raw materials of history. He was prepared to write that in this Theiner surpassed even men like Muratori or Mabillon, and from Acton there could be no loftier praise.

[10] DD, p. 133.

One hindrance to friendship lay entirely on Acton's side. He also began to suffer an obsession.

If authority forced Theiner to stop a mighty work on which his heart was set, the same authority stopped Acton from editing and publishing a Liberal Catholic journal which was the most intelligent Catholic publication of that type in Europe. He was strong in Catholic faith and worship, went to confession regularly, married a devout Catholic wife, and was determined that his children be educated as devout Catholics. But he began to take very unfavourable views of the exercise of Roman authority in the past. He started to search the centuries for occasions when Rome behaved iniquitously. The object of this search was not historical. To him Catholicism also meant freedom and toleration. We must unveil the moments of persecution in their horror, unconcealed, so that never again will Catholic authority dare to fall into such wickedness. Acton was far too good a historian to be a pamphleteer or propagandist misusing sources to a contemporary moral end. But because he was what he was, the moral end could not but affect his historical judgement.

This concern for persecution and tolerance was not yet a King Charles's head like Theiner's hatred of Jesuits. Acton was younger than Theiner. The concern took some fifteen or sixteen more years to flower; until at the end of his life, when he was a Regius professor of modern history, the undergraduates of Cambridge University said that he had persecution on the brain. For the sake of protecting an institution, the Pope or the clergy, for the sake of the earthly power of a Church, authority concealed evidence; and this evidence must be uncovered, the documents must be wrested from their hiding places, from the housetops we must shout the truth about Index or Inquisition or intolerance; until the new archival study of history acts like a swab, cleansing the Church by nauseating Catholic minds with the deeds of which Christian men were capable when acting on illiberal principles.

Wrest the truth from the archives – but his new-found friend

Theiner controlled access to the most important collection. Theiner was a watchdog as well as a historian. Acton admired the historian and resented the watchdog. From an early moment in their alliance this started to complicate their lives.

But for nearly four years they were colleagues; working together, the young man admiring the old and famous, and understanding his difficulties, the old scholar flattered that an English aristocrat should work on similar themes, and struck by the tremendous drive to research which in those years domi-nated Acton's heart. The friendship was never free, partly from difference in background – Theiner began German letters to Acton with the words *Your high-born Lordship* – partly because Acton suspected that the rigid rules of the archives were not uncongenial to the archivist, who liked to have the documents to himself, and partly because Theiner for all his liberties, was a little too papalist for Acton's stomach. Living near the heart of the Vatican for a quarter of a century, devoting every day to the history of an institution at the centre of the past of Christendom, and still with the self-dedication of a convert, Theiner stood in reverence towards the Papacy; a reverence hardly intelligible to the young half-English historian with his assured inherited Catholicism and his intellectual roots in the European enlight-enment.

Theiner agreed to give Acton copies of the much-coveted archive materials on King James II of England and the Glorious Revolution. At this point Acton became aware that Theiner was not a free agent. Before he gave Acton these documents he showed them privately to Archbishop Manning of Westminster, to ensure that he could not accuse him of improper communi-cation of papers; and found that Manning was in favour of their publication. In the autumn of 1866 Acton was conscious that the Jesuits were pressing Theiner against the release of documents. He had heard (in outline) how the publication of Trent was postponed.

Acton was not in the least surprised to find people trying to hide archives, he would have been surprised if he found the contrary. But soon afterwards he began to suspect something more ominous: namely that Theiner himself, in printing documents, suppressed passages discreditable to the Church. Within a year or two suspicion became certainty. Theiner tampered with his texts. So far from Theiner being a man struggling to publish truths which his cardinals preferred to conceal, Theiner was as guilty as his cardinals.

Acton's suspicion was aroused by a study of the massacre of St Bartholomew. No moment of Church history touched Acton's soul more painfully. The killing of the Huguenots in Paris, and the approval of mass murder by some churchmen, he saw as a terrible lesson of the consequence of intolerance. He wanted to find out how far approval went – whether the Pope knew beforehand, whether he sanctioned the coup, whether the assassinations were premeditated or were the sudden results of unexpected events. In October 1869 his article entitled 'The massacre of St Bartholomew' appeared in the *North British Review*. Naturally the article has not survived the test of subsequent inquiry, but remained one of his best-known essays. Though he already had a body of intelligent writing to his name, he had never before printed an essay which proved its author to be in the first rank among European historians.

The evidence which (in Acton's eyes) damned the ecclesiastics, was contained in the reports of the papal nuncio in Paris at the time of the massacre, Antonio Maria Salviati. He thought that the use of Salviati's reports was the chief originality of his essay.

Theiner printed most of these reports in the appendices of documents which he added to the first of his three vast folio volumes on the pontificate of Pope Gregory XIII.

Anyone who begins to work on Theiner's extracts from the nuncio Salviati is at once afflicted with doubt. Part of Salviati's letters, though only a little part, was printed before in an unexpected place – the appendix to the third volume of the *History of England* (1825–40) by Sir James Mackintosh. Though the continuator of Mackintosh selected so few paragraphs, these few paragraphs contained matter which Theiner's transcript of the letters did not contain. Sometimes these omissions were of negligible interest. But occasionally, and especially to a man with Acton's bias in favour of disclosing what discredited, they staggered.

Salviati wrote a letter to Rome on 24 August 1572, the very day of the massacre. Theiner printed long extracts, Mackintosh short extracts. But Mackintosh had paragraphs not found in Theiner, and even put a shocking passage into italics:

I am as happy as I can be that God has been pleased to promote the good of this Kingdom so happily and honourably, at the beginning of the pontificate of His Holiness; and that he has taken under his protection the king and the queen-mother, who have been able to extirpate the poisonous roots with such prudence, at a time when all the rebels were shut up in their cage.[11]

Theiner left out the passage. His transcription shows no mark that anything is omitted. In his text, however, he drew attention to the existence of those transcripts which Mackintosh printed.

Therefore anyone, working on the massacre as a historian and interested in Salviati's reports, must want Theiner's text to be checked. Thus dawned the suspicion about Theiner which henceforth perturbed Acton.

He knew that a check was possible.

Sir James Mackintosh was in Paris during Napoleon's Empire, and worked in the archives. Then or later he found copies of Salviati's letters made by Chateaubriand, and from them made his selection. Acton applied to Paris for the full text of the Salviati letters as copied by Chateaubriand, with notes on whatever Theiner omitted. These copies, which he received before writing his article, are still among the Acton papers. 'I had the means', he wrote later, 'of controlling Theiner.'[12]

Acton was not yet indignant, partly because his obsession was not yet grown and partly because he still worked with Theiner.

---

[11] Mackintosh 3, 354; Theiner, *Annales Ecclesiastici 1572–85*, I, p. 328.
[12] DD, p. 135.

A man who writes the history of a Pope will not print all the reports of all the Pope's ambassadors, and will have a different aim in his selection from a man writing the history of a particular event far from Rome. Acton's article on the massacre has a charmingly cryptic sentence about irrelevance, which no reader of that time could understand: 'Theiner ... omitted whatever seemed irrelevant to his purpose. The criterion of irrelevance is uncertain ...' Thirteen years later bitterness swept over him as he contemplated the *conspiracy to deceive*. Among the conspirators he was prepared to name three of the eminent historical minds of the nineteenth century, and first on the list he put the name of Theiner.[13] Another thirteen years after that, he described Theiner as a gross prevaricator.

These harsh judgements were not in the mood of 1866–74. Acton was already critical of Theiner – but not as a manipulator of sources, only as a man who had such affection for popes that unconscious bias led him astray.

The lives of these historians now became entangled with stirring political events, the Vatican Council of 1869–70 and the fall of Rome to the kingdom of Italy on 20 September 1870.

When the Vatican Council met in December 1869, it soon divided into parties on the question of the teaching office of the Church, and the nature of the Pope's infallibility. Nearly all the fathers of the Council believed that the Pope (in some sense still uncertain) was the infallible mouthpiece of Church authority. A sizeable minority, some 150 to 200 bishops, did not want the Council to make a theological definition of this doctrine, because they feared that the conversion of Protestants might be made more difficult, and because they believed it difficult to define in relation to the general authority of the Church. The majority was determined to define it; partly because the age of indifference and secularity and challenge to Christian truth seemed to require that, if they had a successor of St Peter who

---

[13] Conz., III, p. 284.

could speak with a divine authority, this authority should be declared before the face of the world, and partly because Pope Pius IX himself took this view of the matter, and loyalty made some bishops wish to define as he judged right.

The theoretical argument pressed sorest upon the historians. If men started to declare the Pope (in some way) infallible, the historians looked back upon the history of the Church and saw moments when the Pope was wrong, and either inferred that the Pope was not infallible or argued that the doctrine must not be defined in such a way as to cover that error. The leader of the extreme opposition, though not a bishop at the Council, was the historian Döllinger of Munich. In Rome worked two of his pupils, both historians, Acton and Friedrich. The little handful of bishops with a historical training were to a man opposed to definition – Bishop Hefele of Rottenburg, Cardinal Rauscher of Vienna, Bishop Greith of St Gall. One or two of the leaders of the defining party gave the impression that history did not matter. How shall we test an eternal and unchanging truth by the studies of academics who cannot even agree with each other? Archbishop Manning of Westminster, who was specially prominent in favour of infallibility, uttered sentences which certainly sounded antihistorical.

Theiner was a historian, and therefore at this moment uncomfortable. In the division of parties the Pope, and the Pope's men, could hardly think of the other side as fully loyal to Catholicism. In large measure Theiner was the Pope's man. He was not a member of the minority, and had no place in the Council. But in the minds of the majority he was associated with the minority. And they were right thus far, that correspondents from the minority always assumed that he agreed with them when they wrote him letters. He had dedicated an important collection of documents to Strossmayer the Bishop of Bosnia, the most eloquent and outspoken bishop among the leaders of the minority. He was a historian at a moment when historical enquiry was unpalatable. He was a German inside the Vatican at a moment when most German bishops were opposed to what the Pope wanted. Though he was the Pope's man, he became the Pope's man thirty-five years before, in a less beleaguered city.

The company which Theiner kept was no longer congenial to the Curia. Men remembered the kind of visitor who ascended the long winding stair to sup with him in the Tower of the Winds.

The Vatican of 1869–70 was a different place from the Vatican of 1855. In 1855 Theiner was at home in the air of the Curia. In 1870 he no longer had a natural habitation. One example will suffice: the most unpopular or popular letters of the day were the reports from Rome to Munich, published in the *Allgemeine Zeitung* of Augsburg, under the pseudonym Quirinus. These letters contained a brilliant pillorying of the majority in the Vatican Council, and repeatedly used information available to no one else among the journalists. As early as January 1870, Theiner decided that Acton was the unknown author. Theiner was in part, though only in part, right. But the important point was the nature of his reaction to the idea that his friend and historical colleague should be perpetrating these scandalous letters. So far from being shocked, he was reported by Acton to be 'thrilled'.[14]

When the Vatican Council opened in December 1869, its mode of proceeding was instantly a matter of controversy; whether the heads of the Catholic states should have been invited, who should have the right to propose motions, how the debates should be conducted, whether a simple majority was enough to carry a motion. Naturally everyone wanted to know how the last General Council at Trent conducted its business. The Curia did not wish the proceedings of Trent to be prominent. For the debates of Trent were conducted with less control than the debates of the first Vatican Council – for one excellent and compelling reason, that the number of persons present at Rome was often ten times the number of those present at Trent.

[14] Conz., II, p. 58.

An assembly of 60 may behave as an assembly of 600 may not – that is, if useful business is to be done.

Within the first few days of the Council Theiner received orders not to let anyone see his papers on Trent. The order was not specially directed against Theiner. Another Oratorian, Calenzio, who was also working on Trent, likewise received notice to stop. Not to release even the order of business at Trent was a sign of the besieged stance which prevailed among the cardinals during the last days of papal Rome. Sooner or later the opposition would discover the mode of proceedings at Trent. Even if they had known it in detail since the beginning of the Council, that knowledge could have made no difference to the course of events. From all points of view truth would be better than refusal of truth.

In the spring of 1870 opposition bishops were found to possess the order of business at the Council of Trent. They made use of it in argument. The Curia inferred that the knowledge of the document could only have come from the Vatican Secret Archives. Suspicion fell on Theiner.

And now the rumours of his enemies gathered: he was bribable; let rich Protestants into the archives and took no notice of the rule of excommunication; released papers which he ought not to have released to foreigners, even to an Anglican bishop, gave Cardinal Rauscher the materials with which to write an antipapal pamphlet; communicated the order of proceedings at Trent to Cardinal Hohenlohe; communicated the same to Lord Acton, together with a mass of other material which he ought not to have communicated. As early as 4 February 1870, long before the accusations were directly lodged against Theiner, the pseudonymous Quirinus wrote a fatal paragraph:

Father Theiner, prefect of the Papal Archives, has had parts of the first volume of his Acts of the Council of Trent printed. We find there a *Modus Procedendi*, which secures to the Fathers of the Council much more freedom of action than the present regulations ... Theiner has been altogether forbidden, by the management of the Jesuits, to publish his work, and has received the most strict commands not to show the part already printed to any bishop.[15]

How had the Austrian and Bavarian bishops acquired the order of business at the Council of Trent?

When Pope Pius IX accused Theiner in April 1870, he does not seem to have accused him of communicating the procedures of Trent directly. The documents of Trent gave only the final push to Theiner's fall. Acton went so far as to consider that even without the affair of Trent Theiner could not have survived, and that the charge of communicating documents of Trent was 'only a pretext'. Acton was wrong in thinking it a mere excuse. But he was right thus far, that it was not the first grave charge that the Pope lodged against Theiner.

On 12 April 1870 Pope Pius IX suddenly summoned Theiner to his presence. He was excited and angry. He said that Theiner was reported to have taken Lord Acton into the Secret Archives and given him documents for his use. Theiner denied it with decision, and his denial seemed to make the Pope more excited. Theiner then offered to take a solemn oath that it was untrue. The Pope quietened. But he started blaming Acton – 'he is not one of us' – and Friedrich and Döllinger – and then all the German bishops.

When, therefore, the bishops of the minority produced the Trent procedure, Theiner could not survive in charge of the archives. In Munich Döllinger heard from Friedrich of Theiner's 'very painful situation, suspected by the Pope, and accused.' Acton reported from Rome in a series of laconic letters:

4 June 1870 Expect, any day, disquieting news about Theiner. He will almost certainly be dismissed. Today I was with him and will be tomorrow.

5 June 1870 Whitsunday. The storm at last breaks over Theiner's head ... Theiner's friendship with [Bishop] Strossmayer gave them [the Jesuits] the means to stir the Pope to action.

---

[15] *Quirinus* (English translation), p. 194.

Acton to his wife undated. My friend Theiner has fallen into disgrace. I have been much with him the last two days. I am going to fish in these troubled waters.

Theiner's fate was decided a few days before 5 June. He was out at a villa in the country, working tranquilly away at the life of Pope Benedict XIV, and received an order to return. He went to the Secretary of State, Cardinal Antonelli, who informed him what was decided; characteristically adding that he wished him well, but was powerless to help. Theiner said he was innocent, but in vain. He was required (4 August 1870) to give up the keys of the archives. They trusted him now so little that they walled up the door which led into the archives from Theiner's apartment in the tower.

Theiner was not dismissed, that is, he retained the title of prefect of the archives though he was no longer allowed into the archives of which he was prefect. Whether from kindness to an old man who would find it hard to move house, or to avoid scandal among European scholars if so famous a historian were ousted, he stayed in his rooms up the tower and kept his little stipend of 30 scudi a month. He was grieved that if he wanted to see a manuscript he must ask permission like anyone else and was determined not to be so humiliated. But he had little fight in him. He shocked those who thought him anti-papal (and till that moment they included Acton) by signing an address of loyalty from Roman professors to the Pope. But he was left in peace. Acton observed his behaviour in adversity and admired him.

'His consciousness of how his fate had been incurred gave to his bearing under misfortune a patience which was not without dignity and grace.'[16]

Early in October 1873 Acton, who believed that Theiner was now too old for historical work, was astonished to receive a letter from him telling him in strictest confidence that the Acts of

---

[16] *Saturday Review* (1874), 304.

Trent would soon appear – they were published without papal leave under the patronage of Bishop Strossmayer at Zagreb. Acton was excited. 'How astonishing is your vigour, and power of work!' he answered. 'May the world long be enriched by your treasure.'[17]

Theiner died on 9 August 1874, seeking relief from the summer heat by bathing at Civita Vecchia. When Acton heard the news he remembered the defects of character and scholarship and sent a severe anonymous obituary to the *Saturday Review*. But his epitaph rose above this criticism:

In spite of many shortcomings, Theiner had rendered great services to learning, and so far as learning serves religion, to the Church which he so sternly loved. His death leaves vacant among European scholars a place which no one can fill.

[17] *Carte Theiner*, I, p. 3.

3

AT THE FIRST VATICAN COUNCIL

I N December 1869 the bishops of the world, or some six hundred of them, met in Rome for the Vatican Council. The Vatican sounds the obvious place to hold a Council but no previous Council had met there. If the Eastern Emperor was strong they met at or near Constantinople; if the French were strong they met in the Rhône Valley at Lyons, or Vienne; if the German Emperor was strong they met on his southern Alpine borders as at Basle or Constance or Trent. But now there was no Eastern Emperor south of Moscow. Germany was divided between the claims of Catholic Austria and Protestant Prussia, and although the French Emperor was a bad Catholic and kept a garrison in Rome, he had betrayed the Papal States to Italy. The Council could meet in Rome only because French soldiers defended the city – from whom? Garibaldi's guerrillas? – much more likely the Italian government on the pretext of saving it from Garibaldi's guerrillas. No Pope would dream of summoning a Council anywhere now but in Rome. Formerly if in Rome they met at the Lateran. Events of the past made St Peter's and the Vatican much the more sacred and in a modern world which took not much notice of the sacred there was no hesitation where the Council should meet.

The purposes of the meeting were various. There was a political demonstration – amid all the threats to Rome and the Pope, this city is the sacred city to which representatives of all the world come. The Pope was a very religious person and was sure that what the world needed most was a declaration of the supreme authority of the see of Rome in faith and morals – that he is 'infallible' – that in declaring the faith of the Catholic Church he does not need to agree with all the congregations, they need to agree with him. Many bishops thought that the pastoral care of the church was outmoded and must be brought up to date. Other bishops who were lawyers thought the same of church laws.

Acton decided to attend; not of course the sessions, to which only bishops and their theologians could come, but to be in Rome during the meetings and see whether he could influence what happened from behind the scenes. The bishops would not spend eighteen hours a day in meetings, sometimes they would need to have a drink or an evening meal.

This sounds the wildest plan. A layman; with no official status; aged only thirty-six; not a theologian; a suspect British Catholic; known in Rome as the favourite pupil of a suspect German professor – he might receive courtesy but he was more likely to find that bishops avoided his company and that those whom he met shut their mouths. The Vatican had issued the decree that no information of any kind might be passed outside the Council hall which was St Peter's. The Vatican did not realise the law that what 600 persons do cannot be kept secret with such strictness. Still, this rule was likely to deter bishops from indiscreet babble.

To the contrary, he was still very confident in his own intelligence, perhaps over-confident. And although he was no trained theologian, he had a quality which the bishops were going to need and which most of them lacked. He knew history. If there was talk that the Pope was infallible, someone was going to ask about occasions when Popes went wrong or contradicted their predecessors – then history was a sharp knife. Acton could wield it. Of the 600 bishops, only some five could compare with him.[1]

---

[1] Rauscher, Hefele, Greith, Pitra, Maret: three German speakers and two Frenchmen: of whom Pitra, though a cardinal, was not yet a bishop and Rauscher the only one of the five whose see (Vienna) gave him extra stature.

But he had a weighty quality as well as his history. During the sixties he won the admiration of Mr Gladstone, who at the moment of the Council was the British prime minister. He was not yet Gladstone's pocket sage as he later became. But Gladstone already admired him and his knowledge. Here was an English aristocrat who was liberal in politics and especially about Ireland. In the general election of 1866 Acton stood as the Liberal candidate for an English constituency, his home seat of Bridgnorth. Despite cries of No Popery he was just elected; but in the next year the result was overturned on appeal. So in 1869 Gladstone caused the Queen to elevate him to the House of Lords and he became Lord Acton shortly before he left for the Council in Rome.

The British government had an envoy in Rome, Odo Russell, a friend of Acton. He was accredited to the Pope and would hardly be useful in resisting what the Pope wanted to do at the Council. But if it were true that Acton had the ear of the British Prime Minister, he might be very useful indeed.

For the single person in Europe who could stop this Council was the French Emperor. He had only to order the French garrison to leave Rome and the city would be in chaos. Acton had no influence with Napoleon III, whom he detested. But high policy might make the British work upon the French Emperor. It was just conceivable that Acton's influence with Gladstone would be transmitted into Gladstone's influence with Napoleon, to do something drastic about the Council. The bishops at the Council could not treat Acton as if he was just one of the spectators come to watch. He was like one of the ambassadors of the States represented at the council of Trent, with the exception that he knew far more history than ambassadors did, until the next historian of the Papacy, Pastor, was made Austrian ambassador to the Holy See; that though himself a Catholic he did not represent a Catholic power; and that the same power had also an semi-official agent whose light weight was cast gently and cynically into the opposite scale.

Acton spoke four languages fluently. He knew Rome and had

the entrée to much of Roman society. From a short diary which he kept we can see the social circles in which he moved and which gave him the introductions essential to his programme. His base rested upon

1. Roman hostesses especially the British – one, Mrs Craven, had been his mother's closest friend.
2. The Bavarian embassy where his wife's brother Louis Arco was an attaché. It meant access to Cardinal Hohenlohe, brother of the Bavarian prime minister.
3. The Prussian embassy where Count Arnim befriended him; and where he could meet Prussian bishops like Förster of Breslau. This had an oddness because the Prussian government wanted not to interfere in the Council. But that embassy much helped Acton. Count Arnim shared Acton's views. He thought it in the interest of Prussia to prevent the ultramontanes doing what they wanted. That his master Bismarck preferred to do nothing grieved him. Being a Protestant he did not understand the nuances of the question. He knew little history and had small influence over the German bishops. But his embassy became a leakage of confidential information to Acton.
4. Acton's personal knowledge of a few of the French. He was once the pupil of Dupanloup of Orleans who now had the reputation of being the chief French opponent of the definition of the Pope's infallibility; afterwards the friendship cooled, no one could admire Dupanloup for very long, and Dupanloup was offended by Acton's journalism. But in Rome they needed each other. Acton had not before this known the powerful Archbishop of Paris, Darboy, whom after a time Acton came to think the cleverest man in the Council and who was an outspoken enemy of the declaration of the Pope's infallibility.

Acton sketched Darboy's character: 'He had none of the conventional prejudices and assumed antipathies which are congenial to the hierarchical mind. He was without passion or pathos or affectation; and he had good sense, a perfect temper, and an intolerable wit.' This language is the highest form of praise, Acton had such a sense of reality about human beings that he found it difficult to exalt them in his historical judgements. In a private letter to Döllinger he was frank about Darboy, his ability, the scruples he roused:

> His mind is as clear as crystal. You would be astonished to find how reliable his judgment is and at the great-hearted courage and freedom of his mind. He said to me "The people who want infallibility are like a child who damages his father's watch in looking for the little animal inside that is making the tick. Here in Rome we shall find only large animals". But he is not always trivial like that.[2]

But in Rome Darboy needed Acton less, being the master of his own opinion. Dupanloup came very close to Acton. This was partly because of Acton's friendship with M. du Boys, a lay intimate of Dupanloup who shared a house with him in Rome, and partly because Dupanloup needed Acton. On two occasions the Bishop of Orleans even used Acton as his intermediary to give the Archbishop of Paris messages which he did not like or dare to deliver. 'There's a certain opposition', wrote Acton to Döllinger, 'between the two most important French bishops. Each has given himself away to me, but not obviously. Each of them understands the great weight of the other. But they are divided by French politics' (Darboy was for the Emperor Napoleon, Dupanloup was an old fashioned Bourbon royalist) 'and are rivals here; and especially the serenity and coldness of the one compared with the heat and passion of the other hinders any great cordiality. I cannot say that this is very harmful. But if only they were more intimate, the French bishops would be led more forcibly.'

On this base he built a hard-working endeavour, going to parties, drawing bishops aside for conversation, trying to pump them and sometimes with success, sitting through the night writ-

---

[2] Conz., II, p. 186.

ing reports or letters. He worked with an urgency, almost a passion, yet never lost balance and only towards the end failed in his judgement about what was practicable. When he was inspired he was inspiring. All the ability was harnessed to a cause part-political and part-ecclesiastical, in which his love of religion and his sense of history and his sense of duty to his Church were engaged.

Yet the base had curious limits. It was not surprising that he was not intimate with the majority of bishops who were for the Pope, though at first he kept meeting Archbishop Manning of Westminster at parties and Manning and Acton both knew that they were antagonists. Such bishops regarded Acton as undesirable company and kept away. The curious gap is the Austrian bishops. They were openly or quietly on the side of the minority. The bishops in the minority looked upon Cardinal Rauscher of Vienna as their leader. It was odd that Acton had no more than a formal and passing touch with Cardinal Rauscher.

But he came to know three Austro-Hungarian bishops who in their different ways were potent members of the minority. All three came from non-German sees in the Austro-Hungarian Empire. One was the Archbishop of Prague, Cardinal Schwarzenberg; who was one of the tiny handful of cardinals who became a cardinal before Pius IX was elected Pope and was a tremendous aristocrat. The other two were disreputable with the government in Vienna – Haynald the Hungarian of Kalocsa who represented Hungarian nationalism and knew more about modern science than most bishops; and Strossmayer the Bishop of Bosnia (see of Djakovo) who represented Yugoslav nationalists against the rule of Vienna.

Acton's intimacy with Strossmayer was quick to ripen. They first met in mid-December 1869 and by the New Year were firm friends. Strossmayer was a very attractive man, a noble personality, who spoke beautiful Latin and was the most eloquent speaker at the Council. By January Acton knew that this was no bishop of an obscure Slav see but one of the chief speakers at the Council. He took great trouble; in early January he saw him daily – it was fortunately easy as their lodgings were near – wrote to him three or four notes a day, and made friends with his theologian Vorsak. Strossmayer first dined with the Actons on 18 January. Acton found him a truly big person. He talked of the glowing fire in him, the strength throughout his character, his love for souls and for Christian unity, his freedom in seeking reforms needed in Catholic practice and doctrine. By nature Acton did not revere Popes, bishops, politicians, with the exception of Gladstone. Of no other bishop but Strossmayer did he write in such high terms.

Six days after that dinner the British chargé in Rome, Odo Russell, sent to the Foreign Secretary Lord Clarendon a letter that marked Acton's achievement:

Both Dupanloup and Strossmayer admit that the opposition could not have been organized without Lord Acton whose marvellous knowledge, honesty of purpose, clearness of mind and powers of organization have rendered possible what appeared at first impossible. The party he has so powerfully helped to create is filled with respect and admiration for him. On the other hand the infallibilists think him the devil!

I admire his creation, I bow before his genius and I wish the opposition all the success they have so earnestly at heart, but I adhere to my conviction that humanity will gain more in the end by the dogmatic definition of papal infallibility than by the contrary.[3]

The last sentence shows why Odo Russell, though he was a friend of Acton, was little use in his campaign. He did not believe in the campaign and eyed it with an interested amused detachment. He dutifully passed to London information which Acton wished him to pass, and allowed Acton to use his secret diplomatic bag; but made clear his position, that interference did no good, and that the Council must be left to take its own course and the bishops to determine what they willed. Though Acton was British he derived none of his influence at Rome from his friendship with the British envoy.

---

[3] Blakiston, p. 385.

Odo Russell was diplomat enough to play a double game. In his government's interest he must be friendly with Archbishop Manning of Westminster. He saw Manning frequently during the Council, and for a time took him for a walk every weekend. We know that he passed to Manning valuable information about the opposition. He does not seem to have passed Acton information of importance. Yet there is a letter from Odo Russell to Acton dated 22 February 1870 which proves the double game by giving every sign that the author is on Acton's side and asking for his advice on what to do.[4]

That month a saying passed round Rome, 'The opposition is a sword, and its point is Strossmayer's lips, and its hilt is the hand of Acton.'[5] When he heard the saying, Acton saw that so far as it was true it was of that moment and could not last. For one thing, his last three nights had been without sleep and even he could not keep up such work.

These three sleepless nights were caused partly by the need to write a letter to Döllinger which could be published as news from the Council. The use of private, anonymous, letters marked a new departure in Acton's attempt to influence the bishops at the Council.

During 1869 Döllinger began to use the *Allgemeine Zeitung* as the vehicle for hostile comments about the coming Council. The newspaper was an intelligent liberal journal, neutral and detached from Catholicism. From December 1869, during the sittings of the Council, his comments took the form of 'Letters from Rome'. This title had a measure of truth since he garnered his information from a variety of sources, including not only reports but judgements or news sent in private letters by friends in Rome; and of these friends in Rome, Acton quickly established himself as the source of the best news. Several months later all the *Allgemeine Zeitung* letters were collected and published under the title *Letters from Rome* by Quirinus, as the

---

[4] CUL Add. MSS 8119/5/198.
[5] Conz., II, p. 156.

umbrella-name for the different minds which contributed to the reports.

At first the bishops in Rome classed these letters as another example of the scandal and gossip and lies which filled the international press, which must print news about the Council and was forbidden, by the rules of secrecy, to get reliable news about the Council. Roman gossip speculated on the sources of Roman information; and since a connection with Döllinger lay on the face of the letters, gossip soon fastened on the two young men in Rome who stood nearest to Döllinger, his pupil Acton and his lecturer in church history, Johann Friedrich.

Acton's response to this rumour was unexpected. He did not care. A man who was attempting to form a party, and therefore win moderate opinion, would not normally welcome suspicion that he was the anonymous author of letters which moderate men thought scandalous; especially when, at that time, the charge was false. The obvious result of suspicion must be restraint in conversation by those who conversed, and a reluctance of moderate bishops to go into his company. It is possible to detect the withdrawal of certain informants, who resented Döllinger, resented more fiercely the tone of Quirinus, and therefore kept away from anyone who might supply Quirinus with almost the only accurate information to be leaking out of the Council.

Acton did not mind the suspicion that he might be something to do with Quirinus because he adopted the position, not slowly, that outright opposition was the only policy with any chance of success, and that trying to collect moderate votes weakened the campaign.

He had begun by trying to keep his master in Munich informed. Then the master used the information, among other news, for anonymous letters. Acton revered Döllinger and trusted his judgement. He only asked that personal names and details should be omitted where they could be identified with a known source.[6] The difference was not wide between supplying

---

[6] Conz., II, p. 59, cf. p. 156.

scraps of information to an anonymous writer and writing anonymous letters. The letters could be fuller, more coherent, and more influential. Perhaps he thought that since the letters would be published anyway, and would be identified with Döllinger and therefore with himself, it was best to make the letters as reliable, weighty, and well framed as possible. He happened to be the only person in Rome possessing quantities of secret information about the business and speeches in the transept of St Peter's, but not himself under any undertaking to observe secrecy. At no point did doubt enter his mind about the policy of writing anonymous letters for the *Allgemeine Zeitung*. At no point did he doubt whether Döllinger was right to turn away from learned argument with bishops and appeal to the multitude.

Acton had a uniquely advantageous training for what he was now about to begin, the writing of news letters for the press. To be a born scholar is not regarded as advantageous to a journalist. Later his work for the *Rambler*, and *Home and Foreign Review*, and the *Chronicle*, gave him the ease of public expression, and the sensitive way of persuading an intelligent but not very informed public, which was the best equipment for the task which he now began. This is remarkable when we remember that late in his life some highly intelligent readers found his articles so opaque as to be incomprehensible. He became a journalist with more important secret information than any other journalist in Rome and the gift to explain what the world could understand. He was also the only journalist in Rome with the equipment of a historian, the only layman who needed no one to explain the technicalities of theological statements and who understood the force and the context of draft clauses quicker than many of the bishops in Council. He started to turn Quirinus into a more powerful instrument of policy.[7]

When it is said that Acton 'understood' theology, this does not mean that he cared about the nuances of the doctrine of the

---

[7] The mystery of the Quirinus authors is solved by V. Conzemius in *Freiburger Geschichtsblätter*, 52 (1963–4), 252 ff.

teaching authority in the Church. He was against infallibility of the Pope. But he never explained what he meant by the phrase, and was hardly aware that it was variously interpreted by members of the ultramontane party and still more variously by bishops of the opposition party. For him the word infallibility was imprecise. He cared not at all how men interpreted the doctrine. He felt it as a flag or symbol of all the tendencies – towards power and against freedom, towards persecution and against tolerance, towards concealment and against openness – which he hated and from which he yearned to save the Church. This 'sacramental' nature of the word infallibility in Acton's mind helps to explain the force of his leadership. It also made him almost incapable of understanding the nuances and difficulties in the minds of his own allies, and wholly incapable of seeing into the minds of the ultramontanes. At times this made his utterances a guide which future historians trusted at their peril.

The first letter, written by Acton from Rome with the intention that it might be printed as a report, was dated 26 January 1870. The date is important as a sign why he began to write. Two days later, Strossmayer with his beautiful Latin made a speech in the Council which created excitement and was the chief topic of conversation among the bishops. He talked of the need to universalise the papacy, and prevent it being an Italian institution; of the need to reform the Curia and make it more representative of the world-wide Church; of his desire to have General Councils regularly; of the danger of chasm between Catholicism and modern society; of the freedom of the peoples and of freedom as the true basis of the Church's strength. The speech was secret. But Acton evidently felt overwhelming desire that the whole world should know its contents. The first Quirinus letter that he ever wrote contained his summary of Strossmayer's speech.

The second and third letters for Quirinus, which made a single letter, were finished on 11 February and had a different objective. Acton started by wanting to tell the world. This motive remained. But now he realized that these letters printed in Augsburg made such stir that his interpretation of events in Rome could influence the attitudes of the bishops. From the second of his Quirinus letters he began to write with policy as the object.

The cause of this change lay in conversation with the opposition bishops during the three previous days: not only with Hefele, and Dupanloup, but with Cardinal Schwarzenberg of Prague, Greith of St Gall, the Gallican Maret, Landriot of Rheims, Kenrick of St Louis. What disturbed him was growing agreement that the decree of infallibility must be resisted not because it was untrue but because it was inexpedient. Few bishops were prepared outright to say that it was untrue. Moderate bishops were prepared to say that it was inopportune – whether because it could cause schism, or because it was part of a far broader and more complex area of Christian doctrine, the entire doctrine of Church authority, which had not yet been considered. Acton had helped to build an opposition by bringing French and German bishops together. But when the opposition was in being, its members could not agree on the only programme which Acton wanted, and which he believed to be the only programme with a chance of success. 'I don't believe in the staying-power of these gentlemen', he wrote to Döllinger. '. . . For who risks a schism on a question of timing?' 'Our Party', he wrote again (8 February), 'is heaped together out of delicate and incompatible materials. We have to work at them every day, do our carpentry, prop them up, warn them against traps, put courage into the weak and fear into the ill-disposed. Men who were strong yesterday are weak today. They snatch at excuses to compromise . . ..'[8]

The second of his Quirinus letters (Quirinus, no. 20) was written with the intention of showing the bishops of the opposition that inopportunism could never do as a policy. Truth was principle, opportunity was expediency, and truth must ever conquer expediency. (Cf. Quirinus, Eng. trans., pp. 255–6.) He felt that

[8] Conz., II, pp. 80, 142.

he must compel bishops to decide; to stand up and be counted; not to take shelter in so tactful and weak an opposition. 'I have considered carefully', he told Döllinger, 'where they require to be frightened and where encouraged. It is my most deliberate opinion that this letter, turned into good German but not altered, ought to appear as soon as possible . . . The letter will have a great effect upon the bishops. Everyone will know that it is written here, and obviously by me. Do not be afraid for yourself.'[9]

He threw in a little warning to the other side: that the agreements between the French and British governments now made it impossible for the Pope to use Malta as a refuge if he needed to flee from Italian revolution when the French withdrew the garrison. It was not true, or Acton had no means of knowing whether it was true. He hoped that it was true, and declared it as a fact. Thus the element of policy entered his Quirinus letters.

Whether it was wise for a man in possession of confidential information, who was in daily touch with important bishops, to use the information so that several of the bishops must henceforth distrust his company, will be a matter of opinion. Throughout his life Acton had political force but not always political prudence; or, to frame the same idea in another form, he had no doubts about adhering to a course which he believed to be right and moral, and took little notice of sensitive minds who hesitated whether the course was practicable.

The decision is more intelligible if we recognise that at that moment the opposition were in turmoil, partly because they now had knowledge of what was proposed as a draft schema on the Church. Some of them were ready for very strong measures. Strossmayer and Dupanloup (at least before they read the result) more or less approved the step which Acton took.

But Acton misjudged the power of an anonymous pen. Certainly he stood in a unique place: the only man in Europe with secret information which nothing but courtesy could stop him

---

[9] Conz. II, p. 157. The letter was mostly written in English.

releasing and which the world's press wanted. He exaggerated the effect upon the bishops. 'The *Allgemeine Zeitung*', he told Döllinger,[10] – 'is a power in Rome, bigger than many bishops, and much feared – bigger even than many states.' This was true but the letters were not so powerful as Acton expected and hoped.

The business suffered intolerable delays. No precedent could tell the managers how to conduct sensible debate among 500 or more men, who could only half understand the Latin spoken by other tongues and who could hardly hear in the echoing hall. The managers had not foreseen the problems, and how the agenda dragged miserably with nothing achieved. By the end of January some bishops, who felt their presence needed in their dioceses, were vexed that they had spent two months in Rome to achieve nothing. New rules of business were indispensable.

These new rules were given to the fathers on 22 February 1870. They aimed at speeding the conduct of meetings. They gave to the presidents, at the request of at least ten fathers, the right to accept a resolution by simple majority that the debate be closed. This grieved some of the opposition because it further restricted their already confined liberty of speech. But what caused the storm was the principle of resolution by simple majority. This was explicitly directed at resolutions about particular clauses. But if the majority principle applied to clauses, and no other principle was mentioned for dogmatic decrees, the principle of decision by simple majority must be allowed to apply to dogmatic decrees.

A General Council was in essence an assembly of bishops, representing the teachers of their churches and coming together to declare the faith of the whole Church. No one would expect that in any large group of bishops from the world-wide Church an actual unanimity would be achieved except by miracle. Always the eccentric or the obstinate or the heretic would hold against the consensus. But many good Catholics expected that Councils

[10] Conz., II, pp. 157, 163.

would declare the faith with a 'moral unanimity'; partly because the bishops were not making new faith but defining what was believed, and partly because any other course was unthinkable. Just over half the Church could not suddenly force doctrines or devotions on just under half the Church if the lesser 'portion' never accepted them in all history. One attempt to do this very thing from two different sides ended only in the incurable schism between Holy Orthodox East and Roman Catholic West.

The ultramontane majority in the Vatican Council had no desire to force their faith upon half the Church with a bare majority of votes by bishops. For they believed that hardly anyone disbelieved the doctrine of the Pope's infallibility – perhaps a handful of obstinate or heretical men like Döllinger and Acton, Hefele and Maret. They thought that they could safely disregard the minority because the minority which disbelieved was tiny and the minority that counted was concerned only with timing and not with truth. In this belief they laboured under a grievous illusion which was the disastrous misconception of the Council. But, sharing this illusion, they had no nefarious intent to trample upon a large minority of bishops because they fancied no such minority to exist.

Since the managers of the Council shared these illusions, they drafted a set of regulations which in effect allowed decisions to be taken by a simple majority vote.

This question of moral unanimity became the chief interest of Acton until the end of the Council. He said afterwards that these new regulations first made him optimistic about the chance of victory for his side.

He believed a formal protest to be essential. If they accepted the decision, nothing could stop the definition of infallibility in any sense that the majority determined. If they now declared that they could never accept the mere decision of a majority, they had won the campaign, since whatever the Council determined was not thereby to be received as part of the Catholic faith.

He really wished the opposition bishops to refuse to attend

any session until the majority rule was withdrawn – yet simultaneously recognized that the managers of the Council would not or could not withdraw. Acton thought it wonderful ground on which to fight. He wrote Strossmayer a long letter to persuade him to fight.

We should make it a question of faith and not of tactics. The clash with the immoral spirit of arbitrary rule in the Church must sooner or later come. You should save truth by saving freedom. The world, and public opinion, and the powers, would understand this protest, the bishops would support you and Protestantism would be shattered if you confessed the true principle that a definition of dogma cannot go beyond what is in tradition.

He met Strossmayer before he went to the International Committee.[11] Strossmayer said, 'Everything you have said to me is already written in my heart.' But when he found that despite Strossmayer Dupanloup refused to declare that they would not attend sessions till the rule was withdrawn, he was more gloomy. 'The crisis is postponed.' Quirinus letter no. 28, the fourth Quirinus letter written by Acton, made the best of it, or even better than the best, in telling the world. He called the bishops' protest 'like knocking a nail in the coffin of the ecumenical Council' (Quirinus, E.T., p. 336).

No one yet knew who were the authors of Quirinus's letters. Erroneous speculations still circulated in Rome. The Prussian attaché was suspect – but even that showed how students of the letters perceived the importance of information which probably came via the Prussian embassy. Whatever their origins they were written by a person or persons in the Bavarian and/or Prussian groups. Since Acton began to draft letters, they were better informed, more solid, more cogent, but no less the letters of an advocate pleading with all the conviction at his command. By mid March he was coherent in extremism, not minding if the campaign which he led were to destroy papal authority, provided

---

[11] Acton to Strossmayer, quoted in Conz., II, p. 184.

that truth should prevail. He had a feeling that posterity would judge them all in this crisis for Christianity, and that at least they must not fail by silence.

The bishops had no desire to destroy papal authority. From towards the end of March, if not a fortnight earlier, Acton's part in the opposition ceased to be that of a creative link, and became that of a gadfly on one wing of the opposition, trying to push them to be more revolutionary than they wished or thought practicable; still respected by intimates for information and judgement, still utilized when the opposition felt specially oppressed by the majority, still able to command confidential information about the proceedings in the Council chamber; but confined in his circle to a small number of convinced bishops – Dupanloup, Strossmayer, increasingly the Englishman Clifford, Hefele, Connolly of Halifax, and Kenrick of St Louis, occasionally Förster of Breslau. Acton relied more and more upon Arnim and the Prussian embassy. That Acton should begin to rely more on a Protestant ambassador in a Protestant embassy shows how he had moved to the left and how more Catholic sources of information were restricted. But Count Arnim conversely came to rely more and more upon Acton.

This gadfly aspect appeared in the mood of the Quirinus letters which Acton drafted. Though the best letters of Quirinus were drafted by Acton, partly because they had better information and partly because they had better judgement, they began to adopt the colour of the letters not drafted by Acton, the tone of contempt which at first Acton avoided. He started by wishing the world to know how a noble bishop spoke at the Council; went on to try and strengthen the policy of the opposition, then to whip the opposition for its weakness; and ended by wanting to demolish the Council's authority by exposing it to public scorn. He saw his work with Quirinus as the way in which the public opinion of Europe could be brought to bear upon the enclosed Fathers in the Council, a skylight by which fresh air could blow through minds isolated from modern society in the transept of St Peter's.

But though he now stood openly for a radical policy with which hardly a handful of bishops could agree, they still needed him when they wanted help from the powers.

The Foreign Secretary Clarendon likened the appeals of Döllinger and Acton to the cries of drowning men clutching at straws.[12] Those who knew Gladstone were not sure that the appeals could be so vain. His Christian heart was committed to Acton's cause, he could hardly bear to do nothing. In Rome even Archbishop Manning began to worry that Gladstone would act. As late as 6 April he wrote Gladstone a letter warning him how unreliable a guide he had in Acton, and how dangerous to Ireland would be intervention by the British government in Rome. But relations between Gladstone and Manning had long been icily courteous. Gladstone was impervious to warnings against Acton from that source.

How revolutionary Acton now felt in Rome was shown by sudden fear that he was not safe physically. He asked the British government for protection. He knew that he was watched; and part of the historian's difficulty in following his energetic movements and policies through the mass of documents derives from his reluctance to commit details to paper which, he was afraid, might be opened or stolen. He told his step-father Granville that he was regarded as the evil one at Rome and might be in some personal danger. Some years later he told the historian Bryce that he believed the Jesuits to have hired men to assassinate him, but that was probably his way of making the later conversation more interesting.[13] Granville told his Foreign Secretary Clarendon of the danger. Clarendon thought that expulsion was the worst that Acton had to fear, but ordered Odo Russell to 'throw your aegis over him'. Odo Russell replied: 'I have taken steps to protect Lord Acton, but I do not apprehend that he will be molested. He is of course watched by spies but I do not for one moment believe that they will otherwise interfere with him . . .'[14]

[12] Blakiston, p. 413.
[13] Hensley Henson's Journal, 24 October 1912, record of Bryce's utterance to Henson.
[14] Blakiston, pp. 399, 408.

At this point of time, therefore, in early and mid March, Acton's influence *in* Rome was fading. He had done what he could to help mould an opposition, and now they did not need his activity as go-between. He openly stood for a more revolutionary policy than any but two or three bishops were willing to back. They had looked to him to stir the British government to stir the French government; and by mid March even opposition bishops lost faith that intervention by governments, feeble as it must be, could do anything but harm. He still provided four or five bishops with useful information, argued at them to stand firm, encouraged them when they were melancholy, and he had the intangible influence, large but not so large as he hoped, of being the hardest, and best informed, head among the writers of Quirinus. But the main force of his activity was past. At times he became little more than a purveyor of confidential news – to Gladstone, or to Munich, or to the press, or to the Prussian embassy for use with Bismarck.

Nevertheless, as late as 10 April 1870 Odo Russell sent home another glowing testimony to Acton's role at the Council:

> To Lord Acton's marvellous talents, science, energy, and zeal the enlightened opposition in the Council owes its present existence and strength. Without him the Germans, French, Americans and English could not have agreed and acted together, so different are their national theological standpoints. Acton has done what no one else in the world could do and deserves the highest credit for it. Of course if I cannot always follow his able lead it is because he is a Catholic and I am a Protestant and our standpoints differ accordingly.[15]

At moments of March and April Acton had his last successes in Rome.

The opposition bishops protested, early in March, against doctrinal decrees being voted by mere majority. These protests were couched in moderate words, less stern than Acton hoped, but still firm enough to cast a doubt upon the Council if the

---

[15] Blakiston, p. 419.

majority persisted. The question was, what was to happen if the protests received no answer and were relegated to the archives.

The debate in the Council on 22 March contained a concerted effort by the opposition to protest against vote by majority. Cardinal Schwarzenberg of Prague made a strong speech, during which he was called to order. Then Strossmayer made the speech which caused the 'scene' of the Council. Bishops advanced on the rostrum shaking their fists, men cried out at heresy, the presidents silenced the speaker, Strossmayer objected to the preface of the schema which attributed modern unbelief to the Reformation. He praised the Protestants for all they did to resist unbelief. Amid hostile murmuring from all sides, he declared that doctrine could only be taught to the people as Catholic doctrine if moral unanimity reigned among the bishops. The original text of Strossmayer's speech, which the tumult stopped, shows a challenge in the last paragraph. If we proceed by vote of majority,

this generation and posterity will have a handle to declare, this was neither a free nor a true Council ... It is my deep conviction that a Council which proceeds in this way would by that very act destroy the conscience of the Catholic world ...

The scene at the Council caused strong emotion among the Opposition bishops. That Thursday Acton argued at Clifford, and Clifford, persuaded after difficulty, argued at Connolly and Dupanloup. They decided to carry a protest to the presidents at the public sitting. The president agreed to withdraw the preface to the schema for amendment. And the 'naive bishops' (as Acton described them – he meant Dupanloup and Ketteler)[16] believed that they had won a victory.

The preface reappeared on Monday (28th) much improved. That evening Dupanloup came to Acton's house at 7, Clifford came at 8, Strossmayer's theologian Vorsak came at 9. They gave him the materials for a superb Quirinus letter on

[16] Conz., II, pp. 255, 257.

Strossmayer's speech. Dupanloup and Clifford agreed in giving Acton some credit for Saturday's victory.[17] Acton's influence on Clifford was strong through March and April and May.

In the second week of April Acton, now a close friend of the Prussian envoy Arnim, saw the possibility of at last moving Bismarck to act.

Arnim (rightly as the aftermath proved) was afraid of consequences for Germany if the ultramontanes won their way at the Council. Since the opening of the Council he had wanted Prussia to join a common intervention by the powers. Bismarck would do nothing. He did not much care what happened in Rome ('frivolous *Schadenfreude*' was Acton's description of his mood), and so far as he cared he shared an opinion similar to that of Lord Clarendon, that intervention could do little good in Rome and might do harm among Catholics at home.

Now that Acton was an intimate of Arnim, he poured arguments into his ear.

1. If the dogma is defined, the Prussian government must either depose its opponents and become the tool of Rome's tyranny; or it must support them, and resist Rome. Is it not better to avoid such a predicament, through judicious backing of the opposition at the proper time?
2. The Prussian government cannot concern itself with canons and theology (they assured the bishops of this non-intervention); but it can protect freedom and the rights of the minority. This second is the nub.[18]

Strossmayer's famous speech denounced the draft preface to the schema for its attitude to Protestants. Arnim was able to use the same text to rouse the King of Prussia to anger. In two letters of 25 and 26 March he proposed that if the words were accepted, he (Arnim) should be withdrawn from Rome. Bismarck on 30 March telegraphed a reply that if the preface in this way attacked

---

[17] Conz., II, p. 268.
[18] Conz., II, pp. 305–6.

the king's religion and therefore the king, 'to recall you will be unavoidable, and His Majesty must publicly require the return of the North German bishops to their dioceses. Inform Cardinal Antonelli and the German bishops'. By the time this telegram came the offending preface was withdrawn. But Acton had the sensation that this sudden intervention changed Bismarck's attitude. Lord Clarendon's papers show that Clarendon was aware of a change in Bismarck a week earlier.[19]

The truth is, Arnim did not need Acton's advice to act with his own government. The important thing that Acton did for Arnim was to link him with the French, and thereby to bring the weak Prussian threat into uneasy alliance with the weak French threat.

The new attitude of the Prussian government came far too late to be effective.

Between 23 April and 9 May 1870 Acton was ill of fever and nervous exhaustion. For a time the extraordinary activity ceased. His ninth letter written for Quirinus (*Letters from Rome*, no. 39) was dated 23 April and had a melancholy air. He was still trying to make the opposition bishops fight but confident that they would avoid battle. He began work again on 10 May, restarted his service of confidential news to Munich, and already on 13 May provided Döllinger with his tenth Quirinus letter (*Letters from Rome*, no. 44).

Two days later he sent the information for still another Quirinus letter, not without the intention to bring public contempt upon the majority. In mid May he worked again at getting a protest on 'moral unanimity', with an optimism which the event disproved. When the debate on infallibility began in the second half of May, his reports for Quirinus became still more contemptuous, but that was the chief sign that he was beginning to despair of victory in the Council.

So Acton's influence faded. He wrote much now of Quirinus

---

[19] In Bismarck, *Politische Schriften*, ed. F. Thimme, vol. 6b, no. 1545; cf. no. 1538; Conz., II, p. 275; Clarendon to Loftus, PRO 361/153 ff.

and thereby was still weighty in the repute or ill repute of the Council before Europe. He saw much of Clifford and Hefele and Dupanloup, a little less of Strossmayer who had lost hope of victory and wanted to go home.

Bishops began to be more concerned with the wording of the formula which should be defined, and had ceased to campaign to prevent any formula being defined. We should like a diary of this period, for Acton's sense that he was watched by spies made him too discreet about his sources of information.

By early May Odo Russell had lost none of his admiration for Acton's extraordinary feats – 'If he ever turns his attention to public affairs he is certainly called upon to play a great part in the history of Europe'[20] – but was sure that he was beaten. Six months later Acton himself agreed that by 24 April the opposition was finished.

At the time he still had grounds for hope. In his moments of pessimism he expected the opposition to collapse. Strossmayer after all seemed too discouraged. But in later May, as he talked with Hefele, and Dupanloup, and Kenrick, and Clifford, and even Schwarzenberg, he realized that these men were going to stand firm to the end of the Council. By 29 May he decided that he could do no more in Rome and would go home to Tegernsee. His wife and children left Rome on 30 May. On 2 June he wrote his twelfth, thirteenth, and fourteenth Quirinus letters (*Letters from Rome*, nos. 51–4), three of his most important. 'The Opposition, whose existence at first was so boldly denied, and of which there was originally only a germ in the Episcopate, subsequently developed in Council through the clumsy tactics of Rome, places the Roman See in an unwonted and it is thought an intolerable light' . . . 'All is not yet lost', he wrote on 4 June. He thought that the debate would go on so long that the Council must adjourn, and time at least would be gained. He wanted speakers to speak long, and more speakers. This tactic did not please Hefele or Haynald, but Acton thought it right. Acton still had a

[20] Blakiston, p. 435.

mysterious plan up his sleeve. 'I think we can explode the Council', he wrote to Döllinger on 3 June. On 7 June, three days before his departure from Rome, he wrote to Döllinger, 'Between tomorrow and the next day I shall detonate my mine, but I can tell you nothing about it until I am safely over the frontier.'[21]

This 'mine' is still a mystery. That day the majority enforced a guillotine in the debate, to the indignation of the minority, and for a moment Acton believed that they now believed the Council invalid. On 7 June Acton drafted a statement that the bishops would never accept a doctrine unless it was accepted with moral unanimity. He took this statement round to his friends among the bishops; apparently argued that this was the only way to halt the majority in their course; and at first found 'some' bishops willing to sign his statement. We do not know which bishops. Kenrick of St. Louis was one (on 8 June Acton carried to the railway station an anti-ultramontane speech by Kenrick, prepared but not delivered at the Council, so that it could be printed in Naples). Afterwards, he lamented the failure of minority bishops to accept this statement.

They never used the strongest argument – that they would never accept a dogma without unanimous consent.

It might have failed. But it was deluding the Pope with the belief that they would yield, to avoid so carefully saying that they would not.[22]

In retrospect he believed that the Opposition were blind in thinking that they could achieve anything by courtesy, by appeals to conscience. The Pope and his advisers were set upon a course. Nothing could stop them except (what Acton called) *terror*:

All their petitions and audiences were worthless. They ought to have remembered in what light he [the Pope] regarded them . . . as heretics.

---

[21] Conz., II, pp. 402, 417.
[22] CUL Add. MSS, 5542, 48, 58, 487.

... If they had understood the position, and acted accordingly, they would not have approached him, or tried to influence him by anything but a very menacing alternative.

He could not persuade the bishops. His 'mine' never 'exploded'.

His round of farewell visits raised his spirits. He went to Archbishop Darboy of Paris, who said, 'In the long run no one will recognize the Council. It's a frivolous affair – the presidents are sacristans.' He went to Kenrick of St. Louis, who was 'a rock of bronze' and told him that he believed the Council null and void; that the doctrinal decrees would only be effective when the Council had ended and been confirmed, and that day would never come; that he would never recommend the doctrine to his people or defend it to Protestants, because he held it for untrue and impossible ... 'Time will decide for our side.' Both Darboy and Kenrick asked him to go away and publish what he had seen, all that he knew about the Council.

On the eve of his departure, he finished a letter to Döllinger with an epitaph about himself:

'Anyway, I believe I've done my duty in Rome.'[23]

The question, whether this feverish activity did good to the cause, will be answered variously. The most detached observer in Rome, Odo Russell, thought that Acton kept the opposition in being; for on the eve of Acton's departure he wrote to London: 'Lord Acton is going away on Saturday next and as he has been the soul of the opposition, we all expect the body to collapse the moment he goes.' Russell exaggerated, as events proved. But Acton's brother-in-law in the Prussian embassy wrote to him on 18 June that 'we feel your absence here is a calamity for us'.[24]

The opposition was a far wider body, and far more diverse, than the group round Acton. The German and French documents prove how relatively small was the circle in which Acton

[23] Conz., II, pp. 420, 422.
[24] Louis Arco to Acton, 8121/6/484.

moved at Rome. They show also how his advocacy of a cause affected the historiography of the Council. Acton divided men into those who believed in the infallibility of the Pope and those who did not. For the nuances of infallibility he had neither interest nor understanding. If men believed in infallibility but did not want it defined, they were classified as inopportunists – which they were. It is now clear that the class 'inopportunists' hides a multitude of opinions; held not so much by people concerned over political occasion, like offence to Protestants or fear of schism in Germany, as by people concerned that this was a difficult subject enough and ought to be defined only after the full consideration which it had not received. Acton was not solely responsible for this simplifying. Manning and the more extreme ultramontanes (even the official historian of the Council Granderath) imagined that almost everyone believed in the papal infallibility which they professed, and therefore classified all who would not vote with them as inopportunists. Afterwards it was in the interests of both sides to make the division of opinion crude. It was also in the interests of bishops of the minority, returning to their ultramontane dioceses after papal infallibility was decreed, to clear themselves with their priests and laity by declaring that they believed all the time but did not think it prudent. The doctrines of inopportunism helped them to free themselves from suspicion that they had verged towards heresy. Acton is not chiefly to be blamed for clouding the history of the Council for the next sixty years.

But even if Odo Russell were right, and Acton kept the opposition as an opposition, this achieved nothing – at first sight. On 18 July the dogma was defined in language which the minority might reluctantly accept but which they could neither welcome nor approve. All the manoeuvring inside Rome, of which Acton was a main part, gained as little as the exchanges of notes among the European powers. Pius IX was imperturbable.

But in fact, something was achieved, whether by the notes of the European powers or the bishops of the minority. Though they did not frighten the Pope, they influenced the minds of several of his leading advisers. By the middle of May 1870 the course of debate was turned away from those matters which were specially offensive to governments – whether the Syllabus of Errors was to be made obligatory on Catholics, whether the new declarations of Rome affected education, or laws of marriage, or toleration – those controversial issues, prominent at the Council in February, now dropped out of sight, and theology came to the front, and the bishops confined themselves to the question of faith and authority within the Catholic Church. Though the governments, and the minority bishops, and Acton looked to have failed, and knew that they had failed, they achieved more than then they knew. They prevented the outcome of the Council from being that fierce attack upon liberal European society which extreme ultramontanes wanted and at more than one moment came near to winning. And if extreme ultramontanes had got what they hoped, the consequences for Catholicism could not have been other than calamitous.

Acton, in Bavaria on 18 July when the decree passed, had not accepted defeat. He began his campaign to ensure that the decree was not accepted by the Catholic Church.

4

AFTER THE COUNCIL

O N 27 June 1870 Acton wrote from London to his wife at Tegernsee: 'I find that the report of what I did in Rome during the winter has reached this country. Odo seems to have written very strong and friendly things about me.'[1] He told his wife how Odo Russell had said that when the history of the Council came to be written he, Acton, would have a very import-ant place in it.

He also told his wife of Lord Clarendon's sudden death that morning and how Gladstone must therefore seek a new Foreign Secretary. He thought it likely that his step-father Granville would be chosen (his guess was correct). 'Cela me conviendrait beaucoup, as I understand foreign affairs and would have some influence. Moreover I should get at the secrets of diplomacy with respect to the Council. This may be important . . .'

That August of 1870 at Tegernsee he wrote an open letter, ostensibly to 'a German bishop', but actually intended for all the bishops of the minority in the Council and not only the Ger-mans. He finished it on the 30 August and it was printed at Nördlingen during September and very widely circulated and even (for it had only nineteen pages) reviewed. It was one of his most powerful papers. It begins: 'A great part of the Catholic world reveres the minority at the Council as the true witnesses to Catholic faith.' But now the hour of decision is come and

---

[1] 8121/7/947.

these voices are strangely silent. There is a chasm between the speeches which they made at the Council and their silence now. One said that he would rather die than accept the argument for infallibility. Another called it the suicide of the Church. Acton mentioned several bishops by name – Kenrick of St Louis, Olmütz, Schwarzenberg, Cincinnati, Ketteler of Mainz, Dupanloup, Rauscher who said that it was a declaration of war against Christian antiquity. They had spoken of the use of spurious texts by their opponents, of the unrepresentative nature of the Council and its lack of freedom; they have described the majority as a conspiracy against God's truth. Yet now they are being silent and some of them have already submitted to what has been defined. Is it really possible after all that has been said and happened that you also are going to submit like others? 'I believe that you do not forget what you said and will not deny what you did. I put my trust in those bishops – there were Germans among them – who at the very end of the Council warned their colleagues that they must stick out to the end and give the world an example of the courage and endurance which it needs so badly.'[2]

Then the Franco-Prussian War broke out and the French garrison was taken out of Rome and on 20 September the Italian army took Rome and the Council could not meet and was soon adjourned sine die. The bishops were at home and even the most resolute of the opposition submitted to the decree one by one (Strossmayer the last) for the need was now to rally round a prisoner in the Vatican. Acton never forgave these submissions. In his eyes persons who did not believe something and had publicly stated their disbelief now made public profession that they

[2] *Sendschreiben an einen deutschen Bischof* (Nördlingen, 1870), reprinted DD, pp. 228 ff. Ketteler wrote a reply to the *Sendschreiben* which was reprinted in the *Rheinische Merkur*. But Acton reported to his wife that Haynald and Theiner and 'the Schwarzenburg set' are 'delighted' with my letter (8121/7/950 when he is in Munich, undated). A copy went from him to Wetherell in London, and Wetherell forwarded it to Gladstone (Wetherell, p. 190).

believed it because an old gentleman in Rome told them that they must. These prelates, formerly close allies, he now thought to be wicked; and such a condemnation applied in his eyes to Hefele although or because he was a true historian, and Theiner although or because he was a great purveyor of documents. It did not apply to Darboy; for the Archbishop of Paris was murdered by the communards in May 1871. From the besieged city Darboy wrote a private message of submission to the Pope which the Pope regarded as not satisfactory, because not public; but then he died brutally and for Acton he was a martyr. Acton wrote to Marie from Munich on 'Saturday' (which must be 27 May 1871 three days after Darboy's murder):

I have felt it coming ever since Good Friday. I had so much to say to him – for I loved him and I knew that he loved me – and now that he is dead I feel that I am so much nearer to him than when he was in prison, and that he knows the thoughts that I have. Teach Mamy [his eldest daughter, aged five] to say a prayer daily for the good archbishop who loved Papa. They showed me the account in the *Times* yesterday, but I could not read it because I knew I should cry.[3]

His reputation with the Curia was as low as possible. On 18 December 1870 Granville wrote to him about an archbishop-demon. Manning was reported to have said that he had had great hopes of Acton, of distinction in political life and of service to Catholicism. 'In both these things you have failed completely.' – 'Put that in your pipe and smoke it', said Granville.[4]

Nevertheless Acton decided to follow the Italian army into Rome.

On his way to Rome (October 1870) he passed through Vienna. In Vienna he was not optimistic that the Italian government saw clearly the predicament that they were in after taking Rome. 'I fear that they do not understand the very difficult ques-

[3] 8121/7/959.
[4] 8121/6/178.

tion before them, and only hope that I shall be able to be of some use.'[5] So his first idea in going – a singularly wild one – was that he might be helpful to the new lords of Rome.

The Italian government was still in Florence. There he talked with members of the Italian cabinet about the Roman question and how it could be settled. He thought them sensible; that the result was likely to be good both for Italy and for the Church – might even compensate for the damage to the Church done by the Council. They told him that they could not 'settle the Roman Question' but that they could 'put it in a position where it would be secure, both for the Church and the State'.[6]

As he went to Rome he felt it a return 'full of sadness'.

In Rome he went to Strossmayer's aide Vorsak, then to the ambassadors of Prussia and Austria, visited St Peter's in its mournful state, dined with Stirum the Prussian attaché and Pantaleoni the friend of Cavour, talked with four or five Italians who were hostile to the Papal States and wanted the new Italy, and read the dispatches of the British chargé Jervoise who took over when Odo Russell went. On 19 October he saw Theiner but Theiner himself was not allowed into the archives of which he was archivist.

This was the second point of his visit to Rome at this time.

To whom now did Vatican Library and Archives belong? Soon the new government started to appropriate Church property in the city. Were these the archives of the state like the Public Record Office, or were they the letters of a private but sovereign family like the papers in Windsor Castle? Had the Italian army captured the equivalent of the British Museum, or the equivalent of the Lambeth Palace Library? Some Italians wanted the new Italian state to declare Vatican Library and Vatican Archives to be national property, in the same way that it took the Pope's palace on the Quirinal and property of religious orders in the city.

---

[5] Acton to Marie, 8121/7/1079, undated.
[6] 8121/7/952, Saturday, the day before he arrived at Rome where he expected to be five days only; cf. DD, pp. 101–2.

In the first few days (and first few months) after the occupation, wild fears circulated, that the Italians were ready to take over library and archives as national property, or that papalists would try to destroy compromising but precious documents before they fell into the hands of the invader. There were rumours that all the archives were being shipped off to Malta for safety, then it was thought that they would sail for the United States, men expected a raid of troops into the archives to prevent their export. The mood of the time is illustrated by the alleged behaviour of Lord Acton over the *Liber Diurnus*.

In the debates over papal authority inside and outside the Vatican Council during 1869–70, the *Liber Diurnus* was prominent. It was believed to be the daily handbook of the papal chancellery used between about 750 and 1050. In Formulary 84 the authors of the new heresy (Monothelitism) were condemned, among them four patriarchs of Constantinople and Pope Honorius. In this formula, therefore, later popes were believed to excommunicate an earlier Pope for heresy. Hence its importance to the arguments of 1869–70.

As the Vatican Council loomed, the *Liber Diurnus* aroused lively interest. At Döllinger's house in Munich over Easter 1870 it was a main topic of conversation. Döllinger believed the manuscript to be of extreme importance for the question of infallibility. But he did not know whether the manuscript still existed.

Döllinger fired Acton with the importance of *Liber Diurnus* in the mighty campaign which they both led. Acton asked Theiner for it, but to no avail. Acton, who began to take almost fanatical views about the unscrupulousness of his opponents, suspected that they might easily destroy it as the document which was fatal to their cause.

The German historian Theodor Sickel had an extraordinary story. He said thus: On 16 or 17 September 1870, he went to Acton's hotel in Vienna to fetch him out to dinner. In the hotel he was surprised to meet Minghetti, Italian ambassador to

Austria, who was married to Acton's cousin. Acton told Sickel that Minghetti brought the certain news that within a few days Italian troops would occupy Rome. He (Acton) had devised an adventurous plan. He would enter Rome with the Italian forces, go straight to the Vatican Archive, and carry off by force the *Liber Diurnus*.

We have no reason to doubt Sickel's story of the meeting in the hotel. Acton's rash plan perfectly fits the man at that moment of time. We are not told how he thought he would be able to find the manuscript which Theiner had said that he could not find. But Acton knew what could happen to archives in a state of political upheaval. He had worked in the Venetian archives not long before the war of 1866 which caused Venice to be lost to Austria; and, just at the change of power in that year, the Benedictine Father Beda Dudík appeared with a squad of soldiers and removed eighteen big chests of historical papers and one chest of earlier manuscripts, together with an 'arrested' Venetian archivist who tried to resist. Acton was well aware that when public order breaks down libraries are insecure.

According to Sickel, Acton went, as he intended, to the Italian forces about to attack Rome. But Minghetti warned them of his coming. They put him under courteous arrest, and kept him there for the few days until order was restored in Rome. Sickel said that he met Acton again in 1873 and learnt of his failure. On Acton's death-bed in the winter of 1901–2 Sickel visited him in Merano and tried to get him to remember what happened. But Acton was near the end, and his memory was blurred.[7]

The letters of Acton make the story impossible to believe. Acton went to Rome, but nearly a month after the occupation, arriving on 16 October. A letter to his wife describes how he spent his time. No doubt he intended to save what might be saved, and had the *Liber Diurnus* in mind; but he found the city in no disorder, the library and archives shut, and a wall at Theiner's door. He hoped that the Italian government would

---

[7] Sickel, *Römische Erinnerungen*, pp. 135–6.

make the Pope's library national, and open it to scholars of all nations.

The first years of the Italian occupation of Rome were not years when the campaign to get inside the archives could make progress. Papal Rome was in mourning, functions curtailed, ceremonies bare, choirs silent. To keep library and archives under lock and key was one way of asserting sovereignty; and if, from the political point of view, it made another weakness for the Pope by handing an argument to those who maintained how much more useful these books and papers would be if they were nationalized, that was an argument which the ancient Pope cheerfully gave to his critics. The more difficult the Vatican was of access, the more evidently old rights were asserted against intrusive officers or policemen.

Since the road running just past the entrance to the Tower of the Winds was now a public road, the treasures of the Vatican felt insecure. The six or seven years after Theiner's fall were the years when the Vatican Archives were more tightly shut than at any other epoch. An occasional copy of an occasional document was released by special request if a friendly government applied.

The archives were closed, as if against an enemy – for enemies walked the streets of Rome. At this time the Vatican Archive was called *this unapproachable sanctuary*. In the summer of 1877 a Frenchman thought that he was the first (ever) to be allowed to see anything from the archives. In January 1879 a young German thought that he was the first (ever) to be allowed to see anything from the archives; and a story went round that when he asked for the permission the archivist expressed the hope that this would be the last permission to be granted.

The blank years were not so blank as these applicants supposed.

Later in life Lord Acton claimed that he gave the first stimulus to the opening of the Vatican Secret Archives. At first sight the claim is preposterous. After June 1870, for understandable reasons, Acton was not persona grata in Rome. At one point in 1874–5 he came near to excommunication. He never again worked in the archive which during Theiner's last years was the main interest of his life and a chief source of his advance as a historian.

Four years before, when he negotiated with the Master of the Rolls Lord Romilly about the copying of British documents in the Vatican, Acton realized that he needed a copyist, if Theiner would allow access to such a person. Such a copyist must be experienced in old handwriting, and should preferably be a Catholic because he would probably be treated more openly by officials of the Curia. He found the person whom he sought in Joseph Stevenson.

This was a Durham man by origin with the simplicity and singlemindedness of the true antiquarian. In many volumes he edited *The Church Historians of England* and spent many hours in the British Museum. For thirteen years he was also the vicar of Leighton Buzzard but his flock was hardly his first interest. In 1862 he resigned the living and became a Roman Catholic. Thus he exactly filled Acton's needs – a very experienced copyist and editor and a Catholic convert. When his wife died in 1869 he sought training in the college at Oscott and ordination to the priesthood. He was very short of money, and the officers of the Public Record Office persuaded Prime Minister Gladstone to grant him a pension.

The account of Stevenson in the *Dictionary of National Biography* says: 'He was deputed by government, after consent had been obtained from the Pope, to make a detailed examination of the Vatican Archives'. When we know of the fall of Augustin Theiner, and the walling-up of the archives, and the Italian occupation of the city, and the mood that reigned in the Curia between 1870 and for at least seven years afterwards, this looks like an improbable statement. The truth is still more improbable.

The Treasury agreed to modest payments for researches on British history in European libraries. A few days after Acton arrived in Rome, he was told (3 December 1869) that the Treasury sanctioned the arrangement, and that his help was needed.

Acton asked for explanation. The Master of the Rolls left Acton, the originator of the plan, in complete charge of the delicate operation of extracting British history from Roman archives. No pay was in question; only the sum of £350 to remunerate Roman copyists.

But then Acton led resistance to the Pope's wishes in the Vatican Council. His name was entangled with the name of Theiner, his reputation fell with the fall of Theiner. Acton's control of the plan became a liability if the British government wanted documents from the Vatican Secret Archives. For a moment it was almost like inviting Luther to gain them access to the papers of Pope Leo X. This difficulty was not perceived, either by the Public Record Office or by the Treasury. As late as 17 January 1871 the Record Office asked leave from the Treasury to continue the arrangement; and as late as 25 January 1871 the Treasury gave that leave.

No one enlightened them what conditions were like in Rome. This was fortunate. For they authorized a proceeding which looked as though it had no chance of success, and discovered success beyond expectation.

A year after the Treasury authorized under the direction of Acton researches which Acton could never undertake, Hardy of the Record Office wrote to Stevenson that the government proposed to employ him to make transcripts of documents in Rome provided Lord Acton should have no personal objection. On 27 February 1872 Stevenson, not without scruples, accepted the mission. No pay was provided, only the £350 allotted earlier to Acton. Hardy was almost too conscious that the Treasury would not consent to another penny. Stevenson's superior at Oscott hardly thought the plan important, for he refused to release Stevenson until he had finished coaching a young man for a routine examination. Lord Acton declared this mission to Rome to be 'perfectly idle and irrelevant'.

Stevenson arrived at Rome early in July 1872; thinking it foolish to come then because the important libraries were closed until November, but obeying the behest of the Public Record

Office. He intended to gain access, if he could, to the documents of the Vatican Archives, the Vatican Library, and other Roman libraries, beginning with the reign of King Henry VIII. He carried with him several letters of recommendation – Archbishop Manning to Cardinal Antonelli, Bishop Ullathorne of Birmingham to Cardinal Pitra, the President of Oscott to Archbishop Howard and Monsignor Stonor, these last two being the two influential Englishmen resident in Rome. The Foreign Office instructed Jervoise, the British chargé at the Vatican, to do whatever he could to help.

The Master of the Rolls gave Stevenson printed instructions which he could show to the Roman authorities: that he was to begin with the reign of Henry VIII and secure copies of documents issued between 1509 and 1547: that the bundles of nuncio reports would probably be very interesting: that the transcripts should be made in full: that he should not order copies of any documents already printed by Rymer, Theiner, or any other known collection: that he should send a report on his work every six months: that after Henry VIII he should proceed to later reigns: and that when he had finished the reign of James II he should go back to the Norman Conquest. This last sentence shows that the officers of the Public Record Office had no idea what they asked him to undertake. They were as hazy as the Pope when he asked Cardinal Antonelli to get him an index.

Wherever Stevenson went, men poured cold water on his plan. At the English College they advised him that he must work slowly towards gaining access. At the Gesù the Jesuits expressed their surprise at what he wanted to do, and said that a request to make a general search in the archives was unprecedented. When at last he secured an interview with Cardinal Antonelli he was told that no one had as yet obtained such a privilege, that the documents were of the most private character and touched upon matters of 'extreme delicacy and importance'.

Nevertheless, Stevenson was able to begin work on Saturday, 19 October 1872. To be the only person working at the archives was extraordinary. The quiet ingenuous Stevenson showed no sign of finding it extraordinary. He was excited, but by the materials he found, not by the privilege. In his report at the end of six months he mentioned that he was the first ever to gain access to the Vatican Secret Archives. This was not true. But he knew nothing of the reign of Theiner, or nothing that was accurate.

Acton considered whether he should write the History of the Vatican Council, and an article appeared. But he gave up the bigger plan. Until his last years he did not like to talk about it. He did not go to Rome for ten years. He was depressed; determined to stay a Catholic and receive his communion and go to confession and be an example to his children; determined never to accept the Vatican decree; convinced that hierarchs of churches were often wicked. But what depressed him was not only his personal predicament. He believed that the Vatican Council had so raised the gulf that divided Catholic from Protestant that it made it impossible for Britain to govern Ireland successfully and that the future must hold Home Rule and perhaps eventual independence for Ireland.

In the spring of 1871 Döllinger was excommunicated because he refused to submit to the Vatican decree. In September 1871 they held the conference of dissidents at Munich which led to the foundation of the Old Catholic Church; and Acton attended, Döllinger met him at the station. He found the Arco-Valley household uneasy about religion and preferred to stay at a hotel, the Bayerische Hof. He had meant to visit Paris on the way; but 'I give up Paris, because the murder of my dear archbishop takes away my chief motive for going there'.[8]

On 12 September 1871 the eminent Catholic archaeologist Kraus came to stay at Herrnsheim and enjoyed his reception by Lady Acton. Kraus, like Acton, was determined not to be cast out of the Church or go into the Old Catholic schism. But he found that they could not agree. Kraus believed it possible to remain a Catholic by accepting the decree and putting on it a

---

[8] Acton to Marie (from Munich, Tuesday), 8121/7/1029.

sense not intended by those who drafted it. Acton thought it possible to remain in the Church though it was impossible to accept the decree, it was an unCatholic decree. Nevertheless Kraus was full of admiration for Acton – the 'type of an English Lord', who knows his way in the world and yet is an expert among German scholars; 'a man without a trace of lordliness, and talking in terms of equality'; who understands theology, and is warm, and open, and yet speaks diplomatically, weighing every word.[9]

For many years Acton did not like to write or talk about the Vatican Council. He could not do so without reminding his Church of his 'disloyalty' as they regarded it and its memory was sore as the memory of the great failure of his life.

But when he was a professor at Cambridge towards the end of his life thirty-five years later, he found that people asked him about it, it was now history. He began to read again what had been published and even thought again of writing about it. In June 1897 he sat at Trinity College with George Prothero, the Cambridge man who was professor of history at Edinburgh, and started telling him about it; and when the other people in the room heard what was being said they left their chairs and came over – and 'the whole room was absorbed'.[10]

[9] Kraus, *Tagebücher*, p. 299.
[10] Acton to Mamy, 5 June 1897, 7956/188.

5

ACTON AND NEWMAN

E ACH one of this pair was very unusual; both as a person and as a mind. Both wanted the same thing – to make modern Catholicism intellectually respectable in an age when Pope Pius IX looked to the world to be intent on making it intellectually (though not devotionally) disreputable. Since they both wanted the same thing they seemed to be natural allies, they thought for a long time that they were allies, perhaps Newman even thought it until he died though Acton did not.

Acton was a help to Newman in a lasting achievement, the founding of the Oratory School at Birmingham. For several years they were closer than natural allies, they were partners in the enterprise. Since they wanted the same thing in entirely different ways, and reacted in entirely different ways to the events of those decades, they slowly parted, first in attitude and then in sympathy; until one regarded the other as the sad case of a person who had gone off the rails and the other regarded the one with mortal hostility and abused him as a corrupter of the truth. We see the unusual picture of two friends who for the highest motives of conscience changed from being friends to being opponents, on one side a bitter enemy.

Britain looks back upon both of them, enemies though they became, as men of stature, and in neither case is that recognition of stature caused because he was a Roman Catholic.

They were both clever. They were both dedicated Catholics, Acton from birth, Newman from about his thirty-fourth year.

They were both well educated at a good university, which was not common for English Catholics in those days. In both, their university was formative, each of them looked back upon their experience as a university student and regarded it essential to his understanding of the world and humanity. Both looked back upon a single person at the university as specially momentous in their formation, and both these persons were church historians, though John Keble at Oxford was a church historian and very much a poet, and Döllinger at Munich was a church historian and very much a man of prose; two different symbolic figures in the intellectual background.

There were natural differences: the age gap – Newman was thirty-three when Acton was born; and that is a generation gap, for in Newman's childhood Britain was dominated by the memory of the French Revolution and in Acton's childhood they were thinking about the Corn Laws and Chartism. That is an important difference. Newman never forgot. Nor did Pope Pius IX who was born in Sinigaglia in the year of the French Terror. Acton had no such memory.

There was a difference in parents' ages at death. Newman had a father until he was twenty-three, that is he was an adult when he became responsible for his mother; and his mother did not die till he was thirty-five. Acton's father died when he was one year old and he had a step-father at the age of six and his mother died when he was twenty-six.

This may be nothing to do with it but there was a difference in early arrogance. You cannot find intellectual arrogance in Newman. The trouble with Newman was intellectual diffidence – he infuriates you by saying, that is too difficult for me to manage, or, we have to leave this problem to people who are more expert than I, or, I am only sketching what I suspect may be true, we must leave it to the competent to test it properly. There are moments when you want to shake Newman, because you know that he was the most competent person to test the theory if he would only take his coat off and roll up his sleeves.

We find no such wish to shake Acton, or not for that reason. The young Acton knew at the age of twenty-three that he had what it took to reform the world and the Catholic Church and was not slow in telling people how they were to set about it. At the age of twenty-two he went with his step-father to the coronation of the Tsar and, we are told, 'made a great impression on statesmen and men of intellectual eminence by a display of knowledge surprising in a youth'.[1] If we are told that he made a great impression we are not told whether this impression was good or bad, because people of twenty-two who show they are clever in the presence of persons aged fifty or sixty are not always the most respected people in society. At the age of twenty Acton was trying to appoint a lecturer at Newman's university in Dublin, and even telling the lecturer what subjects he could very well be lecturing about. This arrogance mellowed as is the way of youth. You can be infuriated with Newman, and you are not in awe of him, but you also feel affection for him and your protective instinct is aroused, you feel compassion. You hardly ever feel angry with Acton (though you sometimes feel vexation that he did not express himself more lucidly) but you do not often feel affection for him until you know him very well, what you find in yourself is admiration and at times awe.

So they started as close allies. He first met Newman when he was a boy of seventeen years and Döllinger brought him to England for a visit to the Catholic leaders and Newman had lately set up the Oratory at Birmingham. Acton came out of his university education with the perception that 'scientific methods' have now been perfected (it was a difficulty for Acton that all his life his fluency in German made him imagine that the word *science* is the correct English translation of the word *Wissenschaft*) and, he said, 'have come to be applied in so cautious and so fair a spirit'.[2] Secondly, he acquired the belief that periodical articles are more influential than books, a belief that was to be almost fatal for

[1] Neville Figgis, in DNB *sv* Acton.
[2] *Home and Foreign Review* (1862), 452–3.

his later intellectual career. This second doctrine led him into financing, and helping to edit, and writing for, three journals in succession. He said how disgusted he felt over the hurry of writing monthly articles and how he found an incongruity between his studies and the popular nature of what he had to put out. But he still thought the doctrine to be true. Newman was the old Oxford purist, do not write for reviews. Of course he created a scholarly journal *Atlantis* for his university at Dublin; but it was Acton as much as anyone who drew him into writing articles for these journals, and no one who surveys Newman's career as a scholarly journalist can suppose that this was his best vocation. Indeed, he tried more than once to persuade Acton to take a less ephemeral attitude, to work at something bigger, to get down to something important historically.

They shared a common ability for forcible phrases. Hence one of Acton's has gone into the folk-memory of the educated English. Newman had the same force. But Newman was more conscious of the effect of words and also of the subtlety of truth. For example, in conversation to Acton he would talk of the 'natural inclination of men in power to tyrannize' or of 'the ignorance and presumption of our would-be theologians'.[3] But he did his best to get Acton not to say such forcible things in print, not to interfere in theology, not to be cutting in what he wrote but always to be good-tempered. It bothered Newman how Acton loved to print the striking phrase – for example *St Augustine the father of Jansenism*. Acton was cross at what he called the ignoramuses who objected; he said he thought the misgivings were foolish.[4]

This difference between Newman and Acton was not just due to the different responsibilities which they bore. Acton was a layman, if he fell into trouble with a cardinal it got no one else into trouble except his fellow-writers. If Newman was in trouble with a cardinal, he had two institutions which he regarded as his

[3] Acton to Simpson, 1 January 1859.
[4] Acton to Simpson, 13 November 1858.

important work, his Oratory at Birmingham and now the Oratory school which depended on it; both of them institutions which were vulnerable. It mattered to other people much more if Newman got into trouble than if Acton got into trouble. But although this was an important difference, and although this difference did affect what they both said and how they both said it, the underlying cause of this difference was deeper in the personality. Newman had more doubt in him. *Augustine the father of Jansenism . . .* it looks obvious but the obvious is not always true without qualification, are we so certain that that is right, or at least that we can say it, as Acton wrote it, without a moment's hesitation? This ex-Anglican theologian was more sceptical about truth, and about the exact meaning of dogmatic statements of the truth, than this hereditary Roman Catholic layman.

All this had a nearly fatal consequence for Newman. To save the periodical *The Rambler* from the assaults of its critics and the bishops, he accepted the editorship; which he had no wish whatever to do, and he was right to have no wish to do; a *most bitter penance* was how he thought of it. The motive was odd. Acton and his colleague Simpson, despite various unnecessary shocks, were doing good work for the Catholic Church in England by raising its intellectual standards, a cause which both Newman and Acton much wanted to foster. The bishops pressed to stop the whole affair. If Newman accepted the seat of editor he could save the better part of their work and moderate the provocative language.

This was a bad idea; almost a mad idea. It is to be explained because at this moment Newman not only believed that what Acton was doing needed doing, but also felt a personal affection for the much younger Acton, an affection which is very evident from the sources.

If Newman had affection for the young Acton, the young Acton found Newman to be one of his heroes. One Holy Week he went to a church where Newman was preaching the stations of the Cross. It was the first time he heard Newman preach. That same evening he wrote a description to his future wife's mother. 'The dark church was full, many Protestants were there, but not a sound was to be heard but the beautiful voice of the great preacher praying in the midst and in the name of the people. Nothing could exceed the touching simplicity of his discourse. I am here among many friends who take great care of me in my little cell, and Newman himself comes and sits with me every day.'[5]

Could you say publicly that the system of seminaries created by the Council of Trent is bad? Nearly everyone knew that some of its effects were not ideal. But it had done much good in various places. Could you say it was now urgently in need of reform? Or if a Catholic said that did he attack an ecumenical council? Newman and Acton could hardly understand each other. When The *Rambler* (July 1860) accepted an anonymous letter saying that the seminary system is bad, Newman was offended that the *Rambler* should publish it. For the first time Acton was really offended with Newman. Why ever could you not say such a thing? What did it matter what Trent had laid down on a practical subject in a different generation?

In the same year they disagreed, though they respected each other, when the Piedmontese army occupied most of the Papal States. The disagreement is unexpected. The more papalist of the two, Newman, thought that it did not matter if the Pope lost his States, they might have done good but if they were in the way he could easily be better without them. The more anti-papal of the two, Acton, thought at first that the Papal States in Italy were one of the defences of human law and liberty against the ravages of modern demagoguy and that it was right for us to campaign against what Louis Napoleon and Savoy were bringing about. The Temporal Power means liberty for the Pope and liberty for the Pope is one of the constituents of the liberties of Christendom.

But by the summer of 1860 they agreed. They were both realists who saw that the old Temporal Power could not now be

---

[5] Acton to Countess Arco, 8121/7/804, fragment.

revived. The Piedmontese were lamentable. But this has happened, and it is a gift which we ought to accept, and use. Acton said so publicly. Naturally Newman did not say so publicly, and Acton thought that he should have been bolder.

In the early sixties Acton was persuaded that Newman's Irish university would not do for the Catholics in England – beginning with the boys who passed out of Newman's school at Edgbaston – and that there ought to be a Catholic university in England. He talked this over often with Newman. He even offered land near Bridgnorth as the centre for the university, and used the argument that the place had the Severn as a big river, was in a healthy environment and was a place where Catholic-Protestant feelings were friendly, and where nearby was a large library, his own. He tried to persuade Renouf, the best scholar among the recent converts, that he should help this wild scheme, and said that they must persuade Newman to join in and bring Paley over from Cambridge.[6] Renouf was a realist and knew that the only solution was in the end to set up colleges at existing non-Catholic universities.

By now Acton was aware, perhaps more aware than was the truth, how he was not welcome among normal English Catholics; how 'my objectivity and indifference is profoundly hateful to the English Catholic mind'.[7] 'For this there is no hope or remedy, because the one thing needful is to accustom people to the method and spirit of truth seeking . . . We are the flying fish who can neither swim with the Protestants or fly in peace with the Catholics.'

In the search for truth he was still convinced that Newman was on his side. Two years later he was saying that Newman had great sympathy for the cause of the Liberal Catholics because he is enlightened and liberal and highly cultivated but he does not really understand what was their theory of an intelligent Catholic journal.[8]

---

[6] Acton to Renouf, 14 November, no year but it is 1862, 8119/8/515/23.
[7] Acton to Simpson, 3, 45.
[8] Acton to Simpson, 3, 172.

Newman continued to admire Acton. He liked what he wrote and he thought he should give up his public life with Parliament for the sake of writing more, he did far more good with his pen than sitting silent in a seat in the House of Commons. When, after the Munich Brief was taken to denounce the claim to scholarly freedoms, Acton decided to cease his journal, Newman was very sorry.

In December 1864 came out the Syllabus of Errors which confirmed most of Europe in the impression that the Roman Curia was going in the wrong direction and worried Catholic intellectuals outside Italy and Spain and the Tyrol. In the spring of 1865 Acton visited Edgbaston and talked with Newman at the inn opposite the Oratory. 'Newman has been more kind to me than ever and we have had a long confidential conversation. He is quite of my opinion about Rome, the Encyclical etc, and seems to agree with me more completely than his last book seems to suggest.'[9] (This 'last book' was Newman's semi-autobiography and defence against Charles Kingsley, the *Apologia pro vita sua*).

In Rome during the spring of 1867 he could not but hear what they thought there of Newman and did not like the sound of it. He found feelings in the Curia very strong against Newman; he found Bishop Brown, who admired Newman, 'in despair'; Cardinal Barnabò ran Propaganda like a dictator and Propaganda ran the Roman Catholic Church in England, and Acton heard that Cardinal Barnabò was 'especially violent' against Newman.

This alliance and friendship might have been ended by the Vatican Council. It was not. Acton thought papal infallibility dangerous because it would canonize persecution – and one should say so loudly. Newman thought that the way the thing was being done was very bad and he did not mean to say so publicly but his letter was leaked to the press. When it was leaked to the press he stood totally by the strong language which he used. But to say that infallibility is being defined in a factious sort of way, when we do not need it defined at all, may be most

---

[9] Acton to Marie, 8121/7/831.

unpleasant to the managers in the Curia, but it is different in attitude from that which says that no amount of definition can make the doctrine part of Christian truth because it is untrue.

There is evidence of Newman being confused for a few months at that time. Sir Rowland Blennerhassett called on him at the Oratory on 10 April 1871 and afterwards wrote to Acton and described Newman's state of mind as 'extremely odd'. Newman spoke strongly against the Archbishop of Munich for pressing at Döllinger and, said Blennerhassett, 'professed his own belief in the new dogma though unable to reconcile it with well-ascertained historical facts'.[10] But Newman's position though troubled, was more coherent than that. The definition was a pain to him. But he had always believed in the infallibility of the Catholic Church. How that is expressed must vary or develop in the life of the Church. Any Church definition needs time and mature reflexion before we can see its full effect and full meaning. Therefore we accept what the Church is doing and later on we shall understand what it means better than we do now. The Church is something bigger than its hierarchy and sooner or later the consensus of the faithful will help to show us the balance in this truth.

This position was impossible for Acton. The definition is a statement which history disproves and no one who knows history can believe. So the only course for a Catholic is to take no notice of it; as he or she may take no notice now of earlier definitions which are obsolete by the passage of time. You can be a lay Catholic and be free to think what you like.

You might expect Newman, who was not truculent, to blame Acton for being truculent. He did not blame him at all. His respect for him was as warm as ever. The amazing sign of this came in 1874 when Acton wrote tremendous letters to *The Times* and demands for Acton's excommunication appear in the Propaganda archives in Rome. Gladstone had said that the definition of 1870 made all Catholics potentially disloyal subjects of

---

[10] CUL Add. MSS 4989; MacDougall, p. 122.

Britain. Answers were abundant, Newman's *Letter to the Duke of Norfolk* was the best answer. Acton's was the most shocking. Since the Church has done frightful things in the past and these frightful things have been approved by Popes, why should we, or why should you, take any notice when the Pope does a wrong but not frightful thing in the present? – it cannot make any difference to our loyalty as British subjects.

It was not only the bishops who were disturbed by Acton. Many lay Catholics came to feel that someone who could write such things was not a true Catholic. Lady Georgiana Fullerton was the sister of his stepfather Granville and so the sister-in-law of Acton's mother, and had been converted to be a Roman Catholic nearly thirty years before; and was the most devout of all the lay converts from the Oxford Movement. She now thanked God that Acton's mother was dead because she could not see, as Lady Georgiana wrote to Newman, her son's betrayal of the Church. Acton lost credibility as a Catholic.

Almost the only Catholic with whom he did not lose credibility was Newman. He wrote Acton a friendly letter by which Acton felt consoled. He thought that Acton had expressed himself badly and that the reason for this was that he was a layman and not a trained theologian. Nevertheless, when you subtracted the provocativeness or clumsiness of Acton's language, there were two truths in what he contended. First, you must face historical facts and state them, that was right. And second, the Catholic Church is far deeper than the individuals who act in its name.

Newman defended Acton to friends. The sympathy which he expressed was important to Acton, who had never felt Newman's friendship so weighty as at this moment when he was under such a heavy attack. Acton explained his position to Newman in words which Newman could have accepted for himself. Thus:

The decrees have never been a difficulty to me, not because I have ever examined them and found that they approved themselves to my judgment but because, be they what they may, I am sure it will be all right, and if it is not evidently all right now, that is not my business, I take it that no interpretation holds that is inconsistent with tradition, and with former decrees. And if one does not see how the new and the old can be reconciled, time will show it, and the new will be digested and assimilated, and will be worked into what was there before . . .

Newman said things like that. Time will get it right for us. But this standing by Acton at his lowest moment, when Newman himself was under suspicion from the authorities, was one of Newman's most courageous acts. Acton wrote to Newman that his sympathy was 'never so valuable as now'.[11] He could not think Newman's accepting position tolerable for himself. He told Gladstone that Newman wrote him very kind but unsatisfactory letters.[12] But Newman continued to defend Acton to other, shocked, Catholics. He cannot be expected to express things rightly, he is a layman and with no training in theology. He told Simpson that so many people said unpleasant things about Acton, in Protestant as well as Catholic papers, that Acton seemed to retire into silence and be out of touch, and he wished to be in touch with him again. He told a correspondent, at present unknown, that he ought not to be saying such hard things about Acton. 'He has ever been a religious, well-conducted, conscientious Catholic from a boy. In saying this, I do not at all imply that I can approve these letters to which you refer. I heartily wish they had never been written.'[13]

Manning was demanding that Acton publicly accept the Vatican decrees. Acton used Newman as the director of his soul to discover what he could morally and honourably and honestly say and what he could not. To find Acton using Newman formally as priest and as casuist is indeed a surprise in view of what was to happen. And the effect at this moment was to raise Acton's admiration of Newman to the summit. He vastly admired Newman's *Letter to the Duke of Norfolk* – at least admired it as perfect for its purpose for he thought that Newman only achieved the effect by saying some things that were not true.[14] He told Glad-

---

[11] Acton to Newman, in Dessain, XXVII, p. 166.
[12] FL 69.
[13] Newman to Simpson, 30 March 1875; Newman to an unknown, 13 April 1876.
[14] Conz., III, p. 142.

stone that he thought this was the greatest of English Roman Catholics since the Reformation.[15] Even in July 1880 he told Mary Gladstone that he rated Newman one of the four finest intellects in England.[16]

Only a few months later we are in a different world. Acton wrote to Mary Gladstone that Newman is 'a very able but evil man'.[17] What had happened?

Döllinger never had Acton's admiration of Newman. Just at this time he wrote a comment:

> He is an unusually able and he is also a deeply religious man; and he writes beautifully. But his ideas of church history are so deficient, and with his theory of development he planted Darwinism in religion; except that when Darwin says the ape developed until it became Caucasian man, Newman says Caucasian man gradually sinks into the ape.[18]

Charlotte Blennerhassett said that when Döllinger talked about Newman he talked about him with a laugh like a sneer.[19] This was superficiality by Döllinger; but Acton still revered Döllinger and what Döllinger thought of Newman must affect Acton's mind still; though not for long. Yet this cannot be the reason for the extraordinary change in Acton's attitude to Newman.

Let us compare Acton on Father Haneberg. Like Döllinger he was a professor in Munich but he was also abbot of the Benedictine house there, St Boniface. Everyone liked him and thought him a good scholar and admired him as a pastor. He went on refusing bishoprics with determination. He was a close colleague and for long a good friend of Döllinger. As part of the German unsettlement over the Vatican Council, he at last accepted the see of Speyer where he died after four years.

---

[15] Cf. Newman's *Letters*, ed. Dessain, XXVIII, p. 183.
[16] Acton to Mary Gladstone, 10 July 1880, 21.
[17] Acton to Mary Gladstone, 14 December 1880.
[18] Conz., IV, p. 597.
[19] CUL Add. MSS 4990/129.

So Acton used him, as he now began to use Newman's name: everyone thinks them Good Men but they are Bad Men. Why? because they have accepted the Vatican Decrees and that means that they have made themselves responsible for inquisitions and what not, immoral acts of the Catholic past. These are not the simple, they are intelligent well-informed minds which once knew better. People may think them good but they have compromised with the fundamental principles of moral right. They have made a public claim that for the sake of the higher aims of the Church the worst means are justified. If they were in the shoes of Pope Pius V they would act as immorally as he did.

To which assertion Döllinger had the excellent retort, how do you know? But what was now raised was the question which troubled Acton as a historian for the rest of his life – the moral law is absolute, can we nevertheless make allowances for the behaviour of people who are in very different circumstances from those that we see in our time?

Acton and Döllinger began to quarrel over this in February 1879. It is possible that what shook Acton out of his old friendship with Newman was the accepting of the cardinal's hat, later in 1879, and so telling the world, I am indeed the Pope's man. If we take the parallel case of Haneberg, it was the acceptance of a see; he had been refusing a see for years and now he suddenly accepted one not because he thought it the right work for himself but because in the alarums of Catholic Germany he could not be seen to refuse what the Pope approved; exactly parallel with Newman, who thought himself totally unsuitable to be a cardinal, he had no understanding of administration, all he wanted was to be left quietly in his Oratory, his first reaction made Manning see too clearly that he felt himself very unsuitable. But he had a motive which was not Haneberg's; in England there was no Old Catholic schism to worry about and he had, what Haneberg had not, a programme of theology in which he wished to persuade the Catholic Church to accept good insights of the modern world; this programme was known to be under suspicion; and if he accepted the cardinal's hat, he could be seen to have an approval which he was never known to have before.

16 June 1882: Acton to Döllinger. 'Newman says, no heretic was ever put to death in Rome, except one mentioned in the life of St Philip, an exception that proves the rule. Here is the brutal liar, and the artful deceiver, who seems so scrupulous, and certainly does his work, the devil's work, best.'[20] In 1874 Acton was deeply grateful for Newman's kindness at a bad time. Less than nine years later without anything having happened except that Newman had become a cardinal, Newman was a brutal liar who was doing the devil's work and doing it cleverly. An artful man, a shrewd man, manifesting the spirit of evil. It puzzled him that Gladstone the Anglican could still admire Newman.

Hoity toity we may say, a tangle somewhere in the psyche.

We may attribute something to the development of Acton's own mind and reading. Freed by the Vatican Council from an enchainment to Catholic authors, he read widely and deeply in German Protestant authors, historians like Ranke, moralists like Rothe, ex-Christians like Scherer. He felt that he found there a liberation for his historical intelligence. He went into a long retirement, at the French Riviera, or at Tegernsee in Bavaria, or in London at the Athenaeum, buying many books, reading many books; for nearly twenty years much more like an Anglican in his outlook than a Roman Catholic. Newman seemed then to be of an age of Acton's life out of which he had grown.

For more than ten years he and Newman did not meet. If Newman was a past phase of Acton's life, Acton was certainly a past phase of Newman's. They met for the last joyless time on 19 July 1887. Newman, some three years from death and aged eighty-seven, knew who he was but hardly more, or so it seemed to Acton. He was 'quite at sea, otherwise' wrote Acton to Gladstone, 'and hopelessly weak'.[21] The meeting is not mentioned in

---

[20] Conz., III, pp. 285–6.
[21] Acton to Gladstone, 20 July 1887, BL; MacDougall, p. 140.

Newman's letters, which by then he could only dictate. But we have an account from twenty years later. Acton took with him to see Newman his only surviving son Richard, then aged seventeen. On 28 October 1906, four years after his father's death and when there was a public question of Acton's very low view of Newman, Richard published in *The Times* a letter which simply said 'I was present at his farewell meeting with Cardinal Newman, the most moving scene I have ever witnessed.'

After Newman died three odd things happened.

The first oddity was that Acton, who had more or less lost sight of Newman, was recalled by his death to a more sensitive charity towards his old friend; for example, to Gladstone that 12 October: 'For good and evil he greatly reminds me of Fénelon; but Newman was the stronger man'.[22]

The second oddity was that as a result of the death he developed such an interest that he thought of writing a study of Newman's life and collected a mass of material for the purpose on that famous card index now at Cambridge. The *Dictionary of National Biography*, then in its early progress, invited him to write its article on Newman. He refused. He told Gladstone that he could not get access to the necessary papers (for the Oratory at Birmingham which controlled the papers would not dream of allowing such a disreputable person access to their precious possession – but then they had fits of nerves about allowing anyone whatever to see these letters); and, he told Gladstone, 'I cannot discover the secret of his quarrel with Manning, typical of his quarrel with ecclesiastical authority generally.'[23]

Still, he had the idea of a biography. This, like so many other books planned by Acton, came to nothing. Some of the cards in the index have severe comments on Newman, so the recaptured interest did not mean a posthumous reconciliation. But we must not take all these cards too seriously. Several times Acton records on a card that Newman told him how a Dominican had said that

---

[22] FL 67.
[23] FL 76.

he wanted to burn Acton and Richard Simpson and that he, Newman, agreed with the Dominican. Some historians have shaken their heads gravely over this utterance. They have supposed it proof that Newman by then regarded Acton as a wild and dangerous heretic. But if we imagine the scene in three dimensions, it sounds very different – Newman saying in conversation to Acton, a Dominican wants to burn you and Simpson and I think he is quite right. Newman had a little gentle humour in him.

Acton's cards for Newman's biography, like all his card-indexes, were piled up as they came to him – quotations from Newman, quotations about Newman, his own reflections on Newman, Newman's letters to him, extracts from the critics of Newman like Pattison and Froude and Newman's brother Frank but also from admirers of Newman like R. W. Church and Hutton – never purely factual cards, always with a little slant, pointing by their context to a case to be made out, like the fight against liberalism, or ultramontanism, or attitude to the Temporal Power of the Pope. The notes are enough to show what sort of a biography this would have been. It would have been interesting and bad, and it would have contained many reflexions so profound that even now those cards have made people think seriously on various aspects of Newman's mind.

The biography would have been bad for more than one reason. The first is lack of sympathy between author and subject. The second is that the author has no interest in the theology of the subject, who thought of his main work as theology. Acton possessed a copy of *A Grammar of Assent* but the pages stayed uncut till his death. Stephen Dessain always used to say that the best of Newman's theology is to be found in the *Pastoral and Plain Sermons* while he was an Anglican. I do not believe that Acton ever read many of these sermons, or I think that he did not do more than dip into them, for just occasionally a quotation from them appeared in the card index.[24] The book on *The Idea*

---

[24] CUL Add. MSS 5463/2.

of a University was not important to him, for it contradicted the ideal of a university to which Döllinger had brought him up. And Acton had no interest whatever in Newman the poet. Newman was a devotional writer of the first rank. This never occurred to Acton; or if it did, he did not think it an important thing to be.

He read R. W. Church's history of *The Oxford Movement* before it was printed – in which the Anglican Newman was the hero – and liked the book. 'Newman was not a great academic personage, and he may have done harm as well as good to the University. But he was great enough to obtain national celebrity'.[25]

When his son Dick went up to Oxford, Dick, whose Catholicism was liberal like his father's, became engaged in an undergraduate movement to create a Newman Society, and consulted his father. Acton felt it to be awkward. On one side was the pride of Trinity College in Newman as one of its eminent graduates; and of Oriel too, connected as it was 'with the period of his fame'. But on the other side Newman still had enemies in Oxford and they no small men – Max Müller 'probably' his worst, but perhaps Jowett also, and then several secular minds. His advice to Dick on this matter was 'Do nothing too conspicuously'.[26]

He thought that Oxford grossly mismanaged the question of a statue to Newman. He thought the site proposed bad because it suggested that the burning of the Protestant bishops was not so wicked after all. He suggested that they put it at the back of St Mary's near the Radcliffe Camera – there 'it would be like a monument to a general on his greatest field of battle' (i.e. St Mary's Anglican sermons were the triumph of Newman's life).[27]

In these older years Acton thought of Newman as very

[25] FL 73.
[26] Acton to Dick, 8121/10/134.
[27] FL 74.

Roman, a very ultramontane person. He thought that Newman did not wish that to appear, he tried to hide it because if it were known it would lessen his influence with non-Catholics. But this was a veil. Why, he even believed the Church is infallible when canonizing saints; and when you think what murderous persons are among those whom the Church has canonized, this makes you realize the depth of Newman's Romanism. He pretended to have a sympathy for liberal divinity. Actually, he believed in the inquisition.[28]

But, according to Acton, this is a deeply Roman person who had a twist in his personality which made him feel that every sort of authority was against him – the university of Oxford, the Anglican bishops, Faber, Cullen, Wiseman, Manning, Talbot etc. He needed to feel thwarted. He needed to feel that authority was cool.

Partly this was because authority was cool. And partly it was something about Newman's mind. Acton described that mind on a card: 'fervid, anxious and unresting . . . so intense, so little of the rank and file, his mind was so subtle, so dexterous, so original'.

Acton to Gladstone, April 1896; 'I may say: Read Newman; he is by far the best writer the Church of Rome has had in England since the Reformation. And the pupil will come back and say: But do you think his arguments sound, or his religion Catholic? I shall have to say: No, if you work it out, it is a school of infidelity.'[29]

Yet Acton confessed three liberal facets of Newman's mind. The first was the attitude to science. Newman had no fear of scientists. He had no expectation of a conflict between science and religion. He saw nothing wrong with Darwin. That impressed Acton because it was not what he met elsewhere among either most Catholics or most Protestants.

The second was the attitude to the Temporal Power. All the

---

[28] *Via Media*, 1, 1xxxix; CUL Add. MSS 4989/61; 4989/187.
[29] FL 227.

Catholic world was in a ferment about the necessity for the Pope to keep his secular State. At first Acton agreed with the Catholic world – it is necessary that the Pope be not a subject of any secular sovereign. He was surprised to discover that Newman had no such opinion. He made noises as though he agreed with the Catholic world in a lukewarm way, but Acton soon saw that he did not agree – and on religious grounds. Let us trust providence. If the Pope is deprived of his secular kingdom it may help the Church to a higher spiritual mission. If the Pope is deprived of his kingdom it may even be God's punishment that in the past Rome has mingled too much of earth with the things of the spirit. This was not 'liberal' because it was an opinion held on religious grounds and not political. Newman never thought, and never said, 'Absolute government is not compatible with what we now know of human rights, the Pope has an absolute government, therefore his government must go'. His only question was, how can this institution founded by God best do its work for God? Acton was sensitive enough to see this in Newman.

The third bit of liberalism was that Acton tried to interest the English historical establishment in what Newman had done for their subject by the Essay on Development, on the ground that the acceptance of this idea had helped to transform the historians' conception of their task and so distinguishes modern historical study from the old world of classical historians.

Acton had disliked Newman's idea of development. To him the idea if misused could justify the Vatican decree.[30] But afterwards he saw this idea as not only transforming for the historians but also vital for the future of the Catholic Church. If the Church can develop an idea of unlimited infallibility it can develop out of it. The balance of truth depends on that deep consensus fidelium in the Church which gradually accepts, or at times gradually rejects, what is proposed to it.

Acton grew obsessed about Newman's idea of development. Card after card shows him thinking about it, repetitive, round

---

[30] DD, p. 105.

and round, often back to the same points, with the absurd lists of names which were the strangest quirk of his historical mind. He knew that this was not liberal precisely because Newman believed not at all in the idea of progress and all the Protestants muddled up the idea of development with the idea of the progress of humanity.

Acton took this unrevolutionary thinker to have a revolutionary force in one idea. The Church is more profound than hierarchs. It is the vessel of a people's prayers. Development means, says Acton on a card, that 'the masses may be right when the authorities are wrong – and have been'.[31]

What the idea of development did for the Church was to allow it to grow out of error; it meant that the consensus fidelium could slowly correct what Popes and councils of bishops had decreed. What it did for history was to make the difference between the old history and the new modern history where everything was in movement all the time.

Neither of these judgements about Newman's idea of development will stand up to critical inquiry. Acton was not getting these doctrines out of Newman but using Newman as a peg on which to hang two things which he thought vital for the progress of human thought.

The emotional lives of both men had a complexity. From an early age Newman felt a vocation to the unmarried priesthood and this never left him. But naturally he was helped by the friendship of women like Maria Giberne or Mrs Wootton. At Littlemore and the Oratory he became emotionally dependent on the friendship of Ambrose St John; so that the last paragraph of the *Apologia*, about Oratory friendships, is one of the most disturbing paragraphs he ever wrote.

Acton fell in love with Marie Arco-Valley and had six children by her and died under her care. But in between, the marriage did not run easily. For quite long intervals they lived apart.

---

[31] CUL Add. MSS 5463/21.

These different emotional circumstances cannot safely be brought in to account for a certain awkwardness in the relationship of the two men.

Neither had any small talk. But though the resulting awkwardnesses in conversation afflicted them both, the two awkwardnesses were very different. Newman was easy if you talked theology. If you talked anything else he could not think what to say and felt embarrassed. Acton was far more learned than Newman, his range of talk was far wider. And he was not shy. On the contrary he was assured. But he also was difficult for some people at dinner. This was not because he had nothing to say but because he thought it too trivial to be worth saying. He would shut up and sit like any oyster. In the silences with Newman it was Newman who felt embarrassed. In the silences with Acton it was the other people and not Acton who felt embarrassed. But at other times Acton was very different. Newman was never inspiring in conversation; he was friendly, wise, sensible, interested; but never brilliant, a quality which, like his master Keble, he distrusted. Acton once described his conversation – 'carefully commonplace' and there was something true because Newman thought it wrong to shine. But in conversation Acton could lift you to the heights; get him on one of his great themes like liberty, and he would carry you away, you would feel the man to be inspired, you would be enthralled at the range and power of his mind.

The link might be put paradoxically that they were both Anglicans though they were not members of the Church of England. The Fathers made Newman a Catholic; not Father Ignatius nor Wiseman nor Dominic Barberi. It was the study of Arius and Athanasius, Ambrose and Cyprian that made him a Catholic. And the Fathers were presented to him through a long tradition of English patristic learning. After his conversion Newman was still essentially a man of the Fathers of the early Church. Even the sense of a developing church had something Anglican in its origins, and this was the reason why the Essay on Development was so unacceptable to the conventional orthodoxy of his day.

The essay *On Consulting the Faithful*, the tang in the way the answer to Kingsley was drafted, the *Letter to the Duke of Norfolk*, all owed their power and some of their persuasiveness to this element in Newman, I do not say Anglican element, but this element in his past which did not derive in any way from the prophets of the Counter-Reformation. This was what gave him his freedom in decades when Catholic minds gained the reputation of getting narrower in response to the European attacks on the Papacy. Of course the Anglican hymn of hesitancy, *Lead kindly light*, had turned into the Catholic hymn of assurance, *Firmly I believe and truly*. Yet there are plenty of signs, even in his last years, that a prayer to be led amid the encircling gloom was still at the essence of his faith.

Acton weighed up two opposite views of Newman; the first by Sir Rowland Blennerhassett, the second by his wife Charlotte. According to Rowland, Newman was clever, enlightened, rational, free in mind, far removed from the ultramontanes because he was so intelligent. According to Charlotte, Newman was not separated from Rome because he was intelligent but because he was so religious, he was a deeply spiritual even mystical person. Acton considered these two opposites and concluded that neither was right. Newman was a man who believed in authority in religion; he was as strong for that authority as Rome itself; so that he was separated from the ultramontanes neither by his intelligence nor by the depth of his spirituality. Why then was he suspect to the authority? Because, Acton believed, of the idea of development – it was 'a revolution', it gave him the air of a person who to satisfy himself demanded a theory specially thought out to suit himself, and which justified his first manner, the attacks, and the slowness of the conversion, up to the time he discovered it . . .'. Wiseman said of him, he was of an impossible arrogance – and development was the reason for the hard *mot*.[32]

Acton was of Europe, and of the German part of Europe, who

---

[32] Acton to Charlotte Blennerhassett, 14 April 1894, no. 665.

like the Emperor Charles V accepted that Popes are less than satisfactory but nevertheless they are necessary to the Church, and who for some of the time kept the rules like confession and the sacrament, and whose formation was as a historian under Döllinger and who remained to the end of his life a Catholic, just Catholic, church historian. He had no Anglican background. He had no patristic background except so far as the training under Döllinger meant reading some of the Fathers.

The man who started filling in cards for a life of Newman never to be written was a more Protestant person than when Newman knew him; Protestant only by intelligence, by attitude to the Papacy, by attitude to hallowed texts, by attitude to tradition and Scripture; but still one who thought the Reformation to be largely a disaster, and who still encouraged his children to their Catholic duties, and who still thought of himself as a lay Catholic.

The last oddity was in the year 1895. He gave his daughter Mamy, the intellectual among his daughters, a Christmas present. It was the complete works of Newman. This is as hard to account for as the change of heart from friendship to aversion fifteen years earlier. He was reading or re-reading Newman's sermon on The Parting of Friends and saying that it was the perfection of Newman's style, and drawing his daughter's attention to the music at the end of the sermon.[33]

This is to be accounted for only by a double tension in Acton. Newman had compromised with the Papacy and so had compromised with the wickedness of the past. And yet – he was a man of the true spirituality, and he did struggle for the truth, and he had a historical sensibility, and he thought that historical facts ought to be stated even when they hurt the Church; he might have illusions about those facts for Acton was aware that Newman was not a learned historian as the historical schools now understood that term; but still his intention was honest;

---

[33] Acton to Gladstone, 28 January 1895, BL MacDougall; to Mamy, 22 March and 28 March 1899, 7956/240–1.

and, perhaps above all, he was the only influential person to stand by Acton at the lowest point of Acton's life. Damn him though he might as one doing the devil's work, Acton never recanted the opinion that this was the greatest Roman Catholic to appear in England since the Reformation.

6

WITH GLADSTONE

THE acquaintance between Gladstone and Acton did not start promisingly. When Acton was a new member of Parliament for Carlow Gladstone was already eminent in the House of Commons and Acton was critical of him. It helped that for part of Gladstone's life Lord Granville was his closest political colleague and Acton was Granville's stepson. Then, while Acton was at the Vatican archives with Theiner, Gladstone visited Rome and Acton became a guide to him. Two years later Acton stood as the Liberal candidate for his home constituency of Bridgnorth, when the disestablishment of the Church of Ireland had become the main plank in Gladstone's policy. Acton's Tory opponent played on the *no popery* prejudice of the constituents. Acton himself issued an electoral manifesto which praised Gladstone to the skies – 'possession as no other English statesman ever yet possessed the capacity to tread untrodden paths and the confidence of the classes whom the Reform Act has raised to influence'. Though he was much liked as the generous local squire, he lost the election and was again out of the House of Commons.

Gladstone did not forget. The battle in Bridgnorth was drawn the more to his attention because the headmaster of the Bridgnorth grammar school, who was an Anglican clergyman and the curate of St Leonard's church, seconded Acton's nomination as the candidate. Members of the congregation of St Leonard's were so incensed when their curate seconded a Roman Catholic as their candidate for Parliament that they refused to go to church when he took services. This teacup storm was not unobserved in London.

Before the end of that December 1868 Gladstone was for the first time prime minister, with a big Liberal majority. Less than a year later he asked the Queen to raise Acton to the House of Lords. Then he admired the campaign which Acton conducted in Rome during the Vatican Council and received Odo Russell's wondering reports about Acton's personal achievement in such difficulties. This finally cemented the friendship. Despite the difference in religious denomination, Gladstone and Acton were found to hold common religious and ethical principles, in a form which was near to holding common intellectual principles. Though one was a Roman Catholic and the other an Anglican, their conceptions of Catholicism were akin. Acton became not only a friend but a much valued adviser. This was not because he was of use in the House of Lords, which he hardly attended. It was as a private wise man behind the scenes that Gladstone enjoyed him. For a time the letters were still formal. Gladstone moved to *Yours ever* in 1880. Not till 1884 did the form of address become *My dear Acton*.

By nature Acton was not a diarist. Occasionally, and for special reasons, he kept a diary. Four diaries of different periods a few months at a time, survive (I do not count engagement-books). These diaries have value as historical notes but do not make good reading. The diary of the Vatican Council, which you would expect to be a historical source of the first importance, is singularly uninformative on many of the matters which the historian most wishes to know. And it is dull.

Once, at a later time when he was important in British politics, he was asked whether he kept a diary. He said that he kept the record in letters to his daughters. It was true. Though he was not a prolific writer of letters to all and sundry, and at least four people complained that he did not answer letters at all, he used letters to certain people as his form of a journal: that is, as a record of what happened and as his analysis of, or views about, what happened.

One *man*, and one man only, he used in this way: his master Döllinger. Victor Conzemius has beautifully edited the three volumes of letters, nearly all in German, which Acton wrote to Döllinger over the years, volumes which have now become the indispensable source for Acton's opinions on religion and church history and church literature. But there was another side to Acton, for obvious reasons less represented in his letters to a professor at the university of Munich: Acton the politician.

Throughout his mature life he seemed to find a need to use a woman as the destination of these letters. Three women in succession became the repositories of brilliant letters.

The first was his wife, Marie Arco-Valley. In the early years of marriage he would from time to time write her letters of political analysis, expecting her to share his interests. Her interests were not political, and she could not respond. An enormous letter survives, page after page of exposition of Italian politics and the Roman question, the reader wonders whether she managed to read to the end. The marriage began with tenderness and loyalty. But it failed to develop common intellectual interests, which were important to him. Acton's posterity told a story that once he and his wife had breakfast together, and he asked his wife, who was reading the newspaper, what was the news. She said, there was nothing important. When she passed him the newspaper, he found that it announced the death of Dr Döllinger. The story must be legend, because on the day when the newspaper announced the death of Döllinger, Acton was separated from Lady Acton by hundreds of miles. But that the children should tell and believe it discloses something of their view of their parents' intellectual relationship.

We can hardly believe that Lady Acton managed to read every word of that never-ending letter which analysed the politics of Italy.

This was not quite satisfactory to Acton. He wrote the letters partly to clarify his own mind. But he needed to feel that the reader of the letters was interested in what he wrote. In the end of the seventies, therefore, his wife ceased to be the recipient of this kind of letter. On a visit to Venice in 1879 he struck up a personal and intellectual relationship with Gladstone's daughter Mary; and from the end of that year she took the place of Marie Acton as the woman who received the letters. She had a big advantage over Marie. Being the daughter of either a Prime Minister or a leader of the Opposition, she was in the know. She understood what he wanted to talk and write about; and, at first with diffidence and surprise that so learned a man should choose so unlearned a woman as the home for his confidences, she began to respond. She found him a marvellous conversationalist and letter-writer, and a very sympathetic personality. The alliance which they struck marked the start of a new and different relationship between Acton and Gladstone.

Judged by English custom, by Gladstonian Lancashire custom, the manners of Acton were too polite. With a German mother and a German education, a German wife and movements in the society of European aristocrats, Acton acquired easily and naturally the infinite courtesy of the eighteenth century which simultaneously enchanted and yet maintained distance. In England it was occasionally said of him that his courtesy was not quite English. He was a little too ceremonious, though this was part of the charm and kindness. The love-letters which he wrote to his wife were written in three different languages, and so far as the husband was concerned could easily have been written in a fourth. Among those love-letters between an English husband and a German wife, the commonest language is French, and throughout her life she almost always used French in her letters to him. This is the inheritance of the Holy Roman Empire of the eighteenth century, when German aristocrats still used French because they found it the language of culture and civilization.

Acton could discuss history, or books, or politics, or authors, or politicians, and the issues which authors and politicians raised. If his company could not share these interests, or if he was tired or bored, or disliked the people sitting next to him, he would remain silent through an evening and be thought a disappoint-ment or a bear – a weakness which helped to make him at last a failure in politics.

John Morley, who regarded him as one of the great conver-sationalists, defined the mind as 'comprehensive as an encyclo-paedia, but profound and rich, not tabulated and dry . . . so deep and unexpected was he in thought, so impressive without empty pomp of words, so copious, exact and ready in his knowledge'. But even Morley reported a rueful experience. Wanting to entertain a friend, he invited him to dinner to meet Acton. The intention was frustrated, because Acton said nothing throughout the evening, and devoted his attention to eating through the courses.[1] 'The oracle proved dumb.' At a party late in life, Morley had to search his memory for the utterance which, in his experience, did most to bring talk to a full stop. He remin-isced how at a meal Gladstone (then well over eighty) had Morley at one hand and Acton at the other. Purcell's notorious *Life of Cardinal Manning* was published not long before, and everyone was discussing it. It had poignant interest for the com-pany, that both Gladstone and Acton appeared prominent in the pages, Acton in the role of Manning's dangerous enemy. Gladstone, finding himself with the best-known biographer then writing, together with the Catholic identified with Catholic resistance to Manning, the two men who by then were his two closest friends, said, 'There are no two men in the world from whom I should so much like to learn their opinion of Purcell's *Life of Manning*,' and gazed at Acton. Acton said: 'I haven't read it.' Morley remembered this remark as (what he called) 'the most complete stopper that could be imagined'.[2] When Morley looked back on the unpredictable nature of Acton's talk or taci-turnity, he wrote of him, 'He had a talent for silence which was sometimes provoking.'

[1] Morley, *Recollections*, I, p. 230.
[2] Mary Drew's notes of a conversation with Morley on 19 November 1920; BL Add. MSS 46244/139.

But with Gladstone, with Bryce, at one time of his life with Odo Russell, even at last with Morley despite the gulf between religion and irreligion, and with two women at different times – Mary Gladstone and his daughter Mamy – he was a marvellous talker. He could bring the full range of European literature and history into a conversation without becoming tedious or opening himself to the hint of being a pedant; and the history which he could unfold was not only the long centuries of the European past, but recent and contemporary history, for he mingled in courts and cabinets, and could introduce reminiscences of statesmen and authors, from popes and emperors downward, yet (because of his background) without any breath of the sin of dropping names. 'I told Bismarck through a friend . . .' – it is a wonderful casual sentence and in anyone else you would think the man was an Oscar Browning, always quoting emperors he had known. Acton lived in an international world, and could impart the atmosphere, without discourtesy and without arrogance and without egoism, at the table of any house where the company interested him.

Not everyone interested him. Even if they did, he might need a spark to set him off. Once, in rain and wind, he walked with Gladstone and his daughter through the woods of Hawarden park. The third person present thought the conversation, in the wind and rain, boring beyond belief; 'utterly unenlivened', she wrote in her diary[3] 'by any spark in the conversation which was almost entirely topographical and geological with a very slight smattering of French politics'.

So Acton could sometimes say nothing, or could talk dully. But when inspiration descended, he could be one of the great talkers of his time. Morley, who had experience enough how unconversable Acton could be, missed a lift in a carriage after a political meeting, and had to walk home with Acton, three or four miles along a moonlit road. Morley happened to say that he had to give an address at Edinburgh on the subject of *Aphor-*

---

[3] Mary Gladstone's Diary, BL Add. MS 46259, 2 January 1882.

isms. At once the flame descended upon Acton, and he poured out information on German, French, Italian and Spanish names 'ample enough', said Morley, 'to carry me through half a score of discourses. I never had a shorter walk.'[4]

It is not therefore surprising that when, during September 1879, Acton turned the rays of his mind upon Gladstone's daughter Mary, she was enchained.

That September of 1879 the Gladstone family went to Munich, primarily to see Döllinger. From 17 September they stayed in the villa on the lakeside at Tegernsee. They rowed on the lake, climbed a mountain, walked the woods. Every meal Mary Gladstone sat by Acton. Every evening, after the others went to bed, they talked into the night; till half-past twelve, till quarter-past one, *only* till half-past twelve, till one o'clock, they talked, or rather Acton talked with occasional interjections from her: of British politics, and Gladstone as a politician, of the scepticism of the age, of Lord Macaulay, of the birth of intolerance, of the influence of great men, of the effect of differences of opinion – those who know their Acton see his favourite themes reappearing laconically but radiantly in the diary of the girl, who unlike ourselves had never seen them in print, and who never had a mind of such power dedicated, for hours at a time, to herself.

From Munich the Gladstones moved southward, and just over a week later Acton joined them in Venice. At tables in the squares, in walks through the streets and round the Grand Canal, on the Rialto, on seats in the open air late into delicious evenings, the talks went on, until the last entry of the diary for the last evening – 'Went home at 11, alas it is our last night – Venice grows in beauty and charms and mystery.'

These meetings of autumn 1879, first at Tegernsee and then in Venice, began the famous exchange of letters.

As history contemplates the rowing-boat of September 1879, with its crew of Gladstone and Döllinger and Acton rowing

[4] Morley, *Recollections*, I, p. 230.

down the lake to the far end of Tegernsee, we wonder whether a touch of inward and secret embarrassment afflicted two members of the party. Earlier that year Döllinger published the words of praise for Bishop Dupanloup of Orleans which shocked Acton to his inmost being, and made him realise that the master, whom he sought to follow, held a view of morality in history, and therefore of morality in anything, which was not his. Students have talked of the breach between Döllinger and Acton from 1879. Acton afterwards regarded such a word as *breach* as too strong for what happened. But he knew the realisation to be an epoch in his life, carrying with it a conviction of his intellectual isolation and throwing all his historical plans awry.

Döllinger and Gladstone went the mountain-walk together and Döllinger returned exhausted. He went in that state to Acton's room, and told Acton that he understood what he meant about moral judgment in history and no longer disagreed with him. Acton looked back upon that moment, after the mountain-walk at Tegernsee, as the only time when he succeeded in making Döllinger understand what he meant.[5] Afterwards he realized that, whatever Döllinger said in the evening after his weary walk, it was not true that he agreed.

This intellectual gap between the two historians, only just visible to them both when they rowed down the lake at Tegernsee, but already widening, probably made a difference to what happened. If Acton felt a need for some one person to whom he wrote frank letters, Döllinger met the need. From 1879, and especially from 1881, the letters to Döllinger changed their character. When they were long, they were sometimes argumentative, occasionally fierce. Döllinger was still the master, Acton knew that to Döllinger he owed almost all. But part of the intimacy so far as it was an intellectual intimacy (and that was its important part) was going.

Mary Gladstone happened upon the scene as the friendship with Döllinger began to alter.

---

[5] Acton to Gladstone, Rome, 8 January 1890, BL Add. MS 44094.

The most important group of letters to her was written between the end of October 1879 and Mary's marriage to Harry Drew in February 1886; though there are several important letters after that date. After 1886 they no longer served Acton's private purpose. He wanted to articulate his opinions, but not in public, and he needed a woman as the receiver. But now a third woman took Mary's place as the confidante – his daughter Mamy, as she reached adulthood (she was twenty in the year that Mary Gladstone married). For all the last years of his life, the letters to Mamy became his chief mode of self-expression. Though his son Dick, after an uncertain start, went to Oxford and carved himself a career in the Foreign Office and shared the political interests, Acton used him only rarely as the destination of this kind of letter.

Did he use Mary Gladstone as a way to her father?

At first sight, the answer to that question is an easy affirmative. Consider for example the following paragraph on British statesmen, taken from a letter written at Cannes on 14 December 1880:

... When our descendants shall stand before the slab that is not yet laid among the monuments of famous Englishmen, they will say that Chatham knew how to inspire a nation with his energy, but was poorly furnished with knowledge and ideas; that the capacity of Fox was never proved in office, though he was the first of debaters; that Pitt, the strongest of ministers, was among the weakest of legislators; that no Foreign Secretary has equalled Canning, but that he showed no other administrative ability; that Peel, who excelled as an administrator, a debater and a tactician, fell everywhere short of genius; and that the highest merits of the five without their drawbacks were united in Mr Gladstone.[6]

In writing letters to a daughter about her father, a man has the licence of the maker of epitaphs, he is not upon oath. The cynic hesitates not an instant, that this high prose was intended for

[6] Paul, p. 34.

other eyes than the eyes of Mary. If he jumps to that conclusion he will be bound also to blame the author as a sycophant; or, if that doctrine is strong to stomach when applied to this Victorian aristocrat, then a Machiavellian who used flattery to the ends of power. We will form our opinion more cautiously than the cynic.

In the first place, Acton believed what he wrote. Whether he should have written it to a daughter is another question. But we shall not understand the bond between the two men unless we recognize that in such utterances Acton was sincere. A man might be predisposed to admire another man who got him a peerage, especially if in the getting he smashed centuries of prejudice against Roman Catholics. A man will be predisposed to admire a statesman of European stature who shares his opinions on certain religious matters which to him are concerns of life and death. A man who thinks Disraeli to be corrupting the political morals of Britain will be likely to admire his giant enemy. For these reasons, and more, Acton thought Gladstone the greatest of English statesmen, equalled only by Edmund Burke. And thinking this, he committed a venial sin, if a sin, in writing it to the daughter.

Secondly, this letter about Gladstone has a history.

Originally it was a conversation, late at night in the villa at Tegernsee. Gladstone, Döllinger, Acton and Mary rowed to the end of the lake, and walked back hastening before a storm; and as they hurried Acton talked to her of her father's retirement from the Liberal leadership four years before, and of its results. Late that evening she brought him back to the subject of her father. She said, she wished she could disengage her mind from its surroundings, and see her father as posterity would see him. Acton said, 'If you choose, you may hear it at once.' She encouraged him to go on; and though in her diary she made only the barest note of what he said, and added at the end, *crept up to bed*, the monologue remained for ever in her mind. In her memory she called this talk *The Judgment of Posterity on Mr Gladstone*.

Later she wrote from England, reminding him of the conversation, and begging him to put on paper what he had said. 'How I retrieved my audacity', he wrote, 'I cannot tell; and it is an awkward matter to recall . . .'[7] However, he obeyed; and the result was a wonderful obituary, written about a man nearly twenty years before he died.

Thirdly, Acton was so exceptional in one respect that neither contemporaries nor posterity were quite able to understand it. The sad story of how after Acton's death Charles Oman looked at Acton's heap of card-indexes and notes, and sighed at the vanity of human endeavour, so much knowledge locked up and wasted, and resolved that he at least would put pen to paper before he died, betrays an attitude which afflicts others who see Acton's notes. A man who collects knowledge only for his private satisfaction and with no desire to communicate, to teach, to advance other people's knowledge, is hard for the average man to understand.

At a time when educated England was reading Shorthouse's novel *John Inglesant* about English–papal relations in the seventeenth century, Mary Gladstone asked Acton what he thought. This produced an immense answer, one of the best known of Acton's letters, analysing with rare perception and rarer learning the historical muddles of the novel. It was an article in itself, a review such as no one else could have written. Mary decided that all this knowledge must be communicated, it would change men's ideas, at once it must be sent to *Macmillan's Magazine*. It *must not remain private property*, she wrote to him (27 March 1882). Acton replied instantly with a ban. He had written only for her, not for the public – *please dismiss the thought; and if you compliment anything, let it be the paper and the handwriting.*[8] With care and trouble and hours of time he sent a unique essay in historical criticism, and it was hard for a young woman to believe it aimed at herself alone. And she was right, because he wrote it also for himself. But he had not written for the world.

---

[7] Paul, p. 33.
[8] Acton to Mary Gladstone, 29 March 1882, not printed by Paul.

Still, we have not answered the question whether he used the daughter to influence the father. If he did so, he was not unique. Others, from Lord Rosebery downwards, used her to the same end.

Early in the exchange of letters she asked leave to show them to John Morley. His reply was quick: *Don't show my letters to others – I need to write freely.*[9] The letters as they came in, and Mary's attitude to the letters, made this rule impossible for her to obey. Here was she, receiving some of the most important letters of her generation, ordered to keep them to herself. She even blamed him, more than once, for hiding his light under a bushel. Just occasionally the letter was so extraordinary that she could not but suspect it to be intended for an eye other than her own. A casual scribbled postscript of hers about a French politician produced a long reply of such curious knowledge and statesmanship that she could not imagine how it could be meant for herself only.

Somehow I feel as if I had no right to it, and had got if from you on false pretences – that you really wrote it for my father, and I think I ought to confess to you that I am not at all a good pipe or sieve or whatever it should be called, not nearly as good as any one of the secretaries because neither his eyes or ears are open to me as they are to him.[10]

In letters to her he could say things to her that he could never say to a secretary. But he had this moral advantage over all the other fry who used the Gladstone family to push opinions towards Mr Gladstone. He liked to write to Mary Gladstone for her own sake, because in her he found the recipient who understood the value of his knowledge and his judgements. Some other men wrote to Mary Gladstone only because she was a Prime Minister's daughter. Acton wrote to her because she was herself and became (if it is not paradoxical to say so) he was also himself.

[9] Acton to Mary Gladstone, 3 October 1880, part omitted by Paul, p. 31.
[10] Mary Gladstone to Acton, 30 September 1880, after receiving Acton's letter from Tegernsee of 27 September, printed by Paul, pp. 28–31.

Little by little the rule of privacy became impossible for her to keep. She refrained from reading passages of praise aloud, but she started to read important paragraphs to her father, and found that he liked it and was helped. This habit grew when she was given a semi-official post as a secretary to her father. As early as April 1881 Acton, knowing that she could not read the German language, recommended to her the study of two books on the history of agriculture, both written in German; and that the suggestion was intended for another reader than herself was shown when, after she told him that she could not read them and her father was too busy, he wrote 'it is really important that the P.M. should set somebody in Downing Street to read Wagner's *Grundlegung* ... I would even venture to ask you to mention it to him, as flotsam from the Riviera'.[11] Early in 1882 he was writing on Irish Home Rule, evidently with confidence that his opinion would be passed on; and henceforth, whenever Mary told him that she read passages to her father, he made no comment. By 1884 Acton consciously wrote letters to Mary Gladstone in the endeavour to persuade the Prime Minister that Canon Liddon ought to be made Bishop of London. On this topic full and fascinating letters were exchanged; the more fascinating to posterity because, amid all the interested discussion, none of the three participants asked themselves what business had a Roman Catholic who lived abroad to be recommending names for bishoprics in the Church of England.

These letters, therefore, which began as private letters, became in time letters also to her father. On 31 October 1892 Acton wrote a revealing letter to his daughter Mamy: 'I have had to resume the old correspondence with Mrs Drew. It is a way of conveying some things I cannot say right off. She was nicer than ever.' *I have had to resume* – the relationship with Mary certainly changed after Mamy grew to womanhood.

In this way friendship between Acton and Mary Gladstone cemented the friendship between Acton and her father. For

---

[11] Paul, p. 7.

Gladstone he became a wiseacre; usually distant in Europe, too often distant; not to be trusted, probably, with the rough-and-tumble of everyday politics, but seeing British politics with the same principles as Gladstone, and seeing them the more clearly, partly because he stood aloof, partly because he saw with European eyes, and partly because of his knowledge and experience.

When Acton stayed with the Gladstones, he did not find it comfortable to be revered as an oracle. He stayed at Hawarden Castle, and wrote to his wife that they treated him 'like a sage, and I had the greatest difficulty last night in persuading Mrs Gladstone to let me play at cards with the children'. He walked with Gladstone, sat up late with him, watched him cut down a tree, listened like an anvil to the old man's pet theories of scholarship and did not always enjoy them – 'Before dinner I had a dreadful hour, listening to Gladstone's theories about Homer, and this morning I have been reading a manuscript book of his, which he is going to publish . . . a hard trial.'[12]

This status of private wise man depended on personality, that attraction of one man for another which is not definable by historians.

Acton admired Gladstone, as man, as religious man, as statesman. Admiration is usually a channel through which influence flows. We might expect Acton to have been influenced by Gladstone. This was not how Acton saw the matter.

He had a feeling that he was the Liberal who understood Liberalism, and saw how the roots of Liberalism were religious and moral. He had a feeling that he was the man who knew where he was in religion. In both these aspects of philosophy he conceived of himself as the anchor, and of Gladstone as moving slowly but steadily towards him; Gladstone as the Tory who became a Liberal by circumstance and then began step by step to discover the true basis of Liberalism; Gladstone as the old high-and-dry Anglican who, first through Newman, and later through Acton, understood more and more of the nature of

---

[12] Acton to Marie (from Hawarden, Wednesday), 8121/7/1018.

Catholicism; Gladstone the religious man who only towards the end came to see that his political axioms were founded on religion. He felt himself to be the theorist, Gladstone to be the man of action who slowly grew in understanding the theory. Whether the feelings corresponded with reality in the mind of Gladstone is another question. Whether Acton's own opinions were so static an anchor is still another. But this was how Acton saw it. When Gladstone died, Acton wrote his daughter a letter (23 May 1898) describing these twin judgements about Gladstone's long development of his standpoint.

One or two of the obituaries said that Gladstone (at the time of the Gorham case in 1850) almost became a Roman Catholic; and Mary Gladstone's clergyman-husband Drew published a denial. Acton understood Gladstone's mind too well to suppose any such story true. Still, when he went to Westminster Hall to view his old chief, lying in state on the catafalque, it touched him that at the foot was a cloth with the words *requiescat in pace*, once embroidered for Archbishop Benson of Canterbury; and it pleased Acton to think that the words, as he declared, 'cast Protestantism to the winds' because orthodox Protestantism had not allowed prayer for the dead lest the practice suggest a purgatory after death.[13] More and more Gladstone came, he thought, to understand Catholicism as he came to understand Liberalism, and this deepening was a single process.

Till 1879 Acton and his family lived at their seat of Aldenham in Shropshire. Then they moved to the French Riviera, first to Mentone, then to Cannes, giving as reason for the moves the children's health.

Life at Cannes, or Tegernsee, was a disadvantage to someone who through the Gladstones turned into an eminence of the Liberal party. Gladstone kept at him to come 'home':

The great gifts which have been given you will not easily find their full application without your coming home, and the fields are so white

---

[13] Acton to Mamy (from Athenaeum), 27 May 1898, 7956/212.

to the harvest and the labourers at least the capable labourers so few that one cannot but grudge the lengthened furloughs of those who are most capable among them. [Gladstone 1879]

You will also I hope tell me of the approaching close of your banishment from England – since you I suppose cannot fully perform your work without certain material conditions fulfilled. [1880]

I thought there would be 52 peers [i.e. instead of 51] to vote with the Government, but Lord Granville says you [are] drinking waters somewhere – what a disappointment. [Mary Gladstone to Acton, August 1880]

Be not I pray you too niggardly in dealing out your days. [Gladstone 1881]

When do you *repatriate*? [1888]

and so on, and on.

The absence had another effect besides its bestowal of letters upon posterity. Acton began to get among some Liberal leaders a reputation which was not to his credit. He stood back; wrote letters; was a critic, an armchair critic – but was not engaged, sat remote from the battle and pointed out where generals went astray. Mary Gladstone had a conversation with Lord Rosebery. After the conversation she wrote Acton a stern letter:

There is in some quarters a general idea that you do nothing but criticise with folded hands – that you are always negative – that nobody knows anything at all about your real opinions – that you continually pull down and tear to pieces, without raising up or edifying (in the true meaning of the word). I cannot say that you have ever been so with us.[14]

Sometimes the reproaches were cast in more delicate but not more veiled words: 'Please tell me what you think about the Arms Bill from your distant high mountain.'[15] He talked vaguely of the health of his wife, the health of his children. He wrote loosely about climate. He did not satisfy. After he came, to their gratification, to stay at Hawarden Castle over the New Year of

---

[14] Mary Gladstone to Acton, 20 June 1880.
[15] Mary Gladstone to Acton, February 1881.

1882, Mary attacked him. Was not an absentee landlord like a clergyman deserting his parish? It looked like neglect of duty. The excuses were 'never enough'[16] she said.

Still [replied Acton after five weeks of silence] in giving up one's home, and country, and friends, and occupations, there is at least a mixture of good motives with selfish ones, and something sacrificed, if there is also a good deal of calculated pleasure-seeking and ease. If I held an appointment abroad, keeping me permanently away from my – very modest – estate, you would say that the Government was insane to offer it, but you would hardly think it wrong of me to accept it. And the duty I have allowed to precede all other duties is one that possesses a strong, and unmistakable, claim on me.

Between my children and my Shropshire neighbours my choice is indeed decided.

Not Shropshire neighbours but Shropshire tenants were the duties that concerned Mary. The argument was a side-issue. Gladstone wanted his vote in the House of Lords, his advice on Irish and Catholic questions, and his guidance in history and literature. Gladstone and especially Mary Gladstone wanted both his company and his conversation. He seemed like a remote hermit who knew everything that men needed to know and communicated the knowledge in parsimonious doses, one of the enchanting personalities in Europe who insisted on staying where there was no one to enchant.

But was this not a scholar, engaged in his study? When the Gladstones stayed at Cannes they went over to Acton's villa at La Madeleine, and Mary Gladstone stayed a few days, and there saw the work room, the books with their marking slips, the little black leather boxes stuffed with notes, the cards of the famous card-index, all the signs of a tome or tomes in gestation.

In that visit to Venice in 1879 he had talked to Mary of his great book. Late in the evening of 8 October she and her brother Herbert walked with Acton in the moonlight to a marble bench

---

[16] Mary Gladstone to Acton, 10 January 1882.

by the shore, the Piazzetta behind them; and there divine inspiration came down upon Acton, and he talked magically, tingling to his fingers' ends as Mary described him, of his dreams of a great History of Liberty which was the heart of the history of man. Like *The Judgement of Posterity on Mr Gladstone* late at night in Tegernsee, this talk in the moonlight on the Piazzetta in Venice was a moment vivid to Mary Gladstone throughout her life. She can be found returning to it again and again in her memory.

Harder heads who heard the plan poured doubt. Döllinger told Acton more than once that men should write books which were possible to write. Acton hardly deluded himself. He did not mind what Döllinger said, he could read everything and therefore was undaunted. On the marble bench in the Piazzetta he carried Mary Gladstone away with the vision. But even in the conversation he doubted himself. For he nicknamed his book on The History of Liberty, *The Madonna of the Future*. And in that name lay more than scepticism; almost tragedy.

Six years before, Henry James published the short story, *The Madonna of the Future*, in an American journal. Then it was taken into a collection of short stories, and at last, in this year 1879, was established in Europe, because it became the first story in a collection of two volumes, and gave a title to the whole.

A visitor went to Florence. Out on the piazza by moonlight he found an artist on the steps of the loggia, who seemed picturesque, fantastic, unreal. They walked the street together; and the artist discoursed of his aim in life, so mastering that all other aims dropped away, to create the portrait of a perfect Madonna, ideal of motherhood; and because that was his goal, he could not hurry, he could afford to wait and wait. The visitor enquired of others and found that none of them believed in this distant goal. Then the artist took the visitor to see the girl his model, and the visitor saw that the model was ageing and grew stout. In the last pages the visitor went to the artist's death-bed, and looked at the easel by the window, and upon the easel 'a canvas that was a mere dead blank, cracked and discoloured by time'. And the dying artist said that in his head was matter for a hundred masterpieces. 'But my hand is paralysed now, and they will never be painted.'

In such terms did Acton describe his own book, in the moonlight on the Piazzetta. Mary could feel the mixture of realism and mysticism as he talked. In her diary she recorded, how *extraordinary* that he 'can sit patient and quiet over wife and children and wait and wait another year before he writes. What an odd man.' But he did not try to persuade her that he was serious, and she did not believe him serious. The title *The Madonna of the Future* became a private joke between them. It remained a private joke all his life; so that when near the end of his days he wrote explaining to her the plan for his *Cambridge Modern History*, he jested to her (23 December 1896) 'This is to be a whole choir of Madonnas.' Only posterity, which knows more of Acton, and sees the beginnings, in that year 1879, of deep inward frustration, a mental break with Döllinger who more nearly resembled a father than anyone else he had known, and a growing coolness in his family life, understands that in his soul he could suffer from a touch of hopelessness, and that for him at least the title *Madonna of the Future* meant something more than a joke.

But as the years passed and his reasons for being abroad went lame, and Mary Gladstone grew vexed, even she began to wonder whether this great book was nothing but excuse and that he never intended to write. She wondered now whether it was like illness, or climate, a pretext for not doing his duty in England. In January 1884 these meditations, and a rumour that he meant to let the Aldenham estate, produced the fiercest of her protests, so fierce as to be ungrammatical:

... It seems to me quite dreadfully wicked to entirely forswear your country and no longer give it any of the benefits which as a landowner and peer [sic] it has a right to expect from you. It is most cool of me saying this, but I am your countrywoman and should have some share in those benefits so I think I may speak. We had a great discussion here the other night started by Professor Stuart of Cambridge, on whether 'best is the enemy of good' and I could not help thinking sadly of the Madonna of the Future, and that it is indeed not in this world that any mortal man can afford to wait for best. The History of Liberty, when will the time ever arrive here when all the light that can be thrown on a subject, has been thrown? Never in this world indeed, and are we to cheat our fellow creatures of what we *do* know because of all that we do not know? Would any great work ever have been done from the beginning if perfection had been waited for – and are there not 2nd and 3rd and 4th editions? It makes me wretched when I picture to myself the little black leather boxes standing on 'my' table stuffed with notes, the books stuffed with marks and markers, and above all the vast treasure of knowledge and thought that is there, shut up in that person, seated at that table, reading and marking those books and writing those notes; and think perhaps we, the hungry and thirsty, may never be fed from those plentiful stores.[17]

This outburst was punished by the strongest letter which Acton ever wrote to her:

You make writing as difficult as living afar, by your unspeakable goodness, but also by the infusion of the contrary quality. If I promise not to attack the government, or to believe in Lord Derby, will you agree not to hit me so hard? I cannot well help doing what I do, taking all things into consideration; and as to my tiresome book, please to remember that I can only say things which people do not agree with, that I have neither disciple nor sympathiser, that this is no encouragement to production & confidence, that grizzled men – except [George Otto] Trevelyan – grow appalled at the gaps in their knowledge, & that I have no other gift but that which you pleasantly describe, of sticking eternal bits of paper into innumerable books, and putting larger papers into black boxes. There is no help for it. But your reproaches were much more distressing to read than you suppose, & make me think them better to read than to hear . . .[18]

The Madonna of the Future – the jest never ceased to pain. When Gladstone died, there was one obvious biographer; only one who had the intimate personal knowledge and the under-

---

[17] Mary Gladstone to Acton, January 1884.
[18] Acton to Mary Gladstone (from La Madeleine at Cannes), 9 February 1884.

standing of Gladstone's religion. Mary Drew, and some other members of the family, would have liked Acton to do the Life. But they saw how his career was littered with books begun and never finished; and in writing to tell him with delicacy that they invited John Morley, Mary used the old phrase, which this time contained nothing but sadness: 'There is one biographer whom I feel we should all prefer, were he not too deliberate a historian to perform this "nimble" task. Alas for the Madonna of the Future.'

The tragedy of Acton was not that he meant to write a book and others knew that he would never write it; but that he was *inspired* to write a book and his uninspired self knew that the inspiration could never be brought between cloth covers.

He gave the reasons for exile, though only by hints, in his one explanation. First, family; second, preference; and third, money – my 'very modest' estate.

His wife Marie did not like living in England. She was never fluent in the English language. His fourth child and second son John died in a train at the age of one and was buried at London. Ever afterwards she was nervous over English climate, for herself and for her children. He wanted to be with her and the children; though, as the years went by, he wanted to be with the children more than he wanted to be with his wife. The end of his self-appointed exile coincided with the growing up of his two eldest surviving children.

The 'modest means' – Acton was a peer with an international position in repute. He lived abroad like so many Englishmen in difficulty, because it was cheaper. Heir to an estate of the Holy Roman Empire, descended from an Italian prime minister, son of a Shropshire baronet, stepson of a Whig grandee, he was believed to be rich, or at least comfortable. It was never quite true, and as the years passed it became false. When he was a child his grandmother spent lavishly from the Acton estate in the effort to help her son (his uncle) Cardinal Acton to maintain the state and the charities expected of a cardinal. The Aldenham rents were important; the castle at Herrnsheim too large an expense; his one extravagance (if it is extravagance) the buying of books and the hiring of copyists. His daughter Mamy regarded the years 1883–6 as 'the lean years'. Rents did not come from Aldenham, and they could not survive. So Herrnsheim must be sold to a leather-merchant, with everything inside it, even a manuscript of Schiller and marvellous damask Dalberg table-cloths; beautiful Dalberg jewels were sold at Christie's including a ruby and diamond necklace which Napoleon Bonaparte gave to Duchess Dalberg.

It was not enough. In the winter of 1889–90 Acton was on the point of bankruptcy, and knew that he would be bankrupt unless he borrowed money. He borrowed a large sum from Lloyds Bank. As securities for the repayment of the loan, the bank insisted upon the house at Aldenham, the diamonds and the books. It was decided, whether by the bank or Acton is not clear but probably by the bank, that the library (now about 60,000 volumes, though no one yet knew how many) must be sold in the summer of 1890 to pay back part at least of the loan and interest. Puttick and Simpson were charged with the sale, printed the first part of the catalogue, and fixed the auction for 16 July and the seven following days.

When the sale was announced, Gladstone first knew the extent of Acton's plight over money. He began to help with tact. 'I had hoped and intended', wrote Gladstone, 'to say nothing to you about the distressing subject. But knowing the *worst*, I have been desirous to know more, and in particular to know the *composition* of the library.'[19] He sent Acton a table to fill up, on the approximate numbers divided by subject, and personally went round to see the auctioneers. 'I think', he told Acton, 'Puttick & Simpson are rather overwhelmed by the magnitude of their task.' 'I feel', he wrote a few days later, 'it is like digging into living flesh.'

[19] Gladstone to Acton, 29 April 1890, 8119/9/69. The Puttick and Simpson catalogue of Part I of the Library is among the Acton papers at Cambridge, and among Gladstone's papers in the BM. Acton's reply of thanks from Cannes, 7 May 1890, BL Add. MS 44094.

Believing that this loss was to Acton like the death of a child, Gladstone made energetic efforts to ensure the best of all worlds. At the beginning of June 1890 he found his benefactor. Andrew Carnegie happened to come to the Hotel Metropole in London. Of all the millionaire's charitable interests, libraries were the chief. Carnegie remembered how, as a telegraph boy in Pittsburgh at two and a half dollars a week, he made his way by getting a book a week from a free library. Since he created the free library at his brithplace Dunfermline eight years before, libraries were known to be what he wanted. Gladstone privately approached him. The next document is a note pencilled in Carnegie's hand, dated 10 June 1890, offering to guarantee to the bank a loan of £10,000 with interest; 'the object being to preserve to Lord Acton his library during his life'. 'P.S. If the Bank positively decline to pay the interest and it is necessary that it be paid annually I shall pay it. Lord Acton not to be called upon in any case for a penny.'

And now came the extraordinary moment of this salvage. Acton was in Munich, working away at the ill-sorted papers of the dead Döllinger, whose life he aimed to write. Gladstone sent Acton a telegram, then a letter, then another telegram, then another letter. He needed Acton in London. Acton refused to come. He was busy. Would Gladstone please write? 'I am excessively sorry to answer as if I did not understand the immense value of the interest you are kindly taking.'

'Not having heard from you', wrote Carnegie to Gladstone on 12 June from his hotel, 'I fear my suggestion has not proved acceptable.' Gladstone (13 June) wrote an impassioned letter to Munich:

... It is a question of keeping your library for life, without solicitation, without charge, and with privacy. I cannot doubt that this outline of the matter will bring you home at once ... There surely can be nothing in the disposal of Dr Döllinger's and Professor Möhler's papers, important as it is, which can be pressing in point of time, or which can compare in urgency with the matter which we can only lay

before you with the aid of speech, and which is even now placed at
some small disadvantage by your absence . . .

The same day Carnegie finally agreed, without seeing Acton
and without Acton's agreement. He made it a condition that no
one should know, because if it got about, it would be 'somewhat
uncomfortable' for Acton.

Acton now arrived in England, and saw Gladstone and his
own lawyer Freshfield, but then went to ground in the Athenaeum. Freshfield was astounded by a cheque for £9,000 arriving
from Scotland, whither Carnegie had gone. He said that he had
never heard of anything like it. In the talk with Carnegie Gladstone suggested that Acton should keep the library for life and
then on his death it should pass to Carnegie or his heirs. Carnegie sent the cheque without any such stipulation. It is far from
certain that this son of a Dunfermline weaver wished to possess
the greatest collection of books on Catholic ecclesiastical history
every assembled by a private individual for his own use. In the
light of what happened later, it is certain that he had no desire
for them. He wished to oblige Gladstone, to keep an eminent
Victorian from the shame of bankruptcy, and perhaps to help a
scholar keep the tools of his scholarship. He could only do so
without offence to pride by buying the books. Gladstone felt in
honour bound to make legal provision in this sense, and ordered
the lawyer Freshfield to draft terms.

Freshfield did not find it easy to draft the terms. First, he
found it difficult to get any sign of life from Acton. Letter after
letter flowed out, and disappeared unanswered. Secondly, securing the library to Acton for life was more difficult than it looked.
What would happen if Acton spent extravagantly, or even if,
without extravagance, he fell again into the margin of bankruptcy? Freshfield had not only to establish Acton's permanent
right to use the library, but to prevent future creditors from
getting hold of it. 'Of course', Freshfield told Gladstone,[20] 'Mr

---

[20] Freshfield to Gladstone, 9 July 1890, BL Add. MS 44510.

Carnegie must rely to a very large extent upon Lord Acton doing no act which shall jeopardise the Library in any way by making it liable to his creditors. In fact, from this point of view, I cannot help thinking that the arrangement may be indirectly as service-able to Lord Acton as it will be directly.'

Freshfield was a pessimist. If the Library now belonged to Carnegie it could not be used to pay Acton's creditors even if Acton used it and it was housed in his rooms. At the end of July Messrs Puttick and Simpson, who lost money by cancellation of the auction but hardly complained, returned all the books to Aldenham. The last document in the case shows Freshfield still trying to extract from Acton answers to unanswered letters.

It is not at all certain that the money was adequate to the real value of the books.

It was the great working library of a single mind, with no desire for rarities for the sake of rarities, or of gems for the bibliophile's trade, but simply bought with the ideal of under-standing the past, and through the past the present. 'The whole collection', he once told Gladstone,[21] 'was made with a single view to understanding the public life of the time and the world I lived in. There are no mere curiosities or fine copies, unless by chance.'

The user of Acton's library therefore feels shock when he reads these papers between Gladstone and Acton, Freshfield and Carnegie. *Acton did not mind*. He wrote the warmest letters of thanks to Gladstone for the 'practically inestimable' offer of his anonymous friend. But he did not much care if the library was sold. He had ceased to use it; left it at Aldenham where he had not lived for twelve years; would not at first even come to London when the question of saving it was in the balance; did not bother to answer the lawyer's letters. Selling the library was in sentiment like selling a house which he could not inhabit; not worse. The idea, of preserving a scholar's tools for his study, is mistaken. He needed other books now – British Museum,

---

[21] Acton to Gladstone, 23 May 1890.

Athenaeum, Bodleian, Cambridge University Library, Royal Library at Munich. Perhaps Gladstone secretly understood this, and wanted to preserve his friend rather from public shame than from the loss of his learned equipment. The library was no longer a working library. It was a valuable asset, like a diamond necklace. Though the library returned awry from Puttick and Simpson, he never bothered to put it back to order, so that it was first restored to good use by the staff of Cambridge University after his death.

Whatever the motive, it was a great act of friendship.

The Carnegie gift on loan did not suffice to relieve the pressure. Early in 1891 Acton's stepfather Lord Granville died. By May it was found that the Granville estate was ruined by the slump in iron and steel, and by the autumn Gladstone was trying to persuade several dukes to make an unpromising investment to save Granville's posthumous name from bankruptcy. Times were hard for nearly everyone connected with the Acton family.

Now comes a question, which is almost beyond the evidence, whether Acton made a difference; whether his advice was followed; whether the relationship between Acton and Gladstone had consequence in British history and not only in English literature.

They discussed everything. To Gladstone he was a sage with the highest of ethical ideals, in religion, politics or private life; and perhaps Gladstone was not uncomfortable to find one, whose ethics he respected, believing that his own policies were ethical, that Disraeli's policies were immoral, and that if that devout Anglican the Marquess of Salisbury became Tory prime minister it was as bad as if the atheist Bradlaugh became prime minister. Acton loathed absolute power. When he talked of liberty, a ring came into his voice, all the long story of progress and growth into human dignity, seen in the perspective of an instant and yet historical eternity, and inseparable from the absolute demand of the conscience; as if, said James Bryce after listening to Acton for only six or seven minutes, 'the whole landscape of history had been suddenly lit up by a burst of sunlight'.[22] Most people felt in Acton this inflexible moral will. Some shrugged their shoulders, some thought it unreal, politicians thought it irrelevant. The stirring thing is that Gladstone, though a politician, accepted it as he might have accepted the counsel of a priest, though this was neither a priest nor even a member of the same denomination in religion. Gladstone once told Acton to his face that he trusted him 'more entirely than any other man.'[23]

The charitable forms of this influence were not political. Gladstone knew a scholar, believed him the best-read man in Europe, and picked his brains continually, first for the names of books and authors to read, but later for drafting his articles – on Goethe, the immortality of the soul, the history of eating pork, Homer, the primitive Christian Church, medieval universities, heresy and schism in the modern Church, Bishop Butler, Tertullian – on anything to which he turned his literary mind the polymath *manqué* asked help of the real polymath. Towards the end the help extended further. A friend of Acton's believed that the better parts of Gladstone's Romanes Lecture (1892) at Oxford were written by Acton. It was not true; but the lecture would have been less worthy without him, for by then the word *Old* in the phrase *Grand Old Man* was ceasing to be complimentary.

Acton's opinion was also sought on political questions. But since he usually agreed in politics with what Gladstone did, we cannot think the effect was often marked. Once his knowledge of Italy saved Gladstone from a small error of judgement. He kept telling Gladstone not to resign, in the frequent moments when Gladstone longed for retirement. But whether Gladstone would have resigned without this backing is, despite everything that he said, improbable. At one time Gladstone thought Lord

[22] Bryce, *Studies in Contemporary Biography* (1903), p. 396.
[23] Acton to Mamy, 23 May 1898, 7956/211.

Granville ought to have a turn at being Prime Minister. It says something for Acton's lack of self-interest that he showed no desire at all that his step-father should become Prime Minister.

Acton believed that he and John Morley were the twin authors of the policy of Home Rule for Ireland. But in a conversation with Acton Morley denied that he had anything to do with injecting the idea into Gladstone's mind, and when he wrote the *Life of Gladstone* went out of his way to repeat the denial. This left Acton believing himself to be sole author of the policy; and if his belief were justified, he was the source of one of the revolutionary changes in modern British politics. He also believed that his advice, given to Gladstone on moral grounds, was a crux in Gladstone's refusal to work with Parnell after the adultery case. Whenever Gladstone's sense of expediency conflicted with his sense of right, Acton stood for the moral policy even when it was inexpedient. He exaggerated his own force in the question of Parnell. Whether or not Acton gave Gladstone advice, Parnell would have fallen. But Swinburne would have had a better chance of succeeding. Tennyson as Poet Laureate if Acton had not worked hard. He admitted that Swinburne wrote the best verses, but was determined to keep him from the laurel.

We should beware of over-estimating the weight of all this evidence.

If Acton advised that something should happen, and then the something happened, Acton usually assumed that it happened because he advised. Other sources show that it often happened by more compelling reasons. We shall not be far wrong if we think of him more as the intangible aura of a mind and spirit than the definable stimulus of a statesman who understands how votes are caught and policy executed.

During the second half of the eighties Acton's visits to England became longer. His son Richard came to Oxford and needed to be settled. His daughter Mamy could be introduced to country houses and society. From the spring of 1892 his life lay mostly in England. After fourteen years of exile, Acton began to be English again in fact as well as by birthright. Most of the time he lived at the Athenaeum, where he found the library excellent for his purposes. He dined everywhere. The summer of 1892 was the most dramatic moment of his career.

That summer he moved with the Liberal leaders through the general election. In June he helped Gladstone draft the Liberal manifesto. In July he went to stay with Lord Rosebery at Dalmeny not far from Edinburgh, where Gladstone habitually stayed for the Midlothian campaigns. This was the moment when John Morley, now almost a rival for Gladstone's personal confidence, confessed that of Acton's society Gladstone could never have too much.[24]

The time at Dalmeny was miserable. Gladstone, arriving there with a usual excess of optimism and expecting a huge victory and the consequent ability to carry Home Rule for Ireland at once, had to bear the evidence of the polls that opinion in the country had fallen from the Liberals and that the majority would be small, certainly too small to do successfully what he wanted to do for Ireland.

Suddenly, for the first time, Gladstone was a liability, a leader who was necessary and yet identified with a now impracticable policy. The harder heads fancied it best if Gladstone took the chance to retire. He was too old, and deaf, and easily tired, his discernment between important and unimportant faded, his judgement was less stable. Instantly therefore, at Dalmeny and in Liberal houses where men imagined what was happening at Dalmeny, everyone started to wonder about Gladstone's successor. Inevitably began that embarrassed jockeying for position which is the painful part of the process of choosing party leaders. Acton was surprised to find himself, as he stayed with Rosebery and Gladstone at Dalmeny, at the centre of Liberal pessimism and uncertainty and embarrassment, if not at the beginning of a veiled struggle for power. He found the company strained; and because of the strain they refrained from talking to each other,

[24] Morley, *Gladstone*, II, p. 549.

and poured their confidence into him. For a moment he stood at the heart of British politics.

The house was not comfortable for anyone, probably Acton was the least uncomfortable. Gladstone felt the electoral failure and became dependent on the advice of others. His wife and daughter were forward to offer that advice and became protective. Politicians started to resent the women as interfering busybodies. Rosebery played his part as host. But since, among the three or four possible but not obvious successors to Gladstone he was the least unlikely, his predicament was the most uncomfortable of all; and he irritated the others by refusing, at this moment of all moments, to talk politics, and by keeping out of the way. Acton thought that Rosebery felt the strain more than any of them. Rosebery would not even join in discussion on the new cabinet. He did his duty as host but, wrote Acton to his daughter, 'nor cordially, avoiding political explanations, and professing a sort of vague indifference'.

In the house at Dalmeny host and chief guest, the two principals of the Liberal party at a crisis in its fortunes, could not, or would not, say to each other a word of politics. It was absurd. Other visitors felt an 'indescribable cloud' hanging over the place, a tension which all the mutual courtesies could not hide.

Acton became necessary. They could not speak to each other, but could speak to him. Rosebery could not say to his chief that he had better step down, but could hint it to Acton.

What lay behind Rosebery's mask no one knew then or knows now. The evidence of his own letters shows only that he was shattered by his wife's death two years before (worse than shattered, on the verge of mental disturbance), and wanted to escape from politics. The evidence of his acts during the election, and after the government was formed, points in a different direction. Probably he was torn apart emotionally, and did not know what to do. Acton, watching him at close quarters, thought him a realist who saw with a clear light that whoever succeeded Gladstone had miserable work. As Acton described his mental state, he knew that he 'would have to follow a failing old man, with no hope of lasting, and little prospect of immediate, success'.[25]

All the Liberal leaders but two saw that if this government were to exist with Gladstone at its head, the Earl of Rosebery must be Foreign Secretary. He had the respect of foreign powers, the confidence of the party, national stature made more national partly by glamour and partly by his horses. The only two who refused to see this were Gladstone and Rosebery. Gladstone found aspects of racing Rosebery uncongenial. Rosebery was in a muddle of the psyche, a state of mind which an observer called *desperately morbid – with many cobwebs indeed obscuring his vision.*[26] For reasons of the heart Rosebery half-wanted to retire from politics. The other half had no wish to join a Cabinet which would be the most frustrated Cabinet of Queen Victoria's reign.

Then if Gladstone started to lead, but could not lead long, Rosebery should have the right of succession, holding at once the Foreign Office and the leadership of the House of Lords. Acton understood Rosebery to make this offer, or condition, and to ask him to convey it to Gladstone. This view of the conversation is impossible to believe in the light of Rosebery's letters and acts, and in the light of a later letter from Acton. Probably Rosebery seriously discussed with Acton what would happen if Gladstone did not retire at once, but would retire soon, and they came upon this scheme of securing a succession. Acton declined to give Gladstone any message which would tell him to resign the leadership.

On the day of the Midlothian election, Rosebery took Acton out for a beautiful drive and poured forth his ideas. It became plain to Acton that Rosebery was going to 'sell his life dearly', that is, he would certainly refuse to serve in Gladstone's government unless he was brought in by the highest possible offer. Acton went to Gladstone and advised him to offer Rosebery the

[25] Acton to Mamy (from Athenaeum), 25 July 1892, 7956/74.
[26] Morley to Gladstone, 6 August 1892, BL Add. MSS 44256/227.

169

office of Foreign Secretary and the leadership of the House of Lords.

Gladstone went to Rosebery, and a conversation took place. One of the signs of Gladstone's old age was vagueness, a reluctance to frame precisely. He thought that he invited Rosebery to be Foreign Secretary. Certainly they discussed foreign policy together, even arrangements, and Rosebery failed to protest. But what Rosebery thought to happen was different. He had no consciousness that Gladstone invited him to be Foreign Secretary. He thought that he was told how Acton pressed Gladstone to invite him to be Foreign Secretary. Rosebery left the room unaware that the troubled old man believed himself to have made an offer, and the offer to be accepted. It could hardly please Rosebery to see that Gladstone really preferred someone else as Foreign Secretary, but came to him because Acton, an intruder into politics, pushed him that way.

Gladstone and his family and Acton went off to stay at Braemar with Gladstone's faithful disciple Armitstead. Rosebery, still acting the courteous host, looked glad to see them go, and went sailing among the Hebrides, evidently to escape. Acton's letters show no consciousness of the tensions and emotions and morbidities in Rosebery's breast. He believed that Rosebery saw a clear aim; if it were humanly possible, to prevent Gladstone from forming the government which he was unfitted by age or health to lead.

At Braemar, Gladstone and Acton set about composing a Cabinet, based on Rosebery at the Foreign Office and Sir William Harcourt as Chancellor of the Exchequer.

Acton the Cabinet-maker in Braemar was put a little off balance by finding himself in power, and by knowing that the leader of the Party would do what he suggested. Suddenly to nominate the members of a new Cabinet was a rare experience. Phrases in his private letters show that for a moment power went to his head. A friend of Acton's heard and commented amusedly, 'Acton considers that at this crisis he is going to govern England through Gladstone.'[27] Acton may have made enmities worse by a touch in his manner. He wrote (26 July) to his daughter Mamy:

You are clever enough to understand that I had an unparalleled opportunity of earwigging the coming Prime Minister, and poisoning his mind; and those who are disappointed will lay the blame on my innocent shoulders. At this moment a quarrel rages, with Morley and perhaps with Rosebery . . .

He thought that at Braemar he was forced to take too much upon himself. He was encouraged because Gladstone told him that he must himself be a member of the Cabinet. This was music to his ears. Ever since 1870 he was a politician *manqué* and now he needed to earn his living. He looked forward to a seat in the Cabinet, and talked of it openly. Something in his manner repelled. To at least two of the spectators he gave the impression of grasping at office.

At first sight the idea was not favouritism, but had political merit. The government must try to carry Irish Home Rule. An overwhelming majority in the House of Lords would reject the bill and could not be coerced by an inadequate majority in the Commons. Therefore the tiny handful of peers who believed in Home Rule were keys to the immediate happiness of the Liberal party. Acton was one of the handful.

This view depended on an act of faith that *somehow* pressure could be exerted on the Lords. Gladstone's colleagues thought this an illusion. When Sir William Harcourt heard that Gladstone talked of strengthening the party in the Lords, he said that you might as well talk of strengthening the ocean by pouring in a little glass of brandy.[28]

Acton was fast making enemies: this court-favourite, upstart, busy-body, intruder, flatterer. Edward Hamilton talked of *the*

---

[27] Sir Rowland Blennerhassett, reported in an undated letter from Wilfrid Ward to his wife: Maisie Ward, *The Wilfrid Wards and the Transition*, I, p. 149.
[28] Gardiner, *Harcourt*, I, p. 183.

meddlesomeness of Lord Acton.[29] The Liberal leader with the strongest language was John Morley. He wanted to be Foreign Secretary and Acton flatly told him that it would not do. He resented it when he discovered how Acton wrote letters to Rosebery. And he appears to have thought that but for Acton's presence to support Mrs Gladstone and the Gladstone daughters, the old man might have been persuaded to resign. When Gladstone wrote Morley a letter with the hint that Acton should be in the Cabinet, Morley did not reply to the point. But he knew what he thought.

Back in London followed comic parties, of which we have in the documents brief notices from opposite angles; Acton going out to dine with Liberal leaders and privately reporting how well the evening went, Liberal leaders privately reporting how ill the evening went and their horror at the freedom of Acton's conversation. On 25 July Acton went to the same dinner-party as Earl Spencer. They drew aside and for nearly an hour ranged over the political issues of the day. Acton enjoyed both Spencer and the talk. Not so Spencer. Next morning he went to Gladstone's house specially to say that Acton was *impossible* as a member of the Cabinet. He said that Acton was politically unknown, and had no political experience.[30]

The following evening another dinner-party, this time with the Gladstones. John Morley also came, and found himself sitting by Acton, two great talkers of England. The talk however was not remarkable. Gladstone's secretary registered that it was a dull evening. Acton thought that nothing out of the ordinary happened. Neither perceived the fire burning underneath John Morley's politeness. Morley afterwards told Harcourt that during dinner he could hardly bring himself to be decently civil to Acton. He listened to Gladstone telling Acton 'all his inmost thoughts on men and things'. He came away angry.[31]

---

[29] L. Harcourt's Diary, 1–2 August 1892, Bodleian Library.
[30] Acton to Mamy, 26 July 1892: *Algernon West's Diaries*, ed. Hutchinson, same day.
[31] L. Harcourt's Diary, 27 July 1892, Bodleian Library.

From the sources stand out all sorts of reasons why they wanted to stop Acton being in the Cabinet. Harcourt was passing through a phase of vituperation against peers being so important in a Liberal cabinet, and fought violently against even the five that were chosen. Soberer men merely thought of Acton's inexperience. The Earl of Kimberley said, 'Acton is an excellent good fellow, and has high literary attainments, but he has made no mark whatever in public life, and if he gets an appointment it can only be because he is poor and one of our few supporters in the Lords.'[32] Professors are never likely to be popular among practical men. Acton was not a professor, but had a reputation for knowing more than it is good to know. Edward Hamilton contemptuously called him at this time *the German professor*.[33]

None of them mentioned the subject of Roman Catholicism. By 1892 the argument was disreputable in a liberal society and a Liberal party. Two Roman Catholics had already taken ministerial office. No profession of Catholic faith could debar Acton from sitting in the Cabinet. But underneath, at the level where such things were hardly spoken, this made it less desirable to have Acton. Sir William Harcourt, who was now the strongest parliamentarian in the party as Gladstone lost that proud position, and therefore had influence at this moment, was a very old-fashioned Protestant who feared Catholics because they were Catholics.

Therefore it was undesirable to include Acton because he was a Catholic. It was even more undesirable because, being a Catholic, he was Acton. The only people who might like another Catholic in the Cabinet were the southern Irish, who would not like Acton because they were men of the Pope and did not see Acton as a Catholic.

These reasons were strong. But they were not to be stated

---

[32] Kimberley to Rosebery, Rosebery Papers, cited by Alan Bell in *Times Literary Supplement*, 8 February 1974, p. 137.
[33] Edward Hamilton's Diary, 25 August 1892.

publicly. It was sufficiently strong to state the objection that did not rest unpleasantly upon religion. His past career gave him neither claims upon the party nor political experience to prove his capacity.

The affair of those so unsuccessful dinner-parties proves that Acton's manner could displease. Probably he expressed his opinions freely if not too freely, decisively if not too decisively. His vast knowledge of books, and his experience of *salons* at Cannes, meant that he was familiar with social situations where everyone in the room knew less than he; and his half-foreign background did not make natural the English convention of saying what you know as though you doubt. But these parties hint at something surprising, in lack of sensitivity to atmosphere. To come away from dinner on two successive evenings believing that you have been a success when you have failed, argues that not all clever and learned men are blest with antennae.

On 14 August Gladstone began writing letters of invitation, and two days later the Cabinet was complete.

They began to think of the minor offices – buckhounds, yeomen of the guard, lords-in-waiting, chamberlain, treasurer of the household, master of the horse, and so on. These offices were traditionally the haven of impecunious Whig peers. They were comic. When it was suggested that Lord Breadalbane should be Master of the Horse, and Rosebery protested that he had never been 'outside a horse' in his life, someone else in the Cabinet said mockingly that his duty would be to ride about in carriages with red footmen and not to ride horses. When young Spencer was asked what he wanted, he replied that he did not mind which office he was given as long as it had money. The humorous nature of these offices offended some who received the offer. When Lord Brassey was offered the Mastership of the Buckhounds, he accepted on condition that he drafted a scheme for the abolition of the office. But when he told his wife she said that he would be ridiculous, and he withdrew. Labouchere, who loathed Rosebery, and was discussing what office he would suit best, said 'I think Rosebery would do very well for the Buckhounds.'[34] Two peers if not three who were offered lordships-in-waiting on this occasion, regarded the offers as insolent when they might have expected ministerial rank, and refused. These reluctances of the less impoverished did not stop a grim scramble for places, both among those who wanted it and among politicians determined to help their clients. Nor must we underestimate the time it took. At a meeting of Liberal leaders on 16 August, the meeting went on longer than was pleasing because the Prime Minister spoke for three-quarters of an hour on how to abolish the Mastership of the Buckhounds.

On the day that the Cabinet was formed, Earl Spencer discussed Acton with Gladstone's secretary Algernon West. They agreed that after all that had happened and been said, after all the expectation that was excited, it would be cruelty if Acton got no office. The quest for something continued; and at last successfully. They secured for Acton the offer that he could become Captain of the Yeomen of the Guard.

Whether this was Spencer's kindness, or Gladstone's insistence, is not known. Whoever caused the offer had no strong sense of the absurd. By its title the office was not so odd as the Mastership of the Buckhounds. But Acton was famous as a historian. The office had an unacademic flavour. And this aspect was lately increased by an opera from the hands of Gilbert and Sullivan, first performed just over four years before.

But it had a stipend. Acton was not sure that he could refuse it. He was instantly uncomfortable. When some of the Liberals heard of the offer they smiled wickedly. The comment in Edward Hamilton's Diary is illuminating for more than one reason:

There is something so comic about the Command of the Beefeaters to a German Professor that I think Acton himself appreciates the humour of it. But pecuniary considerations stand in the way of his refusing it.

Algernon West had no hand in eliciting the offer (except by

---

[34] L. Harcourt's Diary, 9, 17 and 19 August, 18 September 1892.

telling Lord Spencer that he must be offered something) and thought that Acton would be absurd wearing a big helmet and sword. He said so to Acton and persuaded him instead to accept one of the lordships-in-waiting to the Queen, offices which were not paid so much but which were not comic. The new government was so short of peers that it found difficulty in filling these lordships-in-waiting, and Acton's acceptance not only embarrassed him less but helped Gladstone to fill a post then not easy to fill.

Throughout these three weeks during which the new Cabinet was formed, what stands out is Gladstone's weakness. We meet sentences like that of Morley when the old man suggested Acton for the Cabinet, *I put my foot down*. Gladstone said that he took less part in the making of this Cabinet than in any of his others. Though it was a way of self-exculpation, it was true. For the first time since 1868 his political position was weak. He no longer sat there indispensable. If Rosebery refused to serve, or Harcourt refused, even perhaps if Morley refused, the government could hardly be formed. By failing to win sufficient majority, he lost magic in the party. Because several of them preferred to be without him, they were willing to say what a few years ago they were not prepared to risk. The meetings were stormy. A discussion on 14 August was as unpleasant as anyone could remember, Harcourt brutally rude to Gladstone, Gladstone pouring reproaches on Morley's head for backing Harcourt. Gladstone became a chairman instead of a commander. A few years ago they could not so have browbeaten him about the choice of ministers. But a few years ago, he would have sensed the peril of trying to bring in Acton.

The lordship-in-waiting was accompanied by two encouraging utterances from Gladstone. First, he told Acton that if Rosebery had finally refused, he would have compelled Acton to high office.[35] Secondly, he suggested that this lordship-in-waiting was only a beginning – that Lord Granville and other

---

[35] Acton to Mamy, 14 November 1898, 7956/224.

eminent politicians began with a Household office – that he hoped to find something better for Acton later.

That October 1892, occurred the oddest incident of this quest by Acton for a means of earning his living.

At a dinner in Armitstead's house Gladstone, and Rosebery, and Acton were guests. That evening Rosebery had a muddled conversation with Gladstone over the British Legation at Munich and Stuttgart (it was a united office). The relations between the two men were not comfortable, for their very different personalities prevented them from being natural allies, and meetings of the Cabinet were still at times unpleasant. What passed at dinner is not clear. When in August Acton was in danger of commanding the Yeomen of the Guard, Rosebery thought it absurd. Looking round for other possibilities he mentioned the legation at Munich as more suitable. At the dinner in October, Rosebery said to Acton that if the Munich legation were vacated by its occupant Drummond, he would see that Acton was appointed.

Rosebery held the private opinion that Acton was so unique as to make this the only post for which he was fitted. In Munich, unlike Berlin, his Catholicism was an advantage. In Munich, unlike Berlin, his Liberal anti-Prussian attitudes were useful. In Munich, unlike Vienna, hostility to the Pope was no impediment. He knew the leading Bavarians and the decrepit royal family. His wife lived in Bavaria and evidently wished to go on living there, wherever her husband worked. He spoke German like the Germans. 'There, and only there perhaps,' Rosebery once told Lord Kimberley, 'he would be a round peg in a round hole.'[36] At the back of Acton's mind lay less the interest in diplomacy than the chance of a united family and the occasion to continue his book on Döllinger.

Out of the kindness of their hearts, the friends of Acton were unkind. Rosebery mentioned Munich with the best of intentions

---

[36] Rosebery to Kimberley, cited by Alan Bell in *Times Literary Supplement*, 8 February 1974, p. 137.

but had little power to do what he suggested. Drummond, the sitting Minister at Munich, was a quiet, urbane man not able enough to move to one of the big European capitals, and not likely to accept a less important place. Acton, in his most unfortunate letter, suggested to Gladstone that since his wife was American and wanted a title, Drummond might accept an embassy in South America if he were made a knight. Gladstone saw no difficulty about this plot, if a little time were allowed to elapse. Rosebery thought that it would not work. 'That affair would not be furthered by a knighthood. I have it greatly at heart, but it must simmer a little.'

This was the nearest Acton came to the post which he wanted. Rosebery, out of kindness or weakness, kept the hope alive. Eighteen months later Acton still hoped to go to Munich. But Drummond stayed at Munich until after Acton died.

Archbishop Manning thought that Acton destroyed the possibility of a career in public affairs by leading the losing side in Rome. He saw straight.

In January 1894 Acton travelled with Gladstone and Mrs Drew to Biarritz, Gladstone in great pain on the journey. They were splendidly lodged, in a hotel with four drawing rooms; Acton called the town deadly dull; but worse, he had a collision with Gladstone over the timing and method of his coming resignation. When Gladstone set out for Biarritz he had decided to resign though not when; and at Biarritz Acton spent his time trying to persuade him that he ought not to resign in the way that he wanted because it would be bad both for the Liberal Party and for Britain, 'and things became quite unpleasant'. For three or four days he was fascinated by what was going on, with Gladstone consulting him at every step, with all the retinue abusing Mrs Gladstone, and with a magnificent Atlantic storm outside the windows. A week after he arrived he could not bear it any longer and took off for Madrid suddenly although 'I am quite sure he likes having me there'.[37] On the way back from

---

[37] Acton to Annie, nos. 76–8, 81.

Madrid he called at Biarritz and carried dispatches to London; but by that time Gladstone was coming to accept that Acton was right in his objections to the mode of the proposed resignation.

In London Acton observed the declining man. 'At times he is quite himself. At other times he is forgetful, nervous, unstable, impervious to argument. It is time. But he proposed at first to act in a manner which would have been fatal to the party and the cause'. His eyesight was failing, one eye gone, cataract on the other.

When Acton went to do his duty with the Queen, he found that everyone was talking of the succession to Gladstone. He was in the corridor outside when Gladstone went in at the beginning of April to give the Queen his resignation and have his last audience. 'I don't believe she was very amiable.' Afterwards he helped the Gladstones into the royal carriage. Gladstone said nothing. 'And that was the last, last end of the Gladstonian greatness and the extinction of the brightest light in our history, and that is how it was at Fontainebleau.' He remembered it as 'one of the most interesting and memorable days'.[38] The Emperor Napoleon I was forced to abdicate at Fontainebleau.

In the old man's retiring years Acton went on seeing much of him; even to near the end. Five months before Gladstone died he and his daughter Mamy stayed with the Gladstones at a dismal house in Cannes, a dreary time redeemed only by Mamy's singing to them in the evening.

On Ascension Day 1898 he wrote to Annie about Gladstone's death. 'He had said everything he could to me on the last day at Cannes; everything that could prove sympathy and friendship; and I do not think that anyone stood nearer to him in these later years. But he never really understood my thoughts; and I expect that things will now come out that will show it. His death makes a great change to me, as there is no one left that I really look up to, or should care to, consult'.

He helped *The Times* obituarist of Gladstone, Herbert.

---

[38] Acton to Annie, no. 82.

Gladstone died on 19 May 1898. Just two months later (20 July) a group of mourners, his widow and daughter and widow's niece Lucy Cavendish (the murder of whose husband in Ireland bound her close to the Gladstone family) talked about the dead man.

Mary Drew then produced Acton's eloquent obituary sent to her at her request after the conversation late at night in Tegernsee: *The Judgment of Posterity on Mr Gladstone*. She read it aloud to her mother and Lucy Cavendish. Though written eighteen years before, it seemed to be of now, the moment of death. We have no expression in the sources of the gratitude or emotion in the three women but we can imagine it. They seem to have felt it to be like the voice of a prophet speaking noble utterance out of the past, which the years since he spoke proved true. Lucy Cavendish then said, Acton's letters surely ought to be published. She suggested that Mary Drew write to Acton at once to ask his leave. Next day Mary wrote to Acton:

It seems to me a vast pity they should never see the light till after we are dead, and I can hardly imagine any moment when they would be not only of the deepest interest but of the deepest value to the public as at this moment. I am quite aware you may think the idea preposterous – on the other hand you may possibly give permission with all kinds of reservations.

They would in no way poach on the coming biography. But they would, if anything more is needed, whet the appetite for it, and prepare the way.

I can never tell you the extent of my appreciation of the inestimable treasure I possess in these letters. But it is not fair that I should have the monopoly.

It turned out that Mary not merely kept his letters as precious, she copied them into a book, omitting what she called 'all the personal bits (which really are the touch of ill-nature that makes the whole world kin)'. (She was quoting an old phrase of his). She suggested that someone should edit them from the originals.

Mamy Acton was with her father when this letter arrived and could remember the distaste which he felt. Acton had the highest opinion of the historical value of letters. But he thought, first, that letters should lie in archives for a long time; and second, that when at last they were published, they almost always lowered the name of their author. He had no desire that his letters, private letters, not intended for publication, should appear in print while many of the people were still alive. He foresaw trouble and he was right. He kindly replied that it would never do because it would trespass upon the coming biography.

Meanwhile the strong-minded Mary handed the letters to Arthur Lyttelton, former Master of Selwyn. She sent the typed selections to the biographer; for Morley had 'provisionally' accepted the family's invitation to write the Life. In her letter to Morley was a hint that she would go ahead and publish without waiting for Acton's permission. She also sent the typescript to Acton. It did nothing to dispel his alarm. Both Morley and Acton, independently and unknown to each other, advised her not to publish. Morley said that if the object was to keep alive interest in Gladstone it would not do it because the main figure in the letters, though not of set purpose, was not Gladstone but Acton. Acton simply wrote (23 September 1898):

... I am thoroughly persuaded that no bookseller would accept it, and that no impartial friend would advise publication. They will tell you that the literature is pedantic and the politics obscure.

Acton to Mary Drew, 25 October 1898:

Conversations with Morley and Rosebery have made it clearer than ever that these letters cannot be allowed to appear; and even if these were not decisive reasons, I now see the amount of excision and omission that would have been required would have made them useless.

Acton to Mary Drew, 29 November 1898:

Pray allow me to keep the type-written letters, and don't let other copies get about. I don't speak or write as freely as that to anybody now.

Something in Mary Drew was insensitive; or perhaps she saw that she had in these letters an overwhelming possession, a proof to the world that the most learned man in Europe revered her father as he revered only one other statesman in British history. She was determined that they should be published, though of course not in full. But as Acton read them through, he must have thought of the indiscretions of youth – seeing again his ferocity against Popes, the frequent damning references to Lord Houghton, the tremendous condemnation of Disraeli, the side-blows at other men, Morley or Harcourt, George Otto Trevelyan or Swinburne, the panegryic on Gladstone, the affection-ate praise of Gladstone's daughter, the too strong words about Macaulay.

In the face of pressure to publish, Acton took a weak way. He used the excuse of the coming biography, and said that because of it the letters could not be published for three years. It was a feeble reply, from a man who did not want the letters published at all; perhaps only to be explained by the knowledge that Gladstone was the great benefactor to whose family he owed a debt which was hard to repay. Just possibly John Morley moved him. Morley, working through the materials for the biography of Gladstone, came across Acton's letters to Gladstone. Acton was uneasy that Morley would find in them criticisms of Morley, and a leading question to Morley got an answer which did not dispel the uneasiness. But Morley surprised him by telling him that some time the letters might be worth publishing. Perhaps this influenced his judgement on the request of Mary Drew. But perhaps it did not. For his daughter Mamy remembered him as being steadily offended at the idea of publication, and giving way at last only because he felt he must. Probably he thought that the determined Mary would do it whatever he said, so he might as well yield. There is evidence that he thought Mary to need money from the publication. He never had to live with this weakness, or this repayment of a debt to Gladstone. The volume of letters did not appear until two years after his death, and then was edited by Herbert Paul, for Arthur Lyttelton died prema-turely. Despite a direct plea from Mary Drew, John Morley declined to review it.

The letters at once became, and have remained, an important

source for Acton's opinions and philosophy. They proved to the world what a great writer of letters he could be. They also confirmed his fear that if published they would do harm.

Some personal offence was taken. Lady Granville, for example, was grieved that he seemed to estimate his step-father's political ability so low in comparison with Gladstone's. The offence was more than personal. The Catholic world had learnt to regard Acton's anti-papalism as an escapade of youth which the mature thinker outgrew. They discovered that this was illusion, and that the man was still the most Liberal Catholic of them all. Scandal was caused. Gasquet countered the effect by publishing (1906) *Lord Acton and his Circle*, a series of ill-edited letters to Richard Simpson which failed to achieve Gasquet's purpose. The *Tablet* printed a ludicrous panegyric of Gasquet's book, and so provoked a debate of two months on whether or not Acton was a loyal Catholic.

The published letters omitted the most trenchant passages. For example: on page 33 the dots after the names *Midhat and Newman* represent the omitted words *two very able and evil men*. On the same page the dots after the name *Mrs Mark Pattison* represent the words *and who seems to live in these parts because her husband is in England*. On the opposite page the dots before the name *Swinburne* conceal the words *The evil-minded poet* – and so on, though not frequently. Herbert Paul committed the fault of running letters together or printing an extract from a letter under the wrong date. In general Paul's transcriptions are accurate.

Most of these letters were written in answer to letters of Mary Gladstone. They took up points which she raised, replied to questions, commented on her experiences, gave opinions on the political situation. Often the force of the letters is hardly intelligible because the editor refrains from telling the reader what the letters are about. They are still remarkable letters, and often their meaning is plain enough. But at other times they are mysterious. Who would suppose that 'the importunate widow' was a favourite name for Sir Augustus Paget, British ambassador in

Rome? Who would guess from a sentence (Paul, p. 25) about 'those who question the certainty of history' that J. R. Lowell had been arguing the *valuelessness* of history at a dinner and Mary Gladstone had felt the need of Acton as a counter-blast? Who would at once know that when Acton wrote of 'the irrepressible Pall Mall bore whom I wish back in his dungeon' (Paul, 175) he meant the journalist Stead? This feature of the correspondence – that only one side is given, and rarely with an explanation – helped to give the letters the gnomic and allusive air. If both sides of the correspondence are read, Acton was no more obscure than most who write letters on subjects of the day.

The letters to Mary Gladstone misled publishers and public. The volume was successful; it had a second printing two years later, and in 1913 an edition with later more numerous, and in two cases more indiscreet, letters. It was successful partly because it was useful to those who disliked Popes; partly because it was scandalous to those who loved Popes; partly because Acton himself interested the public; but above all, because the condition of inspiration for Acton was fulfilled – a few of the letters were great letters, and they concerned not only dead politics and dead politicians, but living literature like George Eliot or Carlyle or *John Inglesant*.

At dinner parties Acton could be dull. For the gift of great monologues smoke must rise up from the depths to turn him into an oracle. Letters were not different. With Döllinger as with Mary Gladstone, the condition of inspiration existed. To other men or women the letters were like the letters of any man, though at times duller because stuffed with more information.

This is the reason why the collected *Correspondence*, edited by his historical pupils Figgis and Laurence, has volume I on it and no volume II ever appeared. No pair of competent editors ever arranged letters more unwisely. But the failure of the volume, and the fright it caused to publishers, was due to more than the disorderly order of the letters. He could be tedious. He wrote at great length, on subjects that were now dead to the world. After the First World War Llewellyn Woodward went round the publishers trying to find someone to take volume II. They made excuse. Moreover, the second Lord Acton lost enthusiasm before he died. Knowing his father's piety, he disliked the appearance of Mary Drew's volume. He expected that the publication of a fuller correspondence would restore balance. The volume published by Figgis and Laurence served only to confirm the general impression caused by the letters to Mary Drew. Lord Acton began to think that it would be better to pause in publishing his father's papers.

7

DÖLLINGER AND ACTON

DÖLLINGER of Munich and Acton of Cambridge: father and son, teacher and disciple; Acton, as a Catholic critic once said, only a pale reflection of Döllinger. German scientific history in its Catholic form passes by this route and generates English scientific history in its liberal form; an important stage in English historical writing; an important side of German intellectual influence on the English; its new standards of scientific history, its new attention to documents and archives, its encouragement of the polymath as well as of the specialist.

So the more liberal, anti-Prussian side of South German Catholicism helped to generate, not English Catholic history, not English church history, but a big school of British historians, especially those centred upon Cambridge, which flourished between 1902 and 1939. It consisted not only of Acton's direct pupils – R. V. Laurence, J. N. Figgis, G. P. Gooch, J. H. Clapham, G. M. Trevelyan, H. C. Gutteridge. It reached out more widely, so that a younger historian like Herbert Butterfield needed to spend much of his life wrestling with Acton, his personality, his historical outlook, and his moral commitment.

This picture of an influence of German liberal history upon British liberal history by the extraordinary and unlooked-for route of two Catholic minds is only to be countenanced with much hesitation.

When Bishop Dupanloup died in 1878, Döllinger's other extraordinary pupil and disciple, Charlotte von Leyden who

186

became Charlotte Lady Blennerhassett, wrote an appreciation for the English periodical *The Nineteenth Century*. Appreciations of the dead were things which Charlotte Blennerhassett could do with a mixture of critical power and sensitive appreciation. Her notice of Dupanloup said good things about him. She asked Döllinger to write a preface to the notice. He sent her a letter. She printed the letter with the article. It said that the article was original and important; that he had known the bishop personally for twenty-five years, and could vouch for the truth of the appreciation. This amounted to a public statement by Döllinger that he saw a lot of good in Bishop Dupanloup. That was a proposition which an untroubled mind could not fail to accept.

Acton's mind was not untroubled. It took about two years for this utterance to sink into the depths of his consciousness. Any bishop who had been against infallibility and afterwards accepted it with seeming ease was to Acton now a traitor; or rather, a man who pretended to believe something which he did not believe, and therefore was playing with truth. Every such person in Acton's eyes – and some of them were big men, a Newman, a Hefele, a Theiner – was, if not a betrayer, at least corrupt. By convolution of mind he found in his heart the conviction that even his master Döllinger was compromising; and that he was near the doctrine that the end justifies the means. Until 1879 Döllinger was Acton's father-figure, his guru, as well as his historical guide. For the next eleven years till Döllinger died, he was still the dear professor and a friend to Acton. But he had lost the quality of father-figure and guru.

The situation was very curious. It was not intelligible when we first knew about it, and it is still unintelligible now that Victor Conzemius has laid out before us all the letters that passed between them – not quite all the letters because there is more than one obvious gap in the correspondence. The situation was very curious because of Acton's own position. Döllinger, a Catholic priest, had been excommunicated for refusing to accept the Vatican decrees. Acton, a Catholic layman, had not been excommunicated. Archbishop Manning of Westminster wanted Rome to threaten Acton with excommunication. Acton's own bishop troubled him more moderately. Acton wrote letters to the two English bishops which evaded their demands, with verbal honesty, though only just with verbal honesty, in the strong desire to avoid excommunication. The years 1874–6 were the years when we find forcible utterances from Acton that to him membership of the Catholic Church was a matter of life and death. Of course that need not mean what many of the public might take it to mean. Döllinger the excommunicate was quite serene in still being a member of the Catholic Church. The excommunication was improper, illegal under canon law, and certainly (in his opinion) did not eject him from the Church.

Here is the oddity of the unexcommunicated layman being far more bitter against the hierarchy than the excommunicated priest. For the first time Acton began to ask himself critical questions about his master in the science of history; questions not only about his attitude to the Church but about his historical methods.

The oddness of the argument raises the question whether there was some underlying change in Acton's life which was more intimate and personal.

By 1878 he had times of melancholy; derived mainly from the pressure of being a sort of devout Catholic yet not being wanted by his coreligionists. Early that year he wrote to his eldest daughter in that mood:

All people who live in the world have a great many troubles and sorrows and trials. They have their hopes and wishes disappointed; they meet with unkindness and ingratitude from those who ought to be kind to them; they are sometimes laughed at and sometimes insulted, and very often humiliated and made to feel foolish, they are made to be much ashamed of their sins and follies; they lose those they love best; they have to bear a great deal of pain and then to die. To be able to bear all these things, there must be a strength inside us. We must bear them without any help but what we receive from God alone . . .[1]

---

[1] Acton to Mamy, 15 February 1878, 7956/3.

Then the illness of two daughters changed the relationship of husband and wife.

The fourth daughter and youngest child Jeanne Marie, who was nicknamed Simmy, was evidently very ill while she was still at her mother's breast. Acton, in whose arms his son John had died on a train, went tense with anxiety and rushed out into the road in search of help, and saw, of all chances, Sir William Jenner, the most celebrated physician in Britain. He brought Jenner into the house to examine the baby. Jenner advised that she must have a wet-nurse and Acton went out to find such a woman. Marie was not consulted and when she was told she resisted, she would keep her baby at her breast. She told her husband that if the baby was taken away from her she would never get over it. Acton nevertheless believed that he must save Simmy's life and insisted. Then there was a change and without the wet-nurse Simmy began to recover.

Marie did not get over it. She thought that she had a husband who was prepared to sacrifice her best and dearest feelings at the word of a doctor whom she had never seen before and did not like. This changed the relation of husband and wife for quarter of a century.

A worse calamity followed. The third daughter Lily was seven in 1881, the year when the breach with Döllinger was widest. She caught scarlet fever. On 1 October 1881 she died at Tegernsee in Acton's arms. She was a very beloved daughter to him. He destroyed everything in her room, even all her toys. But that was not all. To prevent infection he ordered the other children and his wife out of Tegernsee so that Marie was away when Lily died. She did not even attend the funeral though she came to weep over the dead body. Acton himself could not bear to attend the funeral because he was sure that he would break down in public and allowed his brother-in-law Toni to represent him; but was able to go to the funeral mass afterwards. Acton afterwards said that his marriage had never been the same since the affair of Simmy's wet-nurse but that Lily's death and its circumstances were a still harder strain on the marriage. Marie developed moods of melancholy. She never came to England again until her husband's last four years of life.

The number of letters to Marie which survived and which therefore she kept should tell us something. Far the largest number (seventy-three) are from the year of his engagement and preparing for marriage. Then for two years they were much together and only one possible letter survived. From 1868 there were a few letters every year until 1874; after that fewer letters. Then comes a long gap where two letters only survived – the fifteen years 1882–96; and in the last years of Acton's life the letters again become plentiful.

This is not quite a reliable test because it is possible that in the middle years Marie threw letters away and many letters were not given a date. We possess at least one record, in a letter of Acton to one of his children, of a letter from Marie which is lost.[2]

Therefore, in the background to the hardly intelligible contortions of the new relation to Döllinger, there was an internal unhappiness which was nothing to do with Döllinger. Lily's death was not the cause of the argument which was vehement before she died. Döllinger was at Tegernsee with him over the time of the Lily's funeral; and Acton noticed how gentle Döllinger became to him as he shared his suffering – 'he is very gentle with me now, when we dispute of things on which we don't agree'.[3]

For a year over the time of Lily's death there are no letters from Acton to Döllinger. He first mentioned it to Döllinger seven months later with an apology that he could not come to see him in Munich because his wife could not bear to visit the house where Lily died. He went to Tegernsee in August 1882 and in the evening argued with Döllinger for six and a half hours without stopping. But he hated the stay, everything reminded him of her, he felt that he must make no noise lest he wake her

---

[2] Acton to Mamy, 28 August 1883, 7956/9.
[3] Acton to Mamy, 4 October 1881, 7956/5.

up, and at times he listened for her voice 'that none but the angels hear'.[4]

Happiness, he once told a daughter, 'ended for me at Tegernsee in 1881'.[5] When Acton died they buried him by Lily.

Döllinger was less than tactful in trying to heal the breach. It is chiefly a difference of age, he said. I am forty years older than you. Forty years ago I used to make fierce judgements on people's characters and deeds. You will grow out of it in time. (Acton was already forty-seven years old.) Then, said Döllinger, we are of a different class in society. You were born with a silver spoon in the mouth, a citizen of the world. I was born in a narrow and provincial environment made narrower by hierarchy. I know more about prejudice than you do and so I am readier to forgive when I find it in other historians. Acton was so struck by this sentence that he wrote it down on a card in his card-index for use in that biography of Döllinger which he meant to write and never wrote. Neither conceded anything. Döllinger to Acton, 7 February 1881: 'I am sure you will come to agree with me.' Acton to Döllinger, 11 February 1881: 'I am sure you will come to agree with me.'

As the argument went on – it went on and on and on – a gulf began to appear which was not the original gulf. The original gulf was moral – you taught me when I was young that Catholicism is the truth and now I find you compromising about truth, my idol has thus far feet of clay. The new gulf which began to appear was intellectual. Once we concede that the idol has feet of clay and we start looking at him with a more critical eye, we start to ask not just whether the moral attitude is correct, but whether the truths for which he stands are in fact truths, and whether his methods of historical enquiry are the best methods of historical enquiry.

The difference growing between them rested at bottom in a

[4] Acton to Mamy, 6 August 1882, 7956/7.
[5] Acton to Annie, no. 169, undated but probably 1890.

difference about religion. Döllinger had been cast out of his Church. But he remained a Catholic priest: in feeling, sympathy, doctrine, loyalty. He opened his mind more to other traditional Christian denominations, Lutheran, Anglican, Orthodox, Old Catholic, though he was never much of a participator in Old Catholicism and was blamed by its leaders for his lukewarm behaviour. His chief aims were now the reunion of all the true Catholic churches, and the reformation of moral ideas within the Churches. But Acton, who had not been cast out of the Church, was moving out of orthodoxy; not in feeling, not in attitudes to history and society, and as time went on not in the practice of religion. At no point in his life would he have denied, when he was asked, that he was a Catholic. But he began to profess theories which sat more loosely to tradition than those of any other professed Catholic of the nineteenth century. And it was this very circumstance which helped to turn him into the force which he grew to be upon English Protestant historiography:

Why has this breach between us happened? You, an excommunicated man, wanted not to look like someone out for revenge. And your society in Munich is of good heads and you do not meet humanity in its variety. You lived among Catholics, I among Protestants. The opinions of Rothe or Baur interested me more than the opinion of 500 bishops at a Council, probably because I was less interested in dogma (undated but 1881).

What other Catholic of the nineteenth century could have said that last sentence? Five hundred bishops at a Council nothing to do with truth. Anyway less to do with truth than Ferdinand Christian Baur, who set off the critics of the New Testament on their radical voyage; and Rothe, for whom Churches had almost ceased to matter and political institutions were the moral vehicles of the present and the future.

Or, again, a letter to Döllinger of 15 June 1882: 'men like Möhler, Lacordaire and Newman are much more repugnant to me than the *sancta simplicitas* of some old woman or the tricks of some indulgence preacher.'

It was not superstition that he minded. It was not error. It was the conscious pursuit of power by a church organization.

A letter of the next day is still stronger: 'Respect of the hierarchy could not stand without disrespect for the law of God.' Or again, he wrote that the churchman

is dragged down by the best thing in him ... It is when he is at his best, when he is swept and garnished, that he takes the devil into his soul. He never repents. His conscience is at rest, and his conscience is what he has made it ... I am taking the finest specimens. I do not deal with common, obscure, incapable men, victims of a bad training, of a narrow sphere, of a backward age. I am thinking of men with whom I would not venture to compare myself, in knowledge, or talent, or yet greater gifts of God.

On 16 June 1882 he wrote: 'I find that I am alone.' The phrase and the date may be taken to mark a development important to English history: the mind of Acton, freeing itself, *qua* historian, from the mind of his first master. Of course, he had been learning his history for several years from other masters: Rothe for an ethical view of history, Roscher of Leipzig as a social and economic historian, Ranke as the new type of handler of archives and seeker after objectivity. But until now he had not fully realized what all this study was doing to his mind. In all the later stage of his life it was Ranke and not Döllinger whom he looked back upon as his chief historical master.

The new materials threw out all the old studies of Acton. Ulrich Noack wrote three excellent volumes on Acton's mind, between 1927 and 1932: *Geschichtswissenschaft und Freiheit* (Frankfurt, 1935), *Katholizität und Geistesfreiheit* (Frankfurt, 1936), which was suppressed by the police, and *Politik als Sicherung der Freiheit*, which could not be published until 1947 and then only with the leave of the Allied military. These volumes are still useful. But they try, like all other studies, to draw a unified picture of Acton's mind, so that the Acton of 1863, Liberal and strenuous critic but deeply Catholic, at times half-ultramontane, can be used to illuminate the mind of the Acton of 1888, twenty-five years later – still professing to be a Catholic but poles apart from anything like orthodoxy. No one fully realized, till the work of Conzemius, the gulf between the sixties and the eighties. The earlier Acton was influenced by Ranke, and by Rothe without being a convert. It is certain that the Acton of the sixties could never have the influence on the British mind which was achieved by the Acton of the late eighties and nineties.

There are three lines in which this emancipation from tradition proceeded. The first was theology. He accepted that parts of the New Testament might be legendary; that 'the apostolic age' (he wrote publicly, pointing to the apocryphal texts) 'was rich in poetic and theological fiction'. He accepted that miracles 'crumble' away when subjected to historical inquiries. It made no difference to him. His attitude to religion now rested far more on ethical than on dogmatic consideration. Such scepticism about historical origins was not open to Döllinger who still knew himself as a priest of the Catholic Church.

There is the famous story from James Bryce of his amazement at Acton's reading. There were four historians at dinner: Creighton the historian of the Papacy in the Renaissance, Robertson Smith the historian of Semitic religion, Acton and Bryce. When Creighton talked of Pope Leo X, Acton could cap his evidence – that does not surprise. When Robertson Smith talked of Old Testament history, Acton could cap his evidence. This anecdote from Bryce formerly used to look improbable. In the light of what we now know it is wholly credible, though of course Acton was a master in the Renaissance, and only an omnivorous reader in the scholarship of the Old Testament.

The chief mark of these ethical consequences was the attitude to the good atheist. This was first evident in his enthusiasm for the positivist novelist George Eliot. Döllinger was astonished and amused to find Acton rating George Eliot on the level of

Shakespeare. He disliked Acton's article on George Eliot. On her Acton could write in 1885 what by then was almost a portrait of himself – one needs only to turn the feminine pronoun into the masculine:

It was the problem of her age to reconcile the practical ethics of unbelief and of belief, to save virtue and happiness when dogmas and authorities decay. To solve it she swept the realm of knowledge and stored up that large and serious erudition which sustains all her work, and in reality far exceeded what appears on the surface . . . It is her supreme characteristic in literature that her original genius rested on so broad a foundation of other people's thought.[6]

She was a preacher of morality

far more impressive, more true, more elevated, than any but the very best Christian writers, and capable of reaching those whom no Christian could possibly touch. To me this is one of the most wonderful facts, of the most wonderful feats, in the history of the human mind. Atheism, at the moment of its becoming a permanent and preponderant force, was rescued and redeemed . . .
Atheism as a teacher of life became, roughly speaking, the equal of Christianity in moral dignity when it became its rival in mental power.

In the semi-self portrait, he went on, George Eliot was a woman who abandoned religious faith while she preached the highest standards of morality and contracted a great liking for the solemn services of the Catholic Church. She touched 'the central problem of Catholicism', how 'private virtue and public crime could issue from the same root'. The process of her life had brought her to a supreme point of solitude and neutrality that would have been chilling and fatal to a feebler mind, but gave her the privilege of an almost unexampled independence and mental integrity. Her secluded life had important literary consequences. It estranged her from general society and religious people.
Here is Acton's sense of solitariness reflected. Because a

---

[6] 'George Eliot's Life', *Nineteenth Century*, March 1885.

Catholic rebel, distrusted by nearly all Catholics; because a Catholic at all, distrusted by some Protestants. Meanwhile he was moving towards historical neutrality of mind on all the great issues except moral conviction; and he felt the neutrality to be both a constituent of his solitariness and creative in his historical thinking. Here was a religious man who, without losing a religious sensibility, achieved the experience that a positivist attitude towards the historical sources and the historical controversies was necessary for the objectivity and the true creativity of the modern historian. This union of religious feeling, strong moral conviction, and a positivist attitude towards facts was not felt to be a mixture of incompatibles. He knew where he was. But he also knew himself to be solitary.

The solitariness was fostered by what happened in the German historical school. In the north several of the leading historians moved into nationalism, and Acton did not like it, nor think it other than a corruption of true history; Treitschke as the most nationalistic, 'never-flagging' as Acton called him, 'always vehement, always certain, overwhelming'; Droysen, confessed to be eminent but a pleader for the cause of the Hohenzollern; von Sybel; even Mommsen. These were now Acton's natural allies, the heirs of Ranke. But he was detached from them, partly by his English half and partly by his Bavarian half. He thought of the northerners as a phalanx, or garrison, holding Berlin like a fortress. He admired all the heirs of Ranke for their energy, and their sympathetic accuracy, and assurances of steady advances, and willingness to correct in the light of better knowledge. What he could not bear was their identification of success with providence and their complacency if not their arrogance.[7]

He concealed his radical mind from most. He was frank with Döllinger. He would say to Gladstone, or to R. W. Church, what must have disturbed them coming from a Catholic source. Church was Newman's pupil. He was writing that history of *The Oxford Movement* which was published posthumously and

[7] Acton, 'German Schools of History', *EHR* (January 1886).

became one of the classics of Victorian historical writing. He showed the draft to Acton. It was not a very good idea. To Church, Newman was a hero, to Acton he was as bad as the Grand Inquisitor. What Acton said about Newman and his colleagues was this: 'The trouble is that to these people dogma is too much the whole of religion. They don't understand that the chief measuring rod is moral.' Gladstone believed that good orthodox Christians were best for society. Acton wrote to him, 'What would have become of us all without the Independents and Socinians?' and said that this saying was like a cold douche over Gladstone's body.[8]

Acton's friend Edmond Scherer died in March 1889. Scherer was a French citizen by being born at Lyons, but of a Swiss father and a mother who was half English and half Dutch. A period of study during his late teens in the house of an evangelical clergyman in England turned his mind to theology and he went to the university of Strasbourg. He was a stiff Calvinist, and fundamentalist about the Biblical text. As such he became a professor of theology at a Swiss seminary for training dissenting Protestant preachers. He was militantly orthodox. But in 1848–9 he became uncomfortable in his work. He realized that he no longer believed the literal inspiration of a Biblical text, and was excommunicated, amid passion and polemic in the Swiss press. He went on lecturing in Geneva, though to a very select audience.

He abandoned theology, formally. He marked the revolution by giving away all his theological books, either to friends or local libraries. He moved to Paris and turned himself into a literary critic, with Sainte-Beuve as his hero. Here for the first time he came to know Acton. The acquaintance was slow to ripen. He lived at Versailles and was drawn into politics by the Prussian occupation. After a time in the National Assembly he was elected a senator. He hardly ever spoke. He exercised influence far more by political journalism.

---

[8] FL 201; Conz., III, pp. 398–9.

Meanwhile he had become Acton's principal adviser on all French matters. Acton started to buy his books. Acton acquired the eight volumes of literary criticism, the fierce attack on the notion of infallibility in *Lettres à mon Curé*, the pamphlet against the dangers of too much democracy for France in *La Démocratie et la France*. But he did not read them with diligence. At least he did not make marginal lines on passages which he thought important. It was Acton's habit to put a line against passages which struck him in his books. He marked the passages which agreed with his own cast of mind rather than the passages which best represented all the thought of the author of the book which he was reading.

Soon after Scherer died a friend and pupil, Octave Gréard, brought out a memoir of his life (Paris, 1890). Acton not merely acquired this, he marked passages extensively, from the long quotations of Scherer which Gréard printed. These markings disclose how the friendship with Scherer fitted the radical religious mind which was now Acton's.

For example:

He thought the progress of history the greatest intellectual revolution of our times. The scholars seem to play games with trivial details of the past. Then the works start to make a coherence; then you get general conclusions – and history is transformed; and with history, even the moral perception of humanity.

It is clear that the bond between Scherer and Acton was more intellectual than personal. Yet Acton felt Scherer's death as a personal loss. He wrote to Döllinger:

Scherer's death was a true loss to me. We saw each other every year. For me he was a remarkable whetstone for all things French. They'll soon forget that this was the most learned Frenchman of our age. His intellectual development, rightly analyzed, would be very instructive.[9]

There was a rapport between the minds. The one had come

---

[9] Conz., III, p. 402; cf. p. 321.

out of Protestant ultra-orthodoxy, the other out of Catholic orthodoxy; both had lost faith in authority as any absolute concept; and both saw history as inseparable from the conscience of the human race.

At much the same time he wrote his canons on the writing of history. The included this:

> The ethics of history cannot be denominational. Judge not according to the orthodox standard of a system religious, philosophical, political, but according as things promote, or fail to promote, the delicacy, integrity and authority of conscience.

That is: get out of history a religious cause. Get away from Ludwig von Pastor or R. W. Church. Get out of history the philosophic cause, from Hegel and all his heirs in the historical schools from Ferdinand Christian Baur and Karl Marx onwards. Get out of history the political cause. Get away from the Liberal party politicians like Macaulay or George Otto Trevelyan, or from nationalists like Treitschke or Sybel. 'Anyone who writes with a national or denominational preconception will find no countenance from me.[10]

Get away from all these but to what? Is there a historian's yardstick also to judge conscience?

He was moving into an intellectual agnosticism. This was not an agnosticism about religious practice. He encouraged his son to go to confession, though this was a practice which Döllinger had come to doubt. Acton loved *The Imitation of Christ* as true Catholicism, what he described as more normal Catholicism. But in the traditional sense of faith as applied to dogmatic propositions, he was growing increasingly agnostic. When he defined what was the highest book of Christian teaching he chose the *Fioretti*. And those Little Flowers of St. Francis of Assisi are the vehicle not at all of doctrine but of a pure and childlike moral compassion.

In 1981 Conzemius published the fourth volume of the corre-

---

[10] Conz, III, p. 304; *Historical Essays and Studies*, p. 505.

spondence of Döllinger. This contains the letters to and from Charlotte Blennerhassett. On 11 May 1886 she wrote an important letter to Döllinger about Acton's state of mind. The crucial paragraph runs as follows:

It seems to me that Lord Acton's standpoint then was a little different from his standpoint now. At that time doctrine was not yet a matter of indifference; in comparison to the importance of the ethical problem, which has now become for him the only question that matters, and besides which every other question is subordinate . . .

But no man is so clever that he is cleverer than everyone else put together. Anyone who can't find people to understand him must have gone wrong somewhere. Lord Acton must feel that the spearhead of his argument is sharp against more than Catholicism; just as (and this he sees himself) in the same way the repudiation of Ultramontanism cannot alone get over the difficulty which more and more seems to him insuperable.[11]

On 10 January 1890 Döllinger died at the age of ninety, still with the portrait of Acton by Lenbach hanging above his lengthened high desk, and in his house 2,000 volumes belonging to the Munich State Library, besides his own large collection. The death to Acton was like the death of a father with whom the son's relationship has been chequered. He was in Rome. He wrote to all his children about it. We have the letter to his favourite correspondent Mamy:

And so, on my birthday, came the end of our forty years' unbroken friendship. And it has been more than that; for of all the many priests and prelates I have known in many countries the Professor, now lying dead in the rooms where I was educated, was the one who took the deepest and the most earnest view of Religion. He did not agree with me in many things, and sometimes he was angry with me; but to talk to him was altogether different from talk on such matters with any other man. The void, for me, is a very great one; for I always knew that he knew more than I.

Much nonsense will be written, and I fear you will hear some non-

---

[11] Conz, IV, pp. 686–7.

sense spoken about him. The whole story is in what I have just said. Believe only that.

What makes me sorry now is not his death, at such an age and with such work done, but the sense that he never really understood me and my ways, though I am sure he liked me better, at one time, than any one else. On that account he was not always a good adviser, and he felt sometimes unpleasantly, that there was a gap between us.

My recollection is of the day after he walked with the Gladstones and Dick over from the other lake. He was over-tired and faint, and he thought that perhaps the end was coming. He came up into my room and said very solemnly and kindly that I was right, but that it was hard to adopt and follow lines of thought not one's own. Perhaps, if I had taken the other route from Genoa he would have given me the consolation of saying so once more upon his deathbed.[12]

Something in that letter gives the reader pause, considering that it is a letter written immediately after the death of a father. It is a warm letter and affectionate. Yet also it is extraordinarily detached, in the circumstances; with criticism of the dead man's side in the breach but no expressions of regret for his own part in the breach. Acton did better to Mamy in another letter of 27 January: 'I feel the void in my life more and more. He was a tremendous background; now when I don't understand, there is nobody to go to.'

He began to collect the materials to write Döllinger's life. The letters show that Döllinger's death did not resurrect the old intimacy. Acton was a critic of his former mentor. Half affection, half detachment, was the best condition for brilliant reflection on Döllinger and, more important, on the nature of history, using Döllinger as a peg. The materials lie in fascinating profusion at Cambridge. They are coherent, illuminating, repetitive because never finally sorted, and sometimes profound.

So we have a very curious, at times almost hostile, verdict on a man who once had been his foster-father. Döllinger, according to Acton, was an intelligent and perspicuous man who was not

---

[12] Acton to Mamy, 11 January 1890, 7956/40.

even in the second rank for narrative or description. He was not good at suspending judgement, and sometimes said more than he could be sure of. He suffered from a premature certitude. He could impart knowledge better than learning. Nobody ever learnt from him the mechanism by which history is written. He had a wide-ranging learning, the erudition of centuries.

He was grave and unimpassioned. He preferred books full of information. He preferred books not to raise real problems. He was not an innovator and made little use of the new archives. Everybody felt that the power was out of proportion to the work, and that he knew too much to write. It was so much better to hear him than to read all his books. He stuck too much by the traditional view of the Old Testament. He would not even give up the verses about the woman taken in adultery. He could not be shaken out of the belief that the religion of history was Catholicism. His conversation was worth far more than all his twenty-five books. He cared very little for his books. He outgrew them all.

The extraordinary impact of Acton upon English historical feeling – despite the total absence of any published work which changed anyone's historical view about any particular event – must in good part be seen here. He was telling the English in sometimes strange, and sometimes rhetorical, but always in magnetic language, that they could not be an individual without history and that they could not be a healthy society, politically and constitutionally, without a strong historical apprehension as part of their ethical axioms. He was telling them about the function of history, and the vocation of the historian, as a necessity of social health.

We may divine the sources of this attitude of mind in both aspects of his past – the Catholic and the near-Protestant moralist. In his Catholic life history had been the key to truth, trampling upon the opinions of five hundred bishops who do not even matter. In his moralist life, he had come into the edges of the northern German historical school who were in fact the leaders of scientific history in the Europe of that age: they were associating the vocation of the historian with German national feeling. The circumstances of German reunification made European history a key to the self-understanding of the German people. Acton hated historical nationalism. But since he came into the fringe of that great historical movement, he superimposed its sense of vocation upon his Catholic past where history was already a matter of faithfulness to the conscience, against people trying to compromise about the truth.

8

PROFESSOR LORD ACTON

O N 13 January 1895 the regius professor of history at Cambridge, Sir John Seeley, died. Acton, though he had no book to his name, was one of the famous historians in England, by reason of the articles which he had written and his help in founding the *English Historical Review*. He had no experience of teaching, young or old. But his learning was rare and respected in what was then coming to be, for the first time, the profession of historians. So in himself he was considerable. He worked exceptionally hard at books. For example in 1893: when he was in Oxford he spent nine hours a day at the Bodleian Library. In London he worked hours at the British Museum where they kept looking for the books he wanted from Paris or Leipzig and gave him 'a table in a snug corner with about 100 volumes on it, mostly uncut' where he worked daily until darkness fell, and then he moved to the Athenaeum and continued with another pile of books waiting there.[1]

He had thought himself possible as an Oxford professor of history when the chair there was vacant in 1894; and he would not have imagined things for himself which were out of the realm of the practical.

---

[1] Acton to Annie, 15 December 1893, no. 72.

THE APPOINTMENT OF ACTON

The Cambridge University Calendar for 1894–5 said that the regius professor of history must be a Master of Arts, or of Law, or of a superior degree. This was understood at the time to mean that he must hold a degree from the university of Cambridge. If that was right, it ruled out Acton; he had applied to be an undergraduate at Cambridge, to three different colleges (Magdalene was one, his uncle was there) and was not admitted. From the University of Cambridge he received an honorary doctorate in 1888 and the question was raised whether an honorary doctorate counted for this purpose. So now the statute appeared to exclude him as a possible professor. The same statute appeared to exclude other great names whom Cambridge might want – the name of S. R. Gardiner of *England under the Earlier Stuarts* was mentioned at Cambridge, but apart from the blot of his Oxford origin he had refused the Oxford regius chair the previous year. The name of Thomas Hodgkin, of *Italy and her Invaders*, was talked about in Cambridge but he bore the still worse blot of being a graduate of London. The principal of Newnham, who was Gladstone's youngest daughter Helen, proposed both these eminent names.

None other than Vinogradoff was suggested by Pollock on the ground that he was unhappy in Tsarist Russia but he had the blot that he was a graduate of Moscow. Vinogradoff did not finally settle in England, because his liberal opinions were not acceptable in St Petersburg, until the year before Acton died, and he became a professor at Oxford the year after Acton died.

There were some bad ideas. Two obscure persons without any history in them wanted the job because of their political services to the Liberal Party, and were not ashamed to plead that case.

There was an excellent Cambridge teacher of history George Prothero; but he had only lately accepted the chair at Edinburgh and it was thought impossible for the Crown to try to shift him back so quickly; especially when the principal adviser to the Queen was so eminent a Scot.

So must it be someone now teaching in Cambridge? Mandell Creighton, who surprised everyone when he left his chair at Cambridge for the see of Peterborough, said, 'Really there is no one now at Cambridge except Gwatkin (Creighton's successor as the professor of ecclesiastical history) who can be said to know any history'.

But there was one person in Cambridge who thought he was learned in history and wanted the chair, even thought it justice that he should have it: Oscar Browning, Fellow of King's, famous in the world as a character. This was the cause of panic. All the local people were determined to do their utmost to avert the fate of having Browning as their professor.

Before Seeley died Browning was already planning to succeed him. As soon as Seeley died Browning wrote to the Prime Minister asking to be appointed; and the Royal Archives at Windsor show that his application went higher than the Prime Minister. Browning had a claim and a disadvantage. He was a good teacher of history to undergraduates; and had done something to help found the History Tripos. His disadvantage was that he was the most inaccurate man ever to hold a Cambridge lectureship in history. The apocryphal story about him was that he wrote a book on Frederick the Great of Prussia and everyone was surprised to find him devoting so much military history to the conquest of Siberia; and that afterwards the book had an erratum slip, *wherever Siberia occurs please read Silesia*. He was also an eccentric. He had a huge stomach on very small legs, and the only hairs he had were wavy curls round the collar. But professors may look how they like, and eccentricity is not a quality which is a disadvantage to Cambridge historians who had the poet Gray as their professor. Not so long before, they had Professor Smyth. He was said to give the same course of lectures every year, which was possible because no one came; except when he came to the lecture on Marie Antoinette, to which many people came, to see the professor weep, which he did every year.[2]

Browning admired Acton. He was a member of the Liberal Party and Acton was one of the handful of Liberal peers in the House of Lords. He revered persons with titles and Acton satisfied that affectation. He used to send Acton his articles and Acton kindly corrected the elementary mistakes in them. Four years earlier Browning had tried to get King's College to elect Acton as a fellow. When Mandell Creighton left Cambridge to be Bishop of Peterborough, Browning tried to persuade Acton to stand as a possible professor of church history; and Acton the Roman Catholic replied, 'I should not satisfy the requirements as a teacher of Protestant doctrine'.[3] So when Seeley died, Browning and Acton were close, well known to each other. Acton, who knew a historian when he saw one, did not value Browning as a historian but as his link with Cambridge; Browning valued Acton as a historian and a peer and a Liberal.

The best and the worst that can be said for Oscar Browning came in letters that month to the Prime Minister. The best was from a Kingsman:

The work he has done amongst the younger men is remarkable. He has devoted his time and thrown open his rooms to them from all colleges, and has given conversational lectures to them round his fireside on periods of history, leading them to take an interest in history as throwing light on present day questions, in a way that no one else I have known at Cambridge has done.

And the worst: Henry Jackson the great Greek scholar reported to Harcourt of the panic lest Browning might get it. The words were the stronger because Jackson was a man of such

---

[2] Leslie Stephen's reminiscence, given to Prothero, Prothero's Diary, 5 October 1902, King's College.
[3] Acton to Browning, 6 March 1891; cf. FL 70.

sympathy. 'It is suggested that if he should be appointed there would be two consequences, (1) disaster to the history school (2) disaster to liberalism.'[4]

On 11 February 1895 the Vice-Chancellor, Austen-Leigh, pointed out to the Prime Minister that the axiom was false. The professor had not the least need to be a Cambridge graduate. It used to be so. But in 1861 this statute was repealed. They took a couple of legal opinions to make sure. But before the judge replied, the Prime Minister acted.

Acton was large in Rosebery's mind. They were colleagues in the Liberal party. Acton had tried to persuade Rosebery to send him as ambassador to Bavaria, where was his family's home; without success. Rosebery knew that Acton's financial affairs had been going awry and that he needed a stipend. And he found that some in Cambridge, Henry Sidgwick for example, wanted Acton as professor.

On 15 February 1895 Acton wrote to Rosebery accepting the offer of the chair.

Acton to Oscar Browning 18 February 1895:

I am sorry to be the bearer of strange and unexpected news. It has occurred to Lord Rosebery to offer the professorship to me. Of course I at once told him that I could not entertain or consider a proposal if I was to stand in your way; but I learned that he had been advised to prefer several other candidates in case of a refusal, and that there would be no chance the offer would be made to you. I know not whom he has consulted. The only friend of mine whom he has taken into counsel advised that I should not be appointed – I presume on religious grounds. I mention this that you may be assured I have not put myself forward, but that no friends of mine have employed their influence in my favour to the detriment of your obvious claims . . .

After Acton was appointed Browning welcomed him most kindly and they remained friends of a curious sort. He even wrote to the Prime Minister saying how much he welcomed

---

[4] Pro, R. P. Edgcumbe to Rosebery, 2 February 1895; against, Henry Jackson to Harcourt, 24 January 1895; in Rosebery Papers, National Library of Scotland, 1051/138 and 185.

Acton. But inside Browning remained bitter that no one made him the professor, and he imagined mysterious unknown foes writing false information to the Prime Minister to do him down. Foes did write about him but the information was not all false.

Gladstone was the person not pleased at the appointment. Gladstone wanted Acton's mind on wider fields and thought that to go to a chair at Cambridge would be a narrowing of what he could contribute.[5] Gladstone sounded slightly surprised that otherwise the approval seemed to have been unanimous, for he would have expected bigotry to object to a Roman Catholic being put into such a post. His daughter Mary gave three cheers for the appointment.[6] Gladstone warned him that not all would be well in Cambridge because there is an 'organized group or section of Low Churchmen under a Mr Moule'.[7]

Why was Acton appointed? (1) S. R. Gardiner wanted to write his book. (2) Mandell Creighton had gone away to be a bishop. (3) Thomas Hodgkin had no desire to work in a university and wanted to finish his book. (4) The Prime Minister was liberal and so was Acton. (5) Acton needed paid work, not so easy for a peer in those days. (6) Since an unlearned person inside the university had certain claims even though he had earned some contempt, it was absolutely necessary to bring in a very learned person from outside the university. And (7), it was possible to appoint a Roman Catholic for the first time because the liberal governments had slowly opened public offices to members of every denomination; and this particular Roman Catholic was acceptable to Protestants because on his record he was thought to be not in favour of Popes. The Queen commented on the friendly way he was received at Cambridge – 'what a happy change there has been'; and Acton the courtier replied to her, 'All due, Ma'am, to your Majesty's reign.'[8]

---

[5] Gladstone to Acton, 27 February 1895, mutilated letter.
[6] Mary Drew to Acton, 19 February 1895.
[7] This is Handley Moule, a sweet-natured, non-obstreperous person, afterwards a vague but beloved Bishop of Durham.
[8] Acton to Annie, no. 105.

Not all the London intelligentsia were pleased and had an excuse to say what they thought when he started to lecture. They used strong language: 'an overpowering deluge of verbiage'. 'One catches here and there sentences with gleams of light in them' 'hope he will resign the chair for which he is in no way qualified'. 'Surely one of the indispensable qualifications for the chair of Modern History at Cambridge is that its occupant should be intelligible'.[9]

Acton's first official act was to read a dissertation and advise Cambridge not to print it. He looked for lodgings and found a place like a warren full of students in straw hats and rejected it. He found the Master of Trinity College almost too gushing and his able much younger wife very pleasant indeed. Trinity Hall offered him a Fellowship but he refused it and preferred to be given rooms at Trinity. He described how 'a funny old woman' took care of him and that he had a manservant, an ex-soldier, and he thought it worthy of note that he bore a moustache.

He loved being at Cambridge. He loved being a Cambridge man 'at last'. Some thought these years the happiest of his life. He had been an academic *manqué* and now was no longer *manqué*. Trinity elected him to an honorary Fellowship and he moved into rooms in Nevile's court. Later, as the number of books grew and grew, Trinity added the next door room to his.

THE INAUGURAL LECTURE

He realised that his conception of history was different from Seeley's. Seeley thought that history is politics. Acton said very early that history is not the history of politics – why not? politics pass. 'History compels us to fasten on abiding issues, and rescues us from the temporary and transient.' We need to share the existence of societies not our own.

He gave his Inaugural Lecture on 11 June 1895. It was the

[9] *Spectator*, 15 June 1895, p. 814; *Saturday Review*, 89 (1895), 822.

most famous Inaugural Lecture ever given. It was a calamity for professors because it meant afterwards that they all had to think of giving inaugural lectures. It was an utterance so rare, in places so profound, and in other places so personal, that it can be read again and again without boring the reader. He took the chance to state not only his attitude to history and the past but his philosophy of life and moral being. For unlike most historians he thought that a person's attitude to history and his philosophy of life and morality are not two different attitudes but are the same.

Afterwards he showed his weaker side by adding to the published version too many pages of footnotes. The lecture was printed in seventy-four pages, the notes in fifty-seven; but the smaller print of the notes meant that there were many words more than in the lecture.

The love of unnecessary footnotes is a notorious sin of professors because they are suspected, not of ensuring that the reader can see the sources which justify what they said, but of wishing the world to think that they are encyclopaedias on two feet. But these footnotes were different. During the lecture he stated various historical facts, though not a heap of them; a few of which might be argued about. The notes made no attempt to justify this information from their sources. The notes are extracts from writers whose opinions were like or nearly like Acton's. He had spent years compiling an index of remarkable quotations and the temptation to empty the card index into the back pages of his printed lecture was too pressing to resist. The notes to the Inaugural Lecture are the chief pointer, besides his failure to publish, in support of the critics who think he would have done well to throw some of his card index into the dustbin. It is just possible also, that a new professor of history who had not proved to anyone (but experts) that he knew much history, succumbed to the desire to show his new university that at least this incoming incumbent had read shelves and shelves of books.

But the Inaugural was of a far bigger stature than its notes. It had theory and practice. The theory was a coherent summary of

Acton's historical ideal. The practice was good advice to students on how to learn history.

But he had other aims in his mind. He needed to show this Protestant audience that a Roman Catholic historian is neither of necessity illiberal nor of necessity bigoted against Protestant sects. He went out of his way to stress these two parts of his personal liberalism. All that century Popes had been condemning liberalism and revolution. Acton sang the praises of the extreme dissenters of the seventeenth century because the religious conscience was the foundation of English democracy. He did not quite sing the praise of revolution but he did say that revolutions had done much good for the human race; we have to face it that we owe good results to violence; we owe religious liberty to the Dutch revolution (he does not say more, but notice the implication against Spanish repression), constitutional government to the English revolution, federal republicanism to the American, political equality to the French 'and its successors' (which did he mean?). There was here a contradiction because by its nature revolution breaks with the past and 'abolishes history', as some of the French revolutionaries wanted to do. But Acton, observing the contradiction, tried to show that by freeing society from the tighter hold by the past on the present, the revolution made the conditions for a renewal and flowering of historical study.

Then he needed to prove to the university that history is tough, a worthy training of the mind. He found so many of the traditional professors who regarded it as an easy option for young people not good at Latin and Greek and not able to cope with pure mathematics. This severity of history was easy to show but not easy within parts of an hour. He achieved it in two words – *trust nobody*.

The witnesses lie. Or twist the evidence of what happened to suit their cause or their politics or their Church. Or imagine they say what they did not see. Or did not see aright what they saw. Or were so filled with prejudice that they misinterpreted what happened. Or were so ignorant that they misunderstood what they heard. We only have human witnesses and all without exception are wicked or biased. Such is the human condition and such the first vast problem of the historian. *Trust nobody*. Ask their motives. Try to test their sources of information. Examine their background. See what prejudice they might have.

He added to this a doctrine, which his successor and admirer and critic Sir Herbert Butterfield carried to its limit – a Christian is bound to this distrust of the witnesses by his awareness of original sin.

This distrust applies to more than individuals. Governments are worst of all for hiding, manufacturing, altering evidence. Power needs not to tell the truth or only to tell part of it; and to make propaganda; and propaganda is often a lie or an intention to mislead . . . in this distrust of the powerful we have a vast advantage over all our predecessors. Modern representative governments have opened their archives and their example has persuaded other States to open their archives. This therefore (he told his audience – and he was right) is a marvellous new age for historical study. For the first time in history we can check from the sources what governments used to say.

Therefore history is not prejudice but the cure of prejudice; not compilation but critical training. The past has no edges and so opens a limitless field of research, in which the method of criticism is scientific and learns from contemporary natural scientists in the use of analysis.

Then this historian who never taught anyone before gave them hints on how to train themselves as historians. Some of these hints became so famous that they are still quoted:

Ideas are more influential than individual people. Study ideas in preference to men and women though the ideas are put forward by men and women. This means that history cannot be 'national'. No frontier can keep out ideas. By their nature ideas are international. Then history by its nature is international.

Ideas are the cause of what happens, not the effect of what happens. Therefore, in judging the past, we must condemn the theory more harshly than its results.

(Is it right, so invariably? Is it right, the doctrine, we must condemn the theory more than the results? The chief theorist of Nazi racialism was Rosenberg. He was a contemptible whose work made no difference to what happened. Men sublimated their frustrations about society into a hatred of aliens who were alien because they looked different or had different customs; and then the gut-feeling of hatred took hold of the half-literate and they used Rosenberg's *Myth of the Twentieth Century*, and the theory was an accessory to what was hateful, not the cause of the hatred.)

Because ideas are so powerful, there is, he taught, a certain priority in the study of history to ecclesiastical history, the study of religion; for religious ideas have been the most powerful of ideas in social development.

Further advice to young historians included:

> we easily fail to see what is already printed somewhere but has been forgotten
> learn as much by writing as by reading
> be not content with the best book – seek sidelights from others
> have no favourites
> see that your judgements are your own
> suspect power more than vice
> study problems in preference to periods.

For this last he gave instances and they were all problems of intellectual history – the origins of the ideas of Luther and Adam Smith and Rousseau, the influence of the scientific ideas of Bacon, the consistency of Burke, the identity of the first Whig.

He said that he understood modern history, the area which he would take as his own, to begin with Christopher Columbus and the Renaissance when scholars first learned how to distinguish genuine documents among the forged so plentiful in the Middle Ages; when history was 'full-grown'. In the earlier part of the lecture he almost seemed to imply that ancient and medieval history were not worth studying in comparison. He did not wish to include contemporary history because the archives were not yet open and we had less perspective and therefore the result of inquiry must be further from any certainty. But when he came to the practical training of a young historian he took the opposite view about premodern history. The materials for modern history are too vast. We need to start with areas where the sources are limited. Therefore the best training in historical method comes from studying themes or moments in ancient or medieval history. He gave instances – the sources of Plutarch's *Pericles*, the two tracts on Athenian government, the origin of the epistle to Diognetus, the date of the life of St Antony; areas very limited in scope but they all happen to be of rare difficulty for historians whether young or not; and come from the ancient world. And this led him to a general law – gain mastery by taking a small area of study, do not risk superficiality.

The historian cannot be engaged as a politician. The one indispensable quality is detachment. He never mentioned Döllinger as his master though Döllinger had taught him how to be a historian. Twice during the inaugural he talked in praise of Ranke, once he defined him as 'my master', once he described his last private visit to the old man; Ranke the practitioner of the ideal of absolute detachment, Ranke who taught historians that it was indispensable to get behind the books to the unpublished records. There is an enchanting Actonian phrase: Ranke taught the modern study of history 'to be critical, to be colourless, and new. We meet him at every step and he has done more for us than any other man.'

That word *colourless* history was important. The best history was when the historian did not appear in the pages. Not like Macaulay. Not like Thiers. Not like Treitschke. But like Stubbs. Like Fustel de Coulanges. Acton did not practise what he preached. He loved colour. He enjoyed it when he could illustrate the past by personal reminiscence. But in the inaugural he stated the ideal of detachment very persuasively. By the nature of the work the historian ought to be Olympian. It is duty to put at its best the side which the writer personally thinks the wrong cause; and to avoid pertinacity in defending the cause which the writer personally believes to be right. If a Catholic writes a life of Calvin it ought to be impossible for the reader to know from the text that the author is a Catholic. If a patriotic German wrote a Life of Napoleon no one should be able to infer the patriotism from the book.

He seemed to have no use for philosophies of history. He warned his new university against them. But whether or not he had what may be called a philosophy, he worked with two principles which he thought essential and which could hardly be extracted from a study of the past.

The first was that human society is in progress. This progress is observable. Absolutism is finished. He had no idea that forty years after his death all Europe but Britain and Ireland and Switzerland and Sweden and Finland would have absolute governments. If someone had prophesied it he would have found it incredible. Not all is yet done but he was sure that we are moving to civilized societies. What is a civilized society? He defined it:

representative government
the end of slavery
the security in society of the weaker groups and the minorities
liberty of conscience.

The second general principle was moral, his fight with the unmentioned Döllinger. History is moral judge. We cannot be so detached that we refuse to judge. And when we judge we must not succumb to the temptation of so many past historians of excusing by saying that in those days moral axioms were different. He gave instances – his hero Ranke related how King William III 'ordered' the massacre of Glencoe (is it true?) – yet when he sums up the King's character in admiration, murder is not mentioned. Halifax did not believe in the Popish plot but insisted that innocent people should be executed to satisfy the multitude; and then Macaulay wrote of Halifax as of a forgiving and compassionate temper. Beware of the historian's whitewash.

We must have the ideal of detachment, but not absolutely, because we are the conscience of the human race about its past. That is why history is a moral education as well as intellectual training. So he came to his famous end – 'if we lower our standard in history, we cannot uphold it in Church or State.'

THE LECTURES IN THE FACULTY

Professors needed to lecture to those preparing for examinations, perhaps twice a week. The French Revolution was set for examination. Acton was deeply read on the subject and decided to lecture about it.

To his first lecture (ordinary lecture, not the inaugural) came a full room with two or three undergraduates standing and the Master of Trinity standing and his little wife who opened a book to take notes and Miss Gladstone from Newnham who brought along thirty-two of her girls. Dr Gwatkin afterwards came along to say that there were complaints, that Acton talked too fast and they could not take it all in and they could not always catch the proper names; so for this third lecture, still a full room with three or four standing, and with Lord Kelvin the eminent scientist in the audience, and with the wife of the Master of Trinity still taking down every word in her large notebook, he went more slowly and took trouble about the names and watched the many scribbling pens. One of the girls was evidently bowled over because she came afterwards and said that she felt as if she had read twenty volumes; and Lord Kelvin came up and grasped his hand and said it was the best lecture he ever heard and that he never so much regretted the end of the hour. Acton liked praise, but he specially liked praise from people he admired and he admired Kelvin very much.

He wrote to his daughter Annie about it:

We are not made angry by foolish criticism, and I have less right to [sic] than others. Think how unsympathetic my teaching must be to the philistine, the sordid, the technical, the faddist, the coward, the man of prejudice and passion, the zealot etc. This makes much more than half the world. So I am always surprised at praise, and only wonder at blame, and specially misinterpretation in particular places.[10]

His next lecture that term was on 8 November and at the end when he talked of Marie Antoinette, he reported that there were old dons who hid their faces in their hands and shook with sobbing[11] and that some in the town were reported to say that it was the finest thing they ever heard. The Newnham girls were still puzzled over his inaugural and petitioned to be allowed a meeting to discuss it with him.

These lectures were delivered once a week at 12.15. He always lectured in one of the lecture rooms in Trinity – fee for persons not members of the university, 1 guinea to be paid at Deighton Bell's. He wrote the lectures out in his beautiful hand and was said by a close colleague Figgis to have delivered them as they were written. Internal evidence suggests that this cannot be true; for sometimes they are not long enough to fill the time for a lecture and the lecturer must have taken room to expand off the cuff; and occasionally a sentence is so incomprehensible that it can only be a note to remind the lecturer to expand it orally. He did not make life easy for himself because he could not quite repeat the same lectures next year, so he had to go on worrying at the text and amending. It was a time of exceptionally hard work. 'I accept no invitations to London, and neglect many duties graver than that. It is impossible for me to undertake any writing for a long time to come. I should fail, and it would make me nervous and uncomfortable.'[12] The cards in the Cambridge University Library show the labour that lay behind the lectures. He never took a secondary source for granted but sought to track it down to its original. He did not take pleasure in the delivery of the lectures for he disliked public speaking.

---

[10] Acton to Annie, no. 111.
[11] Acton to Annie, no. 113.
[12] Acton to Henry Sidgwick, 7 November 1895, Trinity College MSS.

Each lecture day at 5 he would be in his rooms in college to give advice to students.

Some who came to pass an examination went away. But others were rivetted. The man was intense about history, at times passionate; it was not a mouth that was talking but a whole being; one hearer calls it, meaning it as a compliment, 'an emotional performance'. A rational university will hardly appoint as the most junior assistant lecturer someone whose lecture is an emotional performance. The same hearer says that the lecture was 'a wonderful work of art' and leaves pedestrians to worry about the secret of turning a lecture about the past into a wonderful work of art.[13]

The man was felt to be, at the time, and we feel him to be now, altogether bigger than the lectures. Behind the lectures lay a coherent intelligence, rich and varied, struggling with truth and of a total integrity.

It is a question whether people should leave behind them when they die the manuscript of their old lectures. During Acton's lifetime not only the Cambridge Press but other publishers both English and American asked for permission to have his lectures to print and Acton refused. Figgis and Laurence published both sets – 1907 and 1910 – though the editors were clear about the defects in them for published purposes. Why did they publish? Because they revered the man – because he had grown even more controversial since his death and they wanted to show him as he was – because they thought that for all the oddity of the lectures they contained serious thinking on bits of modern history – and because they were not difficult to publish since Acton wrote them out in a long hand which was easy to read.

The lectures on the French Revolution have this oddness that they begin with two chapters on the background of thought and

[13] John Pollock, *Independent Review*, 2 (April 1904), 366.

then the rest of the chapters are a detailed narrative of what happened 1789–94.

He spoke epigrams and aphorisms which were rather half-truths than truths but are powerful on the reader – the earth belongs to those who walk on it, not to those who are underneath (FR 33); It is a grave miscalculation to think that a regular army is stronger than an undisciplined mob (FR 66); the army which gave liberty to France was largely composed of assassins (FR 90); the single page of print (that is the Declaration of the Rights of Man) is stronger than all the armies of Napoleon (FR 107).

Undergraduates reading history were taught that history should be dry, unemotional. Acton held that this was what Ranke, whom he so much admired, had taught us that history ought to be. Teachers used to say, *Never use a superlative*. Acton approved this idea of dryness but did not practise it. He spattered superlatives – the greatest scene in modern history (FR 53), Mirabeau was the best debater in French Parliamentary history (FR 53), Talleyrand was to be feared, and hated and admired, as the most sagacious politician in the world (FR 69); 9th Thermidor is 'the most auspicious date in modern history (FR 284). 'There is no record of a finer act of fortitude in all parliamentary history' (it is the personal attack by Cambon on Robespierre, FR 294); 'the most brilliant figure on the battlefield of Europe' this is Murat (FR 344). At times the superlatives are allusive and mysterious – the most celebrated of all the Guelphic writers (= Thomas Aquinas), the ablest writer of the Ghibelline party (= Marsilius), 'the most brilliant agitator among the continental Socialists', 'the most illustrious of the early philosophers' (= Pythagoras), 'the wisest man to be found in Athens' (= Solon), the most distinguished English writer of the twelfth century (John of Salisbury), the most learned of Anglican prelates (Ussher), the ablest of the French prelates (Bossuet), the ablest ruler that ever sprung from a revolution (Cromwell), the most popular of bishops (Fénelon), the purest Conservative intellect (Niebuhr), the most intelligent of Greek tyrants (Periander), the greatest theologian of his age (Gerson), the most famous royalist of the Restoration (Chateaubriand), the ablest of historic men (Napoleon); no tyrant 'ever used his power to inflict greater suffering or greater wrong' than King Louis XIV. These superlatives showed the same habit of mind which made him choose a list of 'the hundred best books'.

He had a genius as an anthologist or selector of the telling quotation and putting it onto his card index. He had a fascination about the odd details of history – how the King of France snored more loudly when he was bored by the discussion than when he was asleep (FR 43); how after Charlotte Corday murdered Marat in his bath they went to her room and found the Bible lying open at the story of Judith (FR 265). He loved extraordinary moments and extraordinary careers. Sometimes if a thing was extraordinary he was inclined to believe it. We do not know how the decibels of the King of France's snoring could be tested. On the evidence it is extremely unlikely that they found the Bible open in Charlotte Corday's room, they are far more likely to have found the story of Brutus murdering Caesar, for she really did admire Brutus; but there is no reliable evidence that they found anything of the sort.[14] Such anecdotes explain why there were persons in Cambridge who criticized Acton as a historian whose qualities combined being a Dictionary of Dates and taking pleasure in scandalous stories.[15]

Sometimes there was grim humour. Collot and Fouché were united in sacred bands of friendship – notice Acton's word *sacred* in the band of friendship. Why were they friends? Because they had joined in putting 1,682 persons to death at Lyons (FR 289). One of Acton's friends said that he concealed much beneath 'a grave irony'.[16]

He could communicate a sense of the immediacy of history. If you have lived through the Second World War it is hard to

---

[14] The reviewer in *EHR* was critical that Acton should accept a story that Danton offered a bribe to Pitt to save the King's life in return for a large British bribe.
[15] Reported by Maitland, 19 October 1902, Maitland's *Letters*, ed. Fifoot, p. 317.
[16] R. Lane Poole, in *EHR* (October 1902), 696.

realize that for most of the people you talk to it is as remote as the siege of Troy – except for the few who have lost a father or mother or uncle or aunt in it and except (a large exception) for those who belong to a people, like the Jews and the Poles, who suffered tragedy. Acton could tell stories which easily bridged this gap in human memory. The procession of the States-General at Versailles on 5 May 1789 being cheered by the crown, a turning-point in European history, what did it feel like at the time? Acton had relatives who watched the cheering of the new liberal Pope in 1846. An Italian lady did not cheer. They asked her why. She said 'Because I was at Versailles in 1789' (FR 55). The anecdote bridged the decades, everyone felt at once how short is time. Acton had a gut-feeling how these actions of the past affect us now – the debate on 8 July 1789 which led to the fall of the Bastille – and, he says, the face of the world was changed, and 'the imperishable effects of which will be felt by everyone of us, to the last day of his life' (FR 83). He treasured these moments which linked him to the past. When he went to work in the archives of Venice in 1864 he was presented to the Signora Inocenigo; and it mattered to him that she had in earlier days rented her house to Lord Byron, and it mattered even more to him that as a girl she had danced with the last Doge of Venice,[17] and he loved to tell the historians of Cambridge about this strange link with a vanished world.

Colourless? He had the sense that history is a drama. His account of the flight of the French kind and queen to Varennes, and their pursuit and arrest, is narrative history in the most gripping form, we do not wonder that George Macaulay Trevelyan was one of his best pupils.

He was sure that reading history makes a difference to one's person; he said once that there are two books which can make an epoch in a person's life – they are Michelet and Taine – that is the glorifying and the demolishing histories of the French Revolution – and this is even though the books are not good

---

[17] DD. p. 129.

books in his opinion, for example he regarded Taine not as a historian but as a pathologist (FR 370). He can hate historians; and as was predictable of a Whig lord like this, the most hated of all the historians was Carlyle.

And the moral sense kept coming through. Was it bad, all that murder in the Terror? Yet it was very bad, it was murder. But – murder goes on most of the time in other ages – murder is not peculiar to any one country or time or opinion; and if it wins then historians come along and praise it – 'the strong man with the dagger is followed by the weaker man with the sponge. First, the criminal who slays; then the sophist who defends the slayer' (FR 92) – historians are nearly as bad as the assassins. If you are an honest historian you prove that everyone is bad – and his last words of advice to his audience in his lectures on the French Revolution, try to deal evenly with friend and foe – but is it possible for an honest historian to have a friend? (FR 373) He solemnly told his hearers to take as a principle of their work, *Never be surprised at the crumbling of an idol or the disclosure of a skeleton*.

The lectures were not so very suitable for undergraduates wishing to pass examinations. Figgis said about them that they 'were not so much a mine of instruction as a revelation of the speaker's personality'.[18] Gooch, though now he lived in London, came up to attend them and loved them. George Trevelyan attended them and there was quite a sprinkling of senior members of the university. Oscar Browning attended them regularly and said that there were not many (male) undergraduates, it was a big audience but a lot of them were townsfolk and the lectures could be understood only by those well qualified in the subject;[19] but we should take this with a pinch of salt for Browning afterwards liked to portray himself as the person who taught nitty-gritty history while Acton was the person whose lesser function was only to inspire. Undergraduates were certainly in the

[18] Preface to Acton's *Lectures on Modern History*, p. xi.
[19] Oscar Browning, *Memories of Later Years* (1923), p. 17.

audience. E. M. Forster the future novelist attended the lectures and wrote down in his *Commonplace Book* (1885), slightly wrong, that striking sentence 'Every villain is followed by a sophist with a sponge'; where the misquotation is kinder to the historians than was Acton's actual text.

The lectures at Cambridge were said by good judges to be 'a very good success'.[20] The delivery was powerful – a solemn dignity, as though this thing called history is a sacred subject, a quest for what is true and truth is the greatest thing in the world, and this truth is bound up with the moral nature of humanity.

Everything is so exciting – the archives are open at last, the libraries are open – the State Record offices, the Vatican Archives – we can get authentic history and not what people think happened and not what interested parties wish us to think happened – he felt it to be a seed-time for a much truer history than had ever been written in the past. It is exciting because at last we are getting history out of the biases that restricted it – the bias of race and the bias of religion and the bias of nationalism and the State. Now at last we can write a history of the Battle of Waterloo that French and English will both accept or a history of the Reformation which Catholics and Protestants will both see to be fair. Truth is above the propaganda and the biases. It is beginning to be reachable. And reachable by the ordinary reading person. We are about to make history independent of the historians.

'These things are extra territorial, having their home in the sky, and no more confined to race or frontier, than a rainbow or a storm' (letter to Syndics, October 1896) – there speaks the poet of history. To us this is naiveté – in 1995 a Bosnian historian spoke of the history of Bosnia and it was passionate and during it some of the hearers imagined a Serb historian describing the same events. History is easily turned into propaganda. Hugh Trevor-Roper gave a lecture on German historians and frightened the audience for he forecast what British historians

---

[20] Balfour in M. Grant Duff, *Notes from a Diary* (1905), I, p. 20.

would all be saying now if Hitler had conquered Britain. Acton thought that we had climbed out of nationalism in history. He sang its ideals like a minstrel and the song had beauty and was blind to reality.

Acton was not a pure partisan – he had rigid principles about conscience and liberty – and never concealed evidence that told against him, he never failed to note down the exceptions which spoke against his argument. The contradiction or wonder in the mind, is that he was always yearning, and can be felt to be yearning, to overcome such things as prejudices and see things as they really were.

Human beings are worse in reality than in their reputations. The people we meet look good because we only see the envelope. But the historian is going to read the letters they wrote and what others report that they did. Readers of Acton's pessimistic view of humanity, and the historian's part in it, realize that to have a biography is one of the worst fates that can afflict a suffering person. About individuals in history he could be depressing. He wrote to the Master of Trinity, H. M. Butler: 'We must always expect our pupils to see, more and more clearly, that the great men of history were not good men. There is no remedy. One can only strive to pick up every striking, or elevating, or edifying fact, and fix it on their minds.'[21] It was a curious contrast, that he held the loftiest ideal about what history could do for human beings, but one of the things it does for them is to depress them about each other. He could dismiss eminent persons with an abusive word: Nelson, 'infamous man'; Bismarck, 'a great man, and a great scoundrel'.

Two pupils who attended his lectures, and were taught by him privately, left their impressions of him as a teacher. These are valuable because most judgements of him came from posterity, those who did not know him and judged him by the posthumous print which he did not mean to publish; through which various

---

[21] Acton to H. M. Butler, CUL Add. MSS 7339/3.

adverse judgements were recorded – that he so loved lists of books that he was less a historian than a bibliographer; that despite his own advice he failed to doubt the evidence enough and hence was too dogmatic; that he was like a mausoleum, impressive to look at but not a guide to the living; that he made history too majestic.

The two pupils took very different views of him. George Trevelyan was not sure. Acton had been doubtful about Trevelyan – in the first encounters he was an enthusiast for this able pupil but when Trevelyan began to write immaturely Acton thought that the work was not as good as he had expected it to be and ought to have been better. Trevelyan reciprocated doubt about Acton. The lectures were delivered, he said, as though the speaker was an oracle. This was a sage talking, who had travelled thither from the antique lands of European statecraft, 'with the brow of Plato above the reserved and epigrammatic lips of the diplomatist'. There is an implied doubt in the sentence. Trevelyan thought afterwards that he would not have been remembered as a historian but for the other qualities which were not historical. But he confessed that Acton helped to make the history school great, especially because he made it respected in the university.

The second pupil whose record we have expressed a very different and more uninhibited opinion. During the years when Acton was at Cambridge the great lawyer Sir Frederick Pollock, himself a former fellow of Trinity Cambridge, was the professor of jurisprudence at Oxford. He sent his son John to Trinity after him. John arrived and read history and found Acton his professor and in his own college. The result was more like reverence than admiration; for a unique person, the biggest historian of them all, not only without parallel in his learning perhaps, but familiar with Western literature, a man of wit and passion, 'with the power to tear the heart from many mysteries', a citizen of the world by birth, without prejudice or fear, 'with a burning zeal for the cause of truth and the triumph of justice'. He carried all this weight of learning with ease and without being heavy – 'one of the richest of human minds'. Acton evidently lent him books, and even his copies of manuscripts. But Pollock found each lecture an experience. 'Never before had a young man come into the presence of such intensity of conviction as was sounded by every word' and it was this which gave the lectures 'their amazing force and vitality'.[22]

THE ORGANIZATION OF HISTORY

While he was on the History Board, the Tripos was divided like other Triposes into two parts. He did not speak much at meetings and he approved rather than led what was done. But he had more weight behind the scenes than this suggests. He regarded the plan for reform of the syllabus as his own and was pleased that when it was debated the members of the Theological Faculty came to stand on his side because they regarded him as the lay defender of religion in the university and thought that religion was helped by his historical scheme. He refused to accept a proposal that he should become chairman of the History Board. According to Browning's memory, he refused this more than once and Browning thought that it was his duty to accept. Maitland once wrote a despairing cry: 'The History Board consumes endless time . . . At present Acton = o. I wish he would bless or curse or do something.'[23] Once when he was out of the room they took the moment to elect him chairman when he could not protest but after he came back he persuaded them that it was not right that he should be made to serve.

He made a friend for ever over the chairmanship. Gwatkin the professor of church history looked odd and sounded odder, and was a militant Protestant. The board was resolute not to have Gwatkin as its chairman. Acton resented what he called their 'dead set' against Gwatkin and the Catholic professor

---

[22] Trevelyan, *Autobiography* (1949), p. 17; *Clio a Muse*, pp. 177 ff, especially 183; John Pollock, *Independent Review* (April 1904).
[23] Maitland's *Letters*, ed. Fifoot, p. 177.

proposed Gwatkin for chairman and carried the motion because they did not like to oppose Acton. It is not probable that the resulting chairmanship was always effective; but thenceforth Gwatkin was dedicated to Acton.

The number of students rose steadily: 1897, 48; 1898, 54; 1899, 106; 1900, 98; 1901, 114; 1902, 129 – nearly three times during those last six years of his life.

THE PUPILS

It hurt him when he came to Cambridge that some of the best scholars in the university regarded history as a second-class subject. If you had a brain you read classics, if you had not you did history or science. That was not just pain, it offended him deeply, he felt it almost as though it was an insult to himself. Figgis thought that Acton was the man who did more than anyone to remove this stain and persuade the scholars that this is a subject which elicits high qualities of the mind and is of fundamental importance to the human race. George Trevelyan agreed. This was what Acton achieved.

When inquirers had a private conversation with Acton about history they felt that the wisdom of the ages was speaking through him; and this came over nearly as powerfully in lectures, except that the wisdom of the ages was cluttered up by historical facts. In a sense Acton was the poet of history. History, he says, is to be 'not a burden on the memory but an illumination of the soul'.[24]

With individual pupils he was excellent, really interested in them, sending them piles of books they had never heard of in languages which they did not know how to translate and with a letter telling them this was only the first batch and that more would follow later. This was almost an obsession with him, he loved lists of books and here was a chance to show people that

[24] Report to Syndics of Cambridge University Press, reprinted in *The Cambridge Modern History* (1907), p. 20.

the list really existed. He was never bored by people who came to ask him questions, he liked questions and never made the questioner feel a fool or an ignoramus. He was patient, accessible, and inspiring in encouragement. He asked them questions, really wanting to know what they thought and perhaps to learn from them.

He could be quite fierce in his reports. Here is a report on one student: 'It would do him good to devote a year to the reign of Antiochus, or the policy of Lysander, or something remoter still, that he may learn to put proof in the place of assertion, and to sit tight on the safety valve of opinion.' He could be 'cruel' at need. One showy, insubstantial essay was abused eloquently. Pollock recorded an experience of an undergraduate who must have been himself. He read Fouché's Memoirs, recently translated into English, and used them to write an essay on Austrian policy in the year of Waterloo, but did not mention where he found his facts. When he read the essay to Acton, he received high praise for it, and then a few light corrections; and suddenly at the end Acton said, 'I think you made some use of Fouché's Memoirs. I suppose you know they are not authentic.' This was not the only time when Acton devastated a pupil. But history is difficult. The undergraduate need not have been so squashed. Fouché's Memoirs were published soon after his death and his family went to court to prove them a forgery and won from the courts the destruction of all copies. All through the nineteenth century they were believed to be a fabrication and were still so believed when Acton listened to Pollock's essay. But at that very moment opinion among historians began to turn to the conviction that total fabrication was impossible and that many pages of them were written by Fouché himself.

Acton asked Oscar Browning to tell his students that he was not formidable as they might think – 'I am a comparatively domesticated animal, and not so wild a beast as I look.'[25]

[25] Acton to Browning, 3 and 22 March 1896, Browning MSS, King's College.

Some of Acton's pupils made big contributions to history later. They did it in Actonian ways.

R. V. Laurence, whom Acton called 'my special pupil', wrote nothing, like his master. Figgis, whom he described as a tutor who has particularly 'attached himself to me' and who helped him with an affectionate care as he moved towards illness, was brilliant on Church and State (which was one of his greatest interests), Gutteridge made a difference not to history but to international law and Acton thought the training of international lawyers a part of the business of teaching history, Trevelyan contributed in an original way to Italian history as well as English, Gooch was a Germanic polymath like Acton, Clapham made advances in economic history, Temperley applied international law to the making of treaties, and Benians took history out of Europe and across the world.

Acton founded the Trinity College Historical Society which still goes on. As a Trinity College Historical Society it had this peculiarity that the members did not need to belong to Trinity – Maitland, Acton's close friend and colleague, professor at Downing College and also of Trinity, was a founder member – but only the members of Trinity had votes, so early on there was a charming mock seventeenth-century petition from the historian Figgis 'from my poor garret, starving for lack of two shillings', who was Fellow of St Catharine's and a member, that this was *taxation without representation* because the subscription was put up from one shilling a year to two shillings a year without him having any say in this tax.

The first volume of the minutes of the Society is in the Wren Library and is fun. Trevelyan was one of the original members, so was Cunningham the founder of economic history in Cambridge, and Maitland. Four other future professors were elected members in the next few meetings and Figgis would have made a fifth if he had not been torpedoed by a submarine. One of the members, outrageously unActonian in his attitudes to history, was Lytton Strachey; but the minutes show that he was an infrequent attender; and perhaps we may think that it was not that he was unActonian because he was an infrequent attender but an infrequent attender because he was unActonian. But – was he altogether unActonian? In Strachey one of the axioms of Acton was carried to excess, even corrupted. The doctrine that conditioned Lytton Strachey's work was this, men and women are worse than their public reputations. Let us then enjoy demolishing those reputations. The difference, unspoken, was this: Acton had a faith that however bad we all are, there is a moral nature in the world which enables us slowly, by fits and starts, to make it less bad. Strachey had no such faith. We are bad and what happens to the world is just what you would expect as a result.

POLITICAL RIGHT

Inside his lecturing was his ethics of politics.

Politics mean compromise. In politics we need to choose the less bad course because it is a practicable course and we cannot achieve a better. Moral right means no compromise, we have to decide for the right and let the practicable take care of itself. This tension between sane political practice and any sound political ideal continually concerned him. He worried over the truth in the saying of the old Greek philosopher Chrysippus that in politics it is impossible to please both gods and men at the same time.

History is the conscience of the human race – these exploiters and murderers die prosperous but they cannot for ever escape because history tells what they were like.

States when they are in crisis demand more power at the centre and the appetite grows until they create absolutist regimes or police States. The most famous quotation from Acton has always been the single sentence, '*Power tends to corrupt; and absolute power corrupts absolutely.*' This was not a passing *mot*, it expressed everything about history that he felt passionately. 'The possession of unlimited power corrodes the conscience, hardens the heart, and confounds the understanding.'

He held that any government by the purest form of democracy – that is direct election by all the people to a single assembly which has sovereign power – was sure to end in tyranny and therefore democracies need self-limitation by some form of mixed constitution. He drew this lesson from Athens. 'The lesson of their experience ... teaches that government by the whole people, being the government of the most numerous and most powerful class, is an evil of the same nature as an unmixed monarchy, and requires, for nearly the same reasons, institutions that shall protect it against itself, and shall uphold the permanent reign of law against arbitrary revolutions of opinion.'

A unanimous meeting of ordinary people is capable of deciding what is wholly wrong or wholly immoral. Therefore there is a standard of right for the ultimate mood of a people which does not depend upon the unanimity of the voters, far less on the majority of the voters. The obvious problem here Acton did not attempt to solve – that consciences can be almost as misled as votes.

His third principle was the supreme value of the individual. All States want to make, as he said, 'the passengers exist for the sake of the ship', 'they prefer the ship to the crew'. All governments if they are to survive must content a majority of the people; and it is easier to make the people happy if government takes less notice of the rights of the minority of the people. Writers had argued that like ancient Athens modern democracy could not exist without being supplemented by a form of slavery; for the particular difficulty of democracy was its tendency to end in a Communism which Acton regarded as a system which rode over the rights of the individual; since the individuals could never preserve their private right and their private freedom unless they were allowed the possession of property. 'A people averse to the institution of private property is without the first element of freedom.'

In his eyes the law of human rights – which was not a phrase he liked to use – was a necessity to any moral form of state. He regarded the general acceptance of moral principles as a necessity if the democracy was to survive. Freedom cannot exist for long in a State unless most of the people have an agreement on moral principles and accept the State as more than a mere instrument for protecting them against enemies or criminals or for promoting their prosperity by a centralized management of money and trade and communications.

This preference for democratic regimes with a mixed constitution was not based upon his early experience of the United States. He travelled to the United States during 1853 and was rather contemptuous of what he found. Five years later he was still unhappy with the constitution of the United States and thought it as defective as the Russian – the Russian system too absolute to be good government and the American system too popular to be good government. But in his maturity he looked back upon the American revolution as the beginning of a new epoch in the history of the world. All previous attempts at democracy ended in some form of tyranny by a majority over minorities. But this, he thought, was a democracy which set limits to the authority even of the sovereign people and succeeded in preserving the rights of minorities. It had carried into the world two ideas which old Europe had found it very hard to accept: first, that a revolution may be an act of justice and help to create justice; and second, that a constitution which tries to give 'rule' to the people, and which had always been regarded as an unsafe form of constitution because it meant putting power into the hands of ignorant or bribable voters, could under certain conditions be a safe way for a State to be organized without losing its effectiveness or its justice as a government. He came in the end to feel that the American constitution was 'the grandest polity in the history of mankind'.

He always saw how fragile a possession is liberty – 'the delicate fruit of a mature civilization'. He was also aware how many enemies it had. States need to go to war – and warring States cannot be free. Illiterate peoples cannot be free because they are at the mercy of propaganda and their superstition will not allow others to be free; as religious majorities in the world still persecute or restrain religious minorities. A starving people will not be free because it needs bread far more than liberty and will care nothing for liberty until it has food. And freedom has lesser enemies in individuals who want power and see the chance of it by control of an army or a police.

Is absolute power sometimes better? Especially in crises? He had a hereditary reason to believe that it might be. In the Bourbon kingdom of Naples his grandfather was a successful prime minister. The King's attitude was that this is a poor and suffering people without enough education yet to contribute to politics. Give them democratic institutions and you create strife and probably murder in the society. It will be far better to keep power, give them a good administration, maintain public order, do all that can be done to diminish their suffering and their poverty, and develop the schools to educate them. Acton could portray the theory of absolutism in all its plausibility and knew that in the corruptions of humanity this method was an illusion and could not work. One wonders what he would have said at the doctrine of the generals in the Algeria or Turkey of our day that if you give the power to an illiterate and fundamentalist society the immediate result is tyranny and all the women thrust back under veils and male oppression. For despite this hereditary reason for thinking that there are cases where absolute power is best, he did not believe it at all. He was sure that no king nor queen nor dictator has the right to rule without the consent of the people and that the people may depose such rulers, even after they came to power by legitimate means, if they turn their power over the people into a tyranny.

This faith in liberty was a basis of Acton's power in the intellectual generation that came after him, even or especially in the generation which astonished itself by meeting Fascists and Nazis when it expected to meet government by the people for the people. He made liberty not just a political expedient but a moral right; and he had a mystical sense that this moral right would slowly conquer the world.

He hated every form of oppression; a class of warriors trampling on the weak; a class of rich grinding down the poor; a class of educated élite exploiting the illiterate. He knew that if we want government by the 'best people' in the State, we can never identify *best* with all the educated or all the property-owners or all the persons with political experience. Some people in the 'uneducated class' will be more responsible in their attitude to the State than some of the educated. Some of the poor will be better at seeking good government than some of the rich because good government might need to tread on the interests of the rich.

This hatred of oppression and corruption keeps coming through in Acton's prose. He was conscious of the danger of a class war and the need to protect the weaker against it. He was sure that experience proved that no single person is to be trusted with power over others. But he was painfully aware of the enigma, how, if you cannot trust any one person with power, you will be able to trust twenty? Or a million? He saw, whether he surveyed the ancient or his contemporary world, famous political philosophers advocating doctrines that were criminal and absurd.

And yet he was a student who wondered at the achievements of humanity. This was another source of his influence. He saw corruption and slavery and crime: and yet could exult in what whole societies had achieved. He could think Socialism or Communism mistaken because they wanted to do without private property which was a necessity for a free society. Yet he could see why they attracted. He could see the weakness and the superstitions of Churches and the exploitation by churchmen and yet be sure that Judaism and Christianity contributed vastly to the development of civilization and the ideas of liberty. He could see ancient Greek tyranny or mob rule or slave society for what it was and yet talk of the generation of those who succeeded

Pericles in Athens as those 'whose works, in poetry and elo-
quence, are still the envy of the world, and in history, philosophy
and politics remain unsurpassed'. He could see that despite the
corruptions there was 'a noble literature', 'a priceless treasure of
political knowledge'. Without having any theory of 'great men'
in history, he could yet feel this admiration for individuals: for
a Pericles himself or a Plato.

He expected that federations were fertile in the civilizing process because if two or more peoples lived within a single
umbrella-State the gifts of each race and culture would affect
the other races and cultures and there would be a healthy development of the whole society. 'It is in the cauldron of the State
that the fusion takes place by which the vigour, the knowledge,
and the capacity of one portion of mankind may be communicated to another'. He thought Britain and Switzerland were
blessed in this way. He preferred Austro-Hungary to national
states in Croatia or Serbia or Bohemia or Slovakia. He would
have encouraged the drive in the nineteen-nineties towards
forms of federalism in Europe. But when a lady pupil said to
him that petty tyranny occurred in small States, he was rude to
her: 'that is the silly thing that vulgar people say'.[26]

He was convinced that the freedom of the press is a necessity
for the development of freedom of the citizen and he had no
conception of the possibility that the freedom of the press could
be abused.

He was convinced that since the conscience is the heart of the
quest for liberty, the religious conscience is the ultimate source
of that quest; he used the evidence of the post-Reformation
struggles after toleration as the historical proof of this belief;
and therefore he was assured that the place of religion in the
State is of the first importance to those who wish for a free
society. 'Religious liberty is the generating principle of civil
liberty, and civil liberty is the necessary condition of religious
liberty'.

[26] Pollock, p. 377.

236

The presence of Acton in Cambridge confronted his Church with a difficulty. Here was a Catholic who now had a public post in the non-Catholic world. It was better if that were used by the Church. But this Catholic was regarded by many Catholics as anti-Catholic – if he still stood by his old opinions.

The parish priest at Cambridge was bothered by the coming of a heretic. By his own confession, he was deeply prejudiced against Acton. He was anxious how to behave to an alleged Catholic who had just been elected a professor amid maximum publicity.

He consulted the Archbishop of Westminster. Cardinal Herbert Vaughan had already acted. As soon as Acton's chair was announced he wrote to him to congratulate him and to say that he felt confident 'in your goodness and fidelity to the Church'.

> I know and understand something of the awful trials you must have gone through in the years past, and I cannot but thank God that you are what I believe you to be – faithful and loyal to God and His Church, though perhaps by your great learning and knowledge of the human – in this same Church – tried beyond other men.

And Vaughan signed it: 'Your faithful and devoted servant.'

It is obvious that Acton was very much moved by this letter. After a quarter of a century of suspicion and coldness from the hierarchy (which he had done almost everything possible to deserve) he found that on being elected to a Cambridge professorship he was not only a forgiven man but forgiven in generous language. He evidently did not know how to reply at first, for although he was down with a congestion of the lungs when the cardinal's letter arrived, he was able to write other letters during the next six weeks in which he failed to reply to the cardinal.

When at last he replied (20 April 1895) he wholeheartedly accepted the olive-branch:

> ... I received from your Eminence the kindest and most consoling letter that it has ever been my happy fortune to possess. If I was not afraid of being presumptuous I would in reply assure you that you have

judged me rightly as well as most graciously, and I beg that you will believe in my sincere gratitude for all you say . . . My Cambridge office is full of interest and promising opportunities; but the danger is that it is almost more a platform before the country than a Cathedra with serious students under it.

And Acton signed himself: 'your Eminence's most faithful and obedient servant.'[27]

On 5 July 1895 Acton even lunched with the Cardinal, who was 'as pleasant as he always is'.[28]

Thus Acton had been put, so to speak, into a state of grace with his Church without any need to recant, or profess anything which he could not profess, or make any declaration about the sense in which he accepted or put up with the Vatican decrees. The hesitation about the reply could only be because he must have wondered whether in accepting the olive-branch he was necessarily giving the cardinal the impression that he was a more conventional Catholic than he was and whether he had a duty of honesty to say so. Vaughan had said that he believed him to be faithful and loyal to God and his Church. That was just what Acton believed himself to be. On reflection he felt no duty to explain in detail to Vaughan that they were likely to hold different opinions on what the faith of a faithful and loyal Catholic ought to be; for Vaughan had shown no disposition to enquire. When the parish priest at Cambridge consulted Vaughan how he was to treat this formidable and heretical figure, Vaughan showed him Acton's letter and told him to treat Acton as one of the faithful. Hence the parish priest invited Acton to carry the canopy over the host in procession, and Acton accepted – coming in academical dress. Hence Vaughan invited Acton to attend the laying of the foundation stone of Westminster Cathedral and to speak at the luncheon afterwards; which invitation also Acton accepted. It was as important to him to be seen

---

[27] Westminster Archives, V/1/13/8; my thanks to the archivist Miss Poyser, Cf. Snead-Cox, *Life of Cardinal Vaughan* (1910), II, pp. 298–9.
[28] Acton to Annie, no. 108, 5 July 1895.

to be a Catholic as not to have to retract. It was the scholarly Jesuit Father Herbert Thurston who was to point out, eleven years later, that Acton had retracted nothing. Yet Acton did tell the parish priest, according to that priest's testimony, that he could now look back upon his trials as on 'a hideous nightmare from which the glory and peace of waking has been intense'.

THE CAMBRIDGE MODERN HISTORY

The historians have said that Acton did not invent the idea of the Cambridge histories, it was invented by the Press Syndicate of 1896 and put to Acton who turned it into a possible reality. The archives confirm that statement. But the archives also show that the Syndics thought of the idea early that year because the presence of Acton in Cambridge had put it into their heads. If Acton had not been there to consult and approach, they would not have proceeded in this form. They had a professor who believed in a universal history and that made them willing to believe in it themselves.

There was a minority on the committee and a majority. The leader of the minority was the classical scholar Leonard Whibley, who did not think the plan practicable. The majority who thought that the plan was practicable provided, and only provided, that Acton led it, were the two most eminent scholars in the room: Maitland and Henry Jackson. Maitland was very important to the plan, and to Acton. He was the historian on the Syndicate who had an absolute confidence about both the plan and its editor. He was also the person on the Syndicate who gave Acton the confidence of feeling that the Syndicate would understand what he was at.

The Syndics had the idea of a history of the world. They kept calling it a Universal History. In discussion with Acton they removed all the world before the Renaissance with the possibility of doing the world before the Renaissance later. But in their minutes they still referred to it for the next three years as the Universal History. Six months before they announced it they provisionally invited Acton to edit it. On 21 May 1896 he wrote the secretary a reply saying yes. 'I have not hesitated as much as I ought to do, on account of the difficulty, because my office here makes it a duty not to be declined, and because such an opportunity of promoting his own ideas for the treatment of history has seldom been given to any man.'

This shows that he was aware of something of what lay ahead. He was not aware how much lay ahead or of how the project was to bring him to his grave.

The plan was announced in *The Times* and *The Athenaeum* on 12 December 1896.

Acton chose the authors. It was not a sinecure. He wrote in his own hand letters consulting people about authors, to authors themselves whom he trusted, second or third efforts at authors who refused, letters to find out whether a proposed author knew the necessary European languages well enough, or to find out whether someone who had done nothing but write about wee moments of history would be capable of a general sweep of history; thinking whether the balance was right, economic or constitutional or the realm of thought and art; arguing whether it was better to choose a famous person who would be offended if you tried to edit his work, or a young person who would do just what you wanted if you edited the text; interviewing those in difficulty in his rooms in Nevile's Court or at the Athenaeum in London; deciding whether if someone did not answer his letters he was refusing or whether he was still thinking about it.

He was amazingly lucky. Because nothing like this had happened before, the proposed authors were interested to take part and many felt honoured that they should be chosen by Acton. Authors might accept the work and then die on him.[29] The loss of Hodgkin they felt very serious (a refusal not a death). Acton was pained at the refusals. Maitland said to Jackson, 'Why does not his omniscient lordship write the whole of the book? He

[29] Maitland's *Letters*, ed. Fifoot, p. 241.

could do it and come up smiling.' Some people applied to take part – Oscar Browning among the first – though his application was very frank, 'I sleep badly and can scarcely read a book.'[30] Acton realised that for local political reasons he must use Browning but had a difficulty thinking of a subject which he could safely entrust to that author; and finally pitched on the eighteenth century because Acton seemed to be under the illusion that less happened in those decades.

Acton loved lists of the best historians in the world and wanted them all to write. One of the most enjoyable occupations in his whole academic life consisted in producing the names of 120 first-class historians for the Syndics of the Cambridge Press to consider. Acton assumed that if you were a first-class historian you could write about any bit of history. His friends had to discourage him from trying to get a famous medievalist to write about King Frederick the Great. He did sometimes have wild ideas about historians: he had the idea that they might hire Westcott, who was a Platonist and the least historical mind in England – he saw everything as a bit of eternity. Acton had the idea of offering Calvin to Hodgkin, who was a Quaker – and Quakers being even more against Calvin than are Roman Catholics, the result was comic. Someone in St. John's College refused with these words: 'I am more than ordinarily ignorant of general history. I have no gift of style, and writing is a long-drawn agony to me ... I have ... no literary power, and no historical bent, much less historical knowledge.'[31]

Still, Acton knew a historian when he saw one. His greatest assets were Firth and the reluctant S. R. Gardiner. There are a lot of charming comments on authors among the papers. There were arguments: some thought a historian was good and some did not – the future Cardinal Gasquet was a case in point. Acton finally believed in him and got him to write but the contribution which he produced gave endless trouble to the editors.

---

[30] CUL Add. MSS 6443/112.
[31] Foxwell, in CUL Add. MSS 6443/156.

There were diplomatic considerations – how you address a person, for instance. Some people who are professors like to be called Professor and others who are professors like to be addressed as Mr. When he compiled the names, the number of Reverends on the list looked too high, so Acton decided to call the economic historian Cunningham Dr. Cunningham and not Archdeacon. Acton kept suggesting Miss Shaw but no one knew who she was. For a time they thought he might be thinking of George Bernard Shaw; but she turned out to be a Miss Nora Shaw who cared about colonial history.

In one way Acton was a marvellous correspondent, he wrote a lot of letters and every letter tells. But he did nothing about letters if he did not know what to do. An American was asked to write. He asked the secretary of the Press to ask Acton to tell him what was wanted. Acton was asked; he did not reply. The American wrote directly to Acton but no reply. The American wrote to the Press begging they push Acton to write.

He was clear about the nature of the enterprise to the secretary of the Press, Richard Wright, 30 May 1897:

The work is to be plain, and smooth, and clear, giving all that a general-educated reader wants but at the same time so scientific and erudite at the base, and in the materials employed and indicated, as to satisfy scholars and experts. The tone to be strictly scientific in the sense that no national, political or religious proclivity will be exhibited, or offended. In this respect, as in respect of fullness and accuracy, every contribution to be seriously revised and checked.

He realised that this would be more difficult than he laid down. 'Our danger will be that some men will not readily pocket their private opinions, in politics, religion, and the like – and we must be enabled to chisel all that down.'

Soon he knew that he needed help. A. W. Ward was of the family of Arnold of Rugby and being educated partly in Germany was good at European history with a Germanic style. It is remarkable that of the two people who did most to create the first *Cambridge Modern History* one had all his university education in Germany and the other had a lot of his schooling in Germany. The Press soon made Ward an assistant editor. Two years later Ward felt that he was doing most of the work and demanded more pay and the title of co-editor. The Syndicate was willing for a bit more pay but would have nothing to do with any editor except Acton and Ward resigned.

All the part-help did not remove the burden. In 1899–1900 Figgis saw that Acton could do nothing else but think about this *History* and feared that the labour of it was going to kill him. Maitland and Charlotte Blennerhassett both thought that this work helped bring Acton to his death. He was not a natural administrator. He had taken on the busiest job of editor yet seen and had small qualities as an editor except the quality of knowing a scholar when he saw one. He was a perfectionist and kept correcting people's texts even after they had already gone through more than one draft.

In January 1900 Acton realized that he could not do it and asked that Ward should be a joint editor and that fees to himself should be reduced or abandoned. The Syndics were not going to lose the selling power of Acton's name and refused this out-right. Acton asked them, if they would not make Ward a joint editor, would they not make Maitland? They did not even com-ment on this last proposal. On 31 March 1900 he wrote a depressed letter to Ward saying that the best thing for the Syndics 'would be that the Chair of History should soon be vacant.'

In April 1901 he suffered a stroke. It was the sort of stroke that brought some paralysis. The Syndicate sent a warm-hearted message of sympathy and good will begging him not to do any more till he was rested and completely recovered. In July 1901 the Syndics received a letter from Acton's son Richard on behalf of his father resigning the editorship.

Among the obituaries, that in *The Times* caused a little disquiet in Cambridge. It said good things and true things: his vast learn-ing, his obscure style, his questionable influence on Gladstone's

politics, his lack of feeling for poetry, his brilliance as a conversationalist, in which he equalled Macaulay, his charm and kindness to everyone; but then it said that he was limited by a certain
mental timidity, a distinct want of national fibre. 'With greater
moral courage and a more sturdy literary conscience Lord Acton
would have made a more striking mark in letters and in public
affairs; but his life, as it was, remains a splendid example of
devotion to study, and historical research, and to the cause of
truth.'

The language made Cambridge doubt. Lack of fibre? Lack of
moral courage? Mental timidity? There is in the library of
Trinity an unpublished letter from Acton's friend and
colleague, Henry Jackson. He wrote it after he read *The Times*
obituary.

I cannot guess who has written it; apparently someone who was
well-informed, but not sympathetic either to Acton or to Gladstone.
Someone told me a little while ago that Acton would be regarded
as Gladstone's evil genius, for that Acton wrote letters about public
affairs to Mary Drew, which she was to read to Gladstone when
she saw a favourable moment. The last words of the article – 'a
splendid example of devotion to study, to historical research, and to
the cause of truth – and especially those which I have underlined,
seem to me quite just. But I think that 'a certain mental timidity'
is a phrase which may mislead. I think he never shrank from the
conclusions to which the premises pointed; but he was not a man
of action, and I think, in general, left others to carry things into
effect.[32]

What the leading historian among his colleagues, Maitland,
remembered was not Acton's books of lectures, for Maitland
died before any of them was published. Even if he had seen the
books, he would have remembered something better still. Acton
was a genius not when he wrote history but when he spoke about
history. What Maitland remembered above all were Acton's talks

[32] Henry Jackson to H. M. Butler, 23 June 1902, Trinity College MSS.

in his home of Chaucer Road on Sunday afternoons. 'I shall never forget the few talks that I had with Acton ... in a short time he did an enormous deal to improve the position of history here and I think his loss irreparable.'[33]

---

[33] Maitland, *Collected Papers* (Cambridge, 1911), III; obituary of Acton in *Cambridge Review*, 16 October 1902; *Letters*, ed. Fifoot, pp. 37 and 323.

9

THE ACTON LIBRARY

LORD Acton had inherited and then collected a huge private library for his own historical purposes. When he died these books though still in Acton's various houses, were owned by the American millionaire Andrew Carnegie who had stepped in to save Acton from having to sell them to make ends meet; of course Carnegie did not want them and gave them to the Liberal politician and writer John Morley.

Morley had known Acton for about six years. They never quite liked each other. They were Gladstone's two closest friends during his last years. Each was bound to the old man by political principle and by those rare literary skills which alone could command Gladstone's admiration. Morley could talk well all the time, Acton could talk superlatively well when moved and otherwise could be dull. Each of them was accused, by those who envied their intimacy with Gladstone, of being his court flatterers. Both of them cared about the ethical in politics, Morley cared not for religion, Acton believed it the basis of ethics and therefore of politics. This fundamental difference Acton characteristically believed to be the real gulf between them.

Their friendship never grew warm. In 1892 Morley feared Acton's influence over Gladstone and thought him an intriguer. Acton resented the mistrust and attributed it to low motives. 'You will like John Morley' he wrote to his daughter Mamy. 'He is not, in the supreme sense of the term, quite a gentleman.

There are some refinements he is not prepared for. He was very angry with me for interfering in the making of the Ministry [i.e. in 1892] and having so much irresponsible influence, because he has a careful game to play . . .'

They found a new and better kinship in the debate round Gladstone's grave. As he worked away at the biography Morley read Acton's letters to Gladstone and found in them cause for self-examination. When Acton was nothing but a historian, and Morley no longer in government, their interests in literature brought them together. While Morley was ill, he beguiled his time by reading Acton's Inaugural Lecture, and afterwards wrote that he now had two masters in history, Ranke and Acton.

Then Acton died and Andrew Carnegie gave to the agnostic Morley his great Christian library. Morley could not want 70,000 books, mainly on parts of history in which he was not interested, and he could neither house them nor care for them. He must give them away but to whom?

Morley was a graduate of Lincoln College, Oxford and thought little of his time there and could not imagine that a small college would have the wish or the money for a library like Acton's. He thought that All Souls was possible for it was well endowed and had a great library and Acton was an Honorary Fellow. He thought of Mansfield College in Oxford which trained nonconformist ministers, for here was the library of a Catholic nonconformist. This was an absurd idea, such a seminary could not possibly find the money to look after so many books. So he came to the obvious answer, that the books ought to be offered to the University of Cambridge where Acton had done so much for history. Noises came to Morley from Cambridge that they would value the library if they were given it.

But Morley saw that he had a weapon. This moment lends a mild justification to Acton's mistrust, for Acton could never have done what Morley now did. He used his ownership of the library to try to influence the choice of Acton's successor. He said that he would not give the library to Cambridge if certain people were chosen to succeed Acton. Was he willing to state whom he would so resent? He was. Acton's friend Sir Rowland Blenner-hassett, the husband of Acton's ablest lady pupil, was one; he was already talked about as a possible replacement. Mahan the naval historian was another. If either of these were appointed he said that he would not give a single chapbook out of Acton's collection to Cambridge.

Balfour the Prime Minister then said that Acton had told him that he would like Maitland as his successor. Balfour said that Maitland was too 'black-letter'. It is hard to imagine what Balfour meant when he called Maitland too black-letter; he must have thought Maitland a pedant or too narrow in interests, which was a mistaken judgement. But whether or not he thought Maitland too narrow, the Prime Minister knew that Acton wanted Maitland to follow him. So on 25 October 1902 he wrote to Maitland to ask if he might recommend him to the king to succeed Acton in the professorship. Maitland refused at once. His reason was decisive. He was already in very bad health from pleurisy, he had to spend long winter months in the Canary Islands, he had twice offered to resign his existing chair of Law and his health could not possibly allow him to undertake a new chair. So Acton's wish was frustrated by health almost as bad as his own.

On 28 November 1902 Prothero saw it in the paper that the chair had gone to J. B. Bury, the classical scholar and Byzantinist, of Trinity College, Dublin. Prothero was disappointed. Oscar Browning was disappointed. Professor Jebb in Cambridge was indignant. Acton would not have been disappointed for he much admired Bury's work. Morley was not disappointed, for the library came to Cambridge.

It has to be faced that this, though in a way unwitting, was the greatest of Acton's contributions to Cambridge history though certainly it was far from being the only great contribution. Those members of that university or other universities who have worked extensively in Acton's library, develop a reverence for the mind which collected it and which often put light marks in the margins of the books.

Morley made the condition that they be kept together as a collection. 70,000 books were not easy to put on shelves in the then Library in the Old Schools building at Cambridge, especially if they had to be housed together. It was agreed that each book should be given the classmark *Acton*. When the new library was built the ground floor of the south-east wing was allottted to the collection.

The basis of Acton's personal library consisted of books which he inherited. He was the squire at Aldenham in Shropshire and some books were in the Aldenham library from long before he was born – for example, Tanner's great study of all the abbeys of England and Wales. His father's father, Prime Minister of Bourbon Naples, and in South Italy, during the last age before they were overthrown by French revolutionaries, he naturally acquired books. Not all these books came to the family seat at Aldenham in Shropshire because Acton's father's brother became a Cardinal and some of the grandfather's books may now be in the Vatican library. But it is possible to trace in the Acton library books which came from the Naples age of the family. One, for example, is the legal decisions of the Rota court when Rome for a short time was under the domination of the king who entitled himself King of Sicily and Jerusalem. The book has in it a draft Naples passport for the young man who later was our Acton's father, to enter Austrian territory.

Acton's mother was a German, a Dalberg. In the days before Napoleon the Dalbergs had been one of the great families of German nobles with their seat at the castle of Herrnsheim near Worms in the Rhineland. Acton's great-grandfather on his mother's side was the brother of one of the eminent men of Europe, the last prince- and Elector-Archbishop of Mainz, who was one of the Germans to back the incoming Napoleon and so was made Duke of Frankfurt. He was an intelligent and cultured man and collected a good library. He had special interests in the histories of Spain and Portugal and of Sweden and Russia. Through his nephew and then his nephew's daughter, his castle and its books came to our Acton.

Hence the base of the library at Aldenham and afterwards at Cambridge consisted of two late eighteenth century libraries, one collected by an Englishman in Southern Italy, the other collected by a German in the Rhineland. Because these two had different interests in what they collected, the range of the library was already unusual. Some of the Dalberg books stayed with Marie, Acton's wife, in the house at Tegernsee. But others of the Herrnsheim books moved to Aldenham; and there Acton had to add a new library to his mansion to house the books which came from Naples and the books which came from Herrnsheim and the books which he collected. During the summer of 1869 a Mr Bohn was hired to arrange the Aldenham library while Acton was at Herrnsheim; it cannot have been a very whole-hearted arrangement because Bohn took only five weeks and at the end reported that there were not enough shelves.[1] Even while the library was being arranged he was buying large numbers of German books.

There was a third substantial source of books which he did not collect himself. Sent to the university of Munich, he started on classics and his professor was Ernst von Lasaulx and he became Lasaulx's favourite pupil. When, after Acton had left the university, Lasaulx died, his books came up for sale and Acton bought them. The collection which Acton thus acquired was very different in interest from those of Naples or Dalberg; these books were of the ancient world, of philosophy especially ancient philosophy and the philosophy of history, ethics whether ancient or modern. Acton's library had increased its range in a third direction. Twelve years after Lasaulx died and probably before, Acton employed a graduate librarian to care for and arrange the books at Aldenham.

Meanwhile he bought steadily. Other books were given to him as presents as they are given to us all – Gladstone, for example, gave him a copy of the Odes of Pindar. There was another

---

[1] Acton to his wife, 8121/7/939.

source of miscellany, that to get what he wanted he sometimes bought in bulk, whole private collections that were up for sale, and such purchases obviously included books in which he had no interest. Yet everyone who uses the Acton library is conscious that this is a unity, a single mind dominates the shelves. It may have been awkward, it was certainly inconvenient to the then librarian, that John Morley should make it a condition that Acton's library must be kept together. The condition had grave disadvantages. But its carrying-out enables the user to find this astounding unity which has been imposed and which could only have been imposed by a person of the deepest learning.

He was not a bibliophile; he did not buy books because they were very rare or because they looked beautiful; he bought them because they were tools towards knowledge. When the university librarian, the sweet-natured Francis Jenkinson, saw the collection which the university had forced him to accept, he told a friend sadly that there was hardly a book in it which interested him; for what he loved were medieval manuscripts or books printed before 1500 or the books of the English sixteenth century – and Acton was not very interested in the Middle Ages (but he did study Peter Damian and Gregory VII and the letters of St Boniface) and his passion was of Europe since the Reformation. Acton liked splendid bindings and interesting old books but these were not his motive, he wanted books because they were doors with fascinating country beyond when they were opened. If a book which he wanted was already in ruins that did not stop him buying it. Already as an undergraduate he began to read booksellers' catalogues and to buy books in second-hand shops. Over the next twenty years or perhaps a little more, when he had plenty of money to spend, he bought largely and steadily and intelligently. Eventually the collection – Aldenham books, Herrnsheim books, Lasaulx books, his massive purchases, made one of the great private libraries of Europe and since people referred to it publicly it became well known and when society talked of Acton they talked of his library.

There is a letter to his fiancée of 1865 (he was aged thirty-one) which explained why he wanted to stop being a member of Parliament during the early years of his marriage.

The one supreme object of all my thoughts is the good of the Church ... The greatest good that I can do is by means of literature, for there I have resources greater than any other person, and have collected materials of an immense extent. The time has come when I ought to make something of these collections, and it is impossible while I am in Parliament.[2]

He had two main aims which were the cause and guide to his purchases. He was a dedicated Whig or Liberal and a believer in progress and he wanted to study how humanity had gained liberty in its constitutions and its social life. Then he was a Roman Catholic by birth. In popular northern opinion in his two countries of Britain and Germany the Roman Catholic Church steadily resisted the coming of liberty, a resistance summed up in the word inquisition. Hence his second interest was the history of the Papacy, from the Counter-Reformation to the French Revolution. To students with such strong views as he held these two themes held ample temptation to propaganda. But Acton was determined to know – resolute not to overlook information that told against the thesis which he wanted to prove – and hence the profundity with which he sought out every corner of his two subjects by means of his book-purchases.[3]

It was a good time to buy. Many monasteries had excellent libraries and they were in a bad way. Houses that once had many monks and scholars among them now had a handful. Catholic States treated monks badly – the French Revolution abolished them in France and Belgium, one consequence of Napoleon's power in Germany was the loss of many monastic libraries, Portugal dissolved them all in 1834 and Spain all in the next

[2] Acton to Marie, 8121/7/851, no date but early 1865.
[3] Henry R. Tedder, 'Lord Acton as Book-Collector', *Proceedings of the British Academy*, 1 (1903–4), 285 ff.

year, Italy most of them from 1866 onwards, Swiss cantons by dribbles during the century, most of the Polish houses vanished under Russian rule. On occasion monks, now desperately poor because their endowments had been seized, had to sell precious books if they were to survive.

Not all these books came into the second-hand market. States could appropriate them for the national library, as was done in Bavaria and Rome. Monks were good at keeping their way of life, by moving to Protestant countries where they would be safer or by moving from one Catholic State to another – out of Spain to France when the Spanish dissolved them, out of France to Spain when the French dissolved them; and some books went with them. But many libraries were for sale in the bookshops. The British Museum had a prosperous time.

In Acton's collection are superb books out of the libraries of monasteries. We can track where various of them came from. A book of 1642 by a Dominican about the inquisition came from the Capuchin house at Castelvetrano near the toe of Sicily; another on the same subject of 1648 from the house of the Franciscans at Bergano. The Discalced Carmelites at Castelvetrano provided him with the *Bulla Cruciatae* of Bardi, Palermo 1656. The Capuchins at Verona supplied Medina on Penitence, 1581. Cardinal Petra's Commentary on the Apostolic Constitutions, published at Venice 1729, came from the house of the Discalced Carmelites in Florence.

Naturally the Bavarian religious houses supplied some of the best. The *Magnum Bullarium* (Lyons, 1692), then the indispensable collection of papal bulls and still for some purposes indispensable, was given to help found a Carmelite house at Schöngau in Bavaria, not far from his wife's home at Tegernsee. There was a Jesuit house at Landsberg in Bavaria, why their books did not go to the Bavarian State library it is hard to say, but several of these Jesuit books ended up with Acton. These were not the only Bavarian books. Durandus' text book on law (Frankfurt, 1592), was in the university library at Ingolstadt, which since the Counter-Reformation had been dominated by Jesuits. When the

Jesuits were abolished by the Pope in 1773, the university library gave the book to the Theatine monks of Ingolstadt; it was not the only one of Acton's books which the university gave to the Theatines during the Jesuit crisis; and then the Theatines in their turn lost their library in the revolutionary age and so the book came to Acton. The regular canons at Gars near Munich had a book, Zunggo's History of the canons 1742–49, which came to Acton, but did not come by the Bavarian route because it passed through a French bookseller. There were books from the very historic Irish house at Regensburg. The oddest of the Bavarian acquisitions is a lovely copy of Mabillon's *Annales*, Paris 1739 onwards – for it belonged to the ducal library in Munich. How did the Duke of Bavaria, after Napoleon turned him into a king, manage to lose so splendid a book? We know that Professor Döllinger borrowed books from the royal library in Munich and that Döllinger freely lent books to Acton. One does not like to think that this was the route by which it came into the Acton library. At least two of the books which Acton acquired, Patricii Senensis' *De Regno* (Paris, 1567) and the Jesuit Mariana's famous *De Rege* (Mainz, 1605), state at the front that this book was a duplicate from the royal library at Munich, so we know that the library sometimes sold books.

The revolutionary Portuguese State had little interest in the past and freely allowed its monastic books into the auction rooms. Quite a number of Acton's books came out of Lisbon, the Oratory there (for example Mansi's Supplement to Labbe's Concilia, Lucca, 1748–50, a still useful book) and more from the Portuguese university town of Coimbra which had been packed with religious houses. The Discalced Augustinians of Coimbra supplied him, eventually, with a good number of books.

The monastic books are on various subjects but the collection as Acton made it contains splendid materials for the history of the monastic orders before the French Revolution.

A few of the books have interesting comments in them – like: Reading this book is banned by decree of the index; or in one case: 'This book belongs to the library of St Dominic at Bologna from which it cannot be removed, the penalty of removing it is excommunication, so Popes Urban VIII and Innocent XII.' There was a Paris book which belonged to the Vincentians but did not come from them into the market because in 1728 the Mazarin College gave it to one of its adolescent pupils as a prize for her knowledge of the catechism.

But mostly he was not buying ex-monastic books, there was a book from the university library at Halle which they found to be a duplicate and sold in the market (it was a 1567 commentary on the Decretals) and Acton picked it up. There was *Thuringia Sacra* (Frankfurt, 1737) which was sold in 1851 by the university library at Leipzig, probably because it was a duplicate, and was bought by C. A. Schnabel and thence bought by Acton. The very good collection on the Protestant Reformation was made by himself, for example he bought when it came out Enders' edition of Luther's German works. What he did get out of ex-monastic libraries were the pamphlets or tracts against Luther – like Catharinus, 1521, which had belonged to the Capuchins, and a 1545 Cochlaeus which came from the Franciscans at Ingolstadt, and the canons and decrees of Trent from the abbey of St George at Villingen in Württemberg.

During the course of their history some of these books must have had an odd time. The Palatine Library was collected in the age of the Reformation by an extravagant Elector Palatine at Heidelberg. When the Elector Palatine who was son-in-law of King James I of England accepted the crown of Bohemia, a Catholic army occupied Heidelberg and sent the Palatine library to the Vatican. A volume from the Palatine library, the life of Pope Benedict XIII, appears in Acton's collection. Perhaps the Vatican library got rid of a few duplicates, or perhaps it left the Vatican by some less reputable route.

There is a book on Concordats (Turin, 1770), which belonged to King Charles Emmanuel III, King of Sardinia and Savoy. During all Acton's life there was still a King of Sardinia though for the later half of Acton's life he was also King of Italy. How did such a royal book come into Acton's possession? The kings of Savoy and the kings of Italy were not ardent readers of books and it is possible to guess that not a single one of them would have read a book on Concordats. Yet it is not likely to have been sold from a royal library. The inference must be that during the conquest of Northern Italy by General Bonaparte the devastation reached even to books.

As he developed his library Acton's interest shifted with a change in his own historical inquiries. Before about 1870 or 1874, when he was in danger of excommunication by Rome, his interest was the Papacy and all Catholicism in Europe till the French Revolution. But now his interest widened – to the society and ethics of Europe, including the beginnings of modern social sciences – for example he bought Karl Marx's *Das Kapital*. The second area in which the library specially developed was in French books and pamphlets. He had inherited fine books from Germany and from Southern Italy and he bought many books out of Spain. But now he turned to the French bookshops and built up, what became an outstanding feature of his collection, a superb library of French history especially of French local history. He was the first English historian to have this rare interest in French local history which brought such valuable results in the decades after his death.

Acton bought in London from C. J. Stewart, King William Street off the Strand; from D. Nutt, Foreign and Classical Booksellers, 270 The Strand; from Stanford, famous to us as mapmakers, and from Bickers and Son, and from Burns Oates, and from Williams and Norgate. In Cambridge from Deighton Bell, and from Arthur Cox who was soon to turn into Galloway. In the Hague from Martin Nijhoff's Librairie Ancienne et Moderne. In Paris from the Librairie Ecclésiastique de Toulouse et Taranne, which despite the name was in Paris, 33 Rue Cassette; and from Ernest Thorin at the Librairie Ancienne et Moderne, 58 Boulevard St Michel; also from the French bookshops Librairie Nouvelle and Librairie Universelle and Librairie Spéciale pour l'Histoire de France; in Munich from Rieger who ran the university bookshop, and big purchases from the bookseller Theodor Ackermann, 10 Promenadeplatz. He bought occasionally in the Hague but there is no sign as yet of any regular purchases from an Italian or Spanish bookseller.

It has been regarded as an established truth that Acton built the main part of his library during the twenty years after he was an undergraduate and that from about 1874 he bought far less. But this cannot be true. What is true is that during the later eighties, as he bought and as his children grew more expensive he had to pause because he had not the money to do it; and he and his advisers reached the conviction that if he was to save himself from the creditors he must sell his books. The London auctioneering house Puttick and Simpson printed in 1890 a first catalogue of Acton's books for sale and issued it to the public, to be sold on six days of sale beginning on 16 July 1890 at 1.10 pm precisely. Although it is only a first catalogue it must have roused the interest of every serious student of history and society.

This was when Gladstone stepped in to save Acton from what he regarded as disgrace and persuaded Andrew Carnegie to buy the library on condition that Acton could keep it until his death. If Acton had refused this offer he would have lost his library. But by accepting it he must have been aware that if he had auctioned the books he would have received far more money than he was given by Carnegie. He preferred to keep the books and to be saved from creditors, to selling the books and being very comfortable.

From the moment he was assured of being able to do so, the buying began again; more modern books now, more German than French. There is a bill from Ackermann in Munich dated 28 December 1896 with a list of books bought and the days when they were bought, and it shows that Acton was sometimes ordering three or four books twice a week, and expensive books – one set was 73 marks, another more than 88 marks. More than one bookseller started to worry. When Ackermann presented his bill to Acton that December it was more than 1,350 marks. We find little notes from booksellers, not only foreign, pleading for settlement of a debt.

And now the burden fell on Jenkinson the university librarian, whose natural world this was not, and who by his generosity, indefatigable labours and wisdom turned the benefaction into one of Cambridge's great possessions.

He had a first difficulty: Aldenham Park was rented out, and it had its (so to speak) 'private' collection of books about the house which must somehow be distinguished from the great library. Many books were in Tegernsee, the same series of volumes might be partly in Tegernsee and partly at Aldenham and partly in his room at Trinity. The books from Aldenham, transported to Cambridge in February 1903 by five vans and 443 packing cases, lay in heaps about the Arts School and the Old Syndicate Room in the Old Schools.

The first sight of them made Jenkinson grateful but also alarmed. The gratitude was due to the realization that he had been given a collection which for its themes was not paralleled in any other library in Europe. The alarm came from a perception of the physical and intellectual problems which faced him. Many books were unbound. There were hundreds of rare pamphlets which would require long research if they were to be catalogued aright. And many series were found to be incomplete – Acton might buy the first two volumes and then fail about the third, or buy in a sale the first and third volumes but had no second; and he was the most generous or imprudent man with books, he frequently took a rare book from his library and thrust it into the hands of an undergraduate and this was one way to find a series incomplete – the habit shows as nothing else how he was not a bibliophile but how the books were tools to knowledge and not more. And did he own all the books on his shelves? As late as 1906 they found at Tegernsee a volume which belonged to the Royal Library at Munich, and two years after that the Royal Library pointed out that they had discovered Acton's signature on a borrower's ticket for four volumes of

Döllinger and where were these four volumes? About that time Lord Stanmore claimed back a privately printed volume of his father's correspondence which he had lent to Acton.

So the first tasks were, (1) to find shelves; (2) to make a preliminary catalogue and find out about rare books and pamphlets – that must need extra staff; (3) to bind what needed binding – they bound 13,791 volumes, partly by the library staff and partly by Gray of Cambridge; (4) to try to find single volumes which could fill the gaps – Jenkinson sent out to the European book trade a list of volumes wanted, and eventually succeeded in buying 1,515 volumes of what he needed (cost £417.12s) – it was beginning to be almost an Acton – Jenkinson library; (5) to decide what to do about two peculiarities – the duplicates with existing volumes in the library; and the discovery that in many volumes Acton's working slips were still in place to mark passages of special importance to him, what was to be done with the slips?

He needed a team. With the aid of Adolphus Ward of Peterhouse he collected an excellent team to research into these books and arrange and catalogue them. Ward had been professor of history at Manchester and there knew Alice Cooke, a Manchester girl who had specialized in the history of monks and friars in the Middle Ages. When she won an assistant lectureship at the university of Manchester, she was one of the first women in England to be appointed to a university post. There she had shown her ability as a cataloguer of the Spencer library at Althorp and the fledgling John Rylands library. She had a quiet friendliness which made her easy to work with. For nearly five years, 1903–7, she worked at the huge task which confronted Jenkinson. The witnesses agreed that she was the best of all the assistants in this task. She left in 1907 only because she won a full lectureship in medieval history at Leeds in a competition when the candidates included the great Powicke. Later she was to return to Cambridge as director of studies in history at Newnham College but by that time the Acton work was done. She was one of those assistants who are indispensable to the work of a great library but receive credit only from the very few of her employers who are in the know.

When she went, Ward's hand was still at work and she was succeeded, 1908–12, by T. A. Walker Fellow of Peterhouse, dean of Peterhouse, bursar of Peterhouse, librarian of Peterhouse and vicar of Cherry Hinton; and despite this busy combination he did well with the Acton books and pamphlets. When he ended, the job was almost done.

Jenkinson must ask himself questions about the utility of what they were doing. Not many classical scholars would now want to use German theses on ancient literature which were printed in the twenties and thirties and forties of the nineteenth century and came from the working library of Lasaulx. In the way in which the collection had been made, on occasion by buying a bulky lot, it was inevitable that Acton bought two or even three copies of the same book. The librarian whom he employed at Aldenham in 1873, Tedder, had as part of his duty the thinning out of duplicates and certainly got rid of more than 1,000 books. When the Acton library reached Cambridge in its vans and packages, it had hardly any duplicates. What it did have was the same book in different editions or languages. Acton did not think himself complete if he had a sixteenth-century edition and then there came on the market a seventeenth-century edition of the same book. One of the oddest is Paolo Sarpi's celebrated history of the Council of Trent. Of Sarpi he acquired the original Italian of 1619, which was printed in London because of the danger of publishing in a Catholic country, the English translation, a French translation, and a German translation of 1761. Acton commanded these four languages. The copy which he read was the German.

That was not Jenkinson's chief problem. It was that the university library already possessed many books of which they were now given another copy. Sometimes the books which they possessed were well bound whereas Acton's copy was not; sometimes the series which they possessed was complete and Acton's was incomplete. Yet the university had accepted Acton's books as a totality to be kept together. He was, so to speak, under an obligation not to get rid of anything. Jenkinson called this the problem of 'surplusage'.

A ruthless librarian, who had not enough space on his shelves, would in a mysterious way have got rid of duplicates, even though his bosses in the university had accepted the library as a unity to be kept together. Jenkinson, though he was the least ruthless of men, did precisely that. First, he asked John Morley the donor whether he would like any of the duplicates apart from the *Biographie Universelle* which he had demanded to keep; for no one could blame the librarian if the donor accepted back some books; and Morley was willing, because eventually they sent him altogether 940 books which they saw no point in keeping. Then he asked the second Lord Acton whether he would like some of his father's books and persuaded Morley to give the new Lord Acton 6,000 books. Even that was not enough. From an early moment in the operation intelligent scholars of other universities realized that there must be duplicates and asked whether their own inadequate libraries might not be passed the duplicates which Cambridge did not want. The librarian at Tübingen university was quick to express a hope that they might get Acton books. No less a scholar than Mary Bateson, for example, asked Ward of Peterhouse, who had helped Acton edit the *Cambridge Modern History* and was now working closely with Jenkinson, whether the unwanted duplicates might not be given to the National Library of Ireland.[4] Ward replied very cautiously. They might not have the power to give away any of the books which they had accepted, and before there could be any question of it a considerable time must elapse. It is impossible to tell whether when Ward talked of a considerable time, he was thinking of the years that must elapse before the collection was fully catalogued and ordered – this took in the end some ten years – and so when they would know what were duplicates and what

---

[4] Mary Bateson to Ward, 13 June 1903. My thanks to John Wells for his help with these papers in Add. MSS 9376.

were not; or whether it also came into his mind that after years have elapsed donors do not grieve so much if gifts are given away by the recipients. It took Jenkinson six years before he felt that the time was ripe for a sale of duplicates – but this sale must be very private, no one must see that the University of Cambridge was getting rid part of a benefaction. He offered duplicates to a bookseller in Tunbridge Wells on the strict condition that no one should know where the bookseller found what he had for sale.

But this diminution of the duplicates, first to John Morley and via John Morley to the second Lord Acton and then to Tunbridge Wells, does not disclose the humanity of Jenkinson. Like every other worker on Acton he was moved by the power of the single mind moving among all this material – that is, he did not want to give away or sell books, even if he had them already, when the disappearance of the book would imply that Acton's range was narrower than it truly was. He kept many duplicates, even though they were duplicates, because their presence in the Acton library illustrated the mind of Acton.

This was particularly important with the slips. Acton often put slips into his books, to mark a sentence or passage which struck him. The passage on that page might also be given a light pencil line in the margin. The slips were systematic in that they were almost all the same size, some two inches by half an inch, and most cut from booksellers' catalogues of second-hand books, usually English booksellers but sometimes German. Because they had lived in the book for years, all were dusty, most were crumpled and some were dirty. Probably most librarians would have thrown all these slips away as worthless. Jenkinson kept them all, at the page where he found them. They illustrated the omnivorous mind of this indirect benefactor of the library. Jenkinson's brother-in-law testified that Jenkinson, the bibliophile for whom Acton's books were not his sort of special affection, was almost more interested in the slips than any other part of what Acton did.[5]

---

[5] H. F. Stewart, *Francis Jenkinson* (Cambridge, 1926), p. 56.

There were a few oddities left in such a unique operation as they had engaged in. As we browse revering in the shelves, and wishing that we had read more than any of us have, we come across J. P. Whitney's *The Reformation*, 1908. It was the best textbook of its time, of a type which Acton dismissed as too outline a textbook to matter. Acton would not have bought it probably, and he did not buy it certainly, because by then he was dead. There could not but be curious turns in the work of making useful such a big monument to a private thirst to know the past.

INDEX

Acquaviva, Cardinal, 38

Acton, Annie, daughter of historian, 7–9, 178–9, 191, 204, 209, 217f, 238

Acton, Cardinal, uncle of historian, 1–3, 27, 159, 249

Acton, Jeanne Marie (Simmy), daughter of historian, 189

Acton, Sir John Francis, grandfather of historian, 1, 17, 20, 50, 159

Acton, Sir John, from 1869 Lord Acton, *passim*: education, 1ff, 79; at Tsar's coronation, 117; advising on lectures at university of Dublin, 117; and journalisms, 11ff; in Parliament, 13ff; marriage, 22ff; and Theiner, 48ff; peerage, 78, 140, 148; at Vatican Council, 70ff; diary of Council, 140; Quirinus, 71ff, 83ff; *Liber Diurnus*, 107; *Sendschreiben*, 103–4; history of Vatican Council, 113; letters to Döllinger, 141, 186ff; moral argument with, 146; proposed life of, 161; the election of 1892, 166ff; lord-in-waiting, 176ff; and Newman, 115ff; and Mary Gladstone, 145ff; *History of Freedom*, 156–7; library, 161–3, 246ff; proposed sale of books, 160–3; the Cambridge chair, 204ff; inaugural lecture, 210ff; 247; lectures, 219ff; political ideas, 231ff; *Cambridge Modern History*, 157, 239ff; personal religion, 65, 113, 199, 237–9; manners, 142; as conversationalist, 142–5, 164–5, 173–4, 244; on aphorisms, 145; portrait by Lenbach, 200

Acton, John, son of historian, 159, 189

Acton, Lady, mother of historian *see* Granville

Acton, Lily, daughter of historian, 189–90

Acton, Mamy, daughter of historian, 25, 105, 137, 144, 147, 151, 153, 160, 165–6, 169, 171, 179ff, 188, 190–1, 200–1, 246–7, 252

Acton, Marie, née Arco-Valley (from 1865 Lady Acton), 3–4, 23ff, 65, 105–6, 108, 115, 122, 134, 141–2, 152, 159, 177, 189–90, 250

Acton, Sir Richard, father of historian, 1–2, 159, 249

Acton, Richard (from 1902 second Lord Acton), 129, 131, 147, 166, 185, 243, 261

Adrian VI, Pope (1522–3), 37

Alciati, 56

Alexander VI Borgia, Pope (1492–1503), 34

Antonelli, Cardinal, 57, 61–2, 74, 112

Aquinas, Thomas, 220

Archives, Vatican, 32ff; transferred to Paris, 39–40; returned to Rome, 41–2; fate after fall of Rome in 1870, 106ff; 224; *see also* Garampi, Marini, Theiner, Stevenson

Arco, Countess, mother of Lady Acton, 23ff, 119–120

Arco, Louis, brother of Lady Acton, 79, 100

Arco, Toni, brother of Lady Acton, 189

Arnim, Count von, 79, 92, 96

Augsburg, Treaty of (1555), 36

Avignon, archives at 33, 39